How To Win The Battle Against Inflation

With A Small Business

Creative proven strategies for the entrepreneur or investor

by
Murray Miller, M.D.
and
Franz Serdahely

ISBN: 0-913864-33-1

Library of Congress Catalog Card No. 79-53799

Published by: Enterprise Publishing, Inc.
            Two West Eighth Street
            Wilmington, Delaware 19801

Printed in the United States of America.

This book is dedicated to Elaine, an entrepreneur in her own right, recounting her experiences in the weekly newspaper field, and her activities in the toy and game industry, and for her innate ability to view problems pragmatically.

–Franz Serdahely

The development of this book as the culmination of my varied experiences in many types of investments has been extremely pleasurable. But, as with anything of effort, it did not occur by or from the authors alone. This dedication is to my parents who raised me to believe in myself, to my uncles who enabled me and encouraged me to start developing my concepts and counseled me when requested, and to my co-author who put the facts and concepts on paper. My deepest thanks, because they know more than I, what they have contributed. This only leads up to my biggest supporter and friend, without whom none of this would have occurred or would have meant anything, my wife Renee.

–Murray Miller, M.D.

Contents

ACKNOWLEDGEMENTS AND CREDITS

The following individuals, corporations, and organizations have been generous with their time and efforts in assisting with the research and writing of this book:

Franklin D. Burke, *Burke Lawton and Co.*, Investments; Lacy D. Hunt, Economist, Sr. Vice President, *Fidelity Bank,* Philadelphia; Vijay Kothare, Editor, *FOCUS Business Newsweekly,* Philadelphia; John Raezer, President, *FIN PAC Computer System*, Narbeth, Pennsylvania; Salvatore Castro, President, *Castro Electronics, Inc.*, Beth Ayres, Pennsylvania; Alan Halpern, Editor, *PHILADELPHIA Magazine; MEDICAL ECONOMICS Magazine;* Robert Kraus, Patent Illustrator; Irving Shier; Tom Styer, *STYER ORCHARDS*; Somers K. Butcher, President, *Butcher Trade Exchange on Barter; Joseph P. Jansen Co.,* Construction, Milwaukee, Wisconsin; *"Topsider" Homes, Inc., Louis Traiman Auction Co.*, Philadelphia; *Wharton School Entrepreneurial Center*, Philadelphia; *Internal Revenue Service*, Philadelphia; *Federal Reserve Bank,* Philadelphia; *Federal Energy Administration; Drexel University Research;* and for valuable guidance and assistance Beverly Horning Natrin, Editor, *Enterprise Publishing, Inc.* and the *U.S. Labor Department* for data and charts.

Foreword

America has come to a crossroads. The signs no longer point to "Prosperity–Two Miles Ahead," or to "Easy Street." The terrain has an edge to it, and across the land we can see the lengthened shadows of The Four Horsemen of the Apocalypse. Inflation, recession, energy crunch, and productivity decline are riding high in their saddles, cutting right through our cherished dreams and aspirations.

These dreams and aspirations are going to be more expensive in the years to come, not only in terms of the dollars and cents that will be required in greater numbers, but also in terms of sweat and tears and tenacity. It takes a sense of urgency to recognize change in the air–drastic change indeed.

The world we leave behind for our children will not be the same one that we inherited. It will be less flexible, more expensive, less compromising, and more demanding. Accommodation with this world of tomorrow will require a drastic change in our lifestyles and in our orientation. America is to come face-to-face with a world that is contrary to all its cherished aspirations. It is on our doorstep. Nay, it may well be in the foyer. It is here. In the kitchen, in the living room. It is the night after the OPEC blackmail. We are hostages in our own homes and in our factories.

You and I have nowhere to turn but to our scrappy individualism. **How To Win The Battle Against Inflation** will be an invaluable aid in nurturing this enterprising spirit within us. There is nobody out there who is going to solve our problems for us. We cannot depend on the government because it has become a dinosaur, stymied by its own inefficiency and sinking rapidly into bureaucratic quagmire. This book will help you to be more self-sufficient, to depend on your most valuable resource–yourself.

We have to take matters into our own hands, short of a revolution. Most of us are still quite fat and contented. A sizable population is living on welfare and the rest of us are working our butts off to keep them in steaks and butter. This is not a proper scenario for a revolution.

I am not advocating a revolution. It takes a mob to make one–a mob that is lean and hungry and mean. We don't have an enemy in the world, but we have become the enemy of all discontented people. We have been suffering from a case of infantile inaptitude. And we cannot be expected to remedy the agony of indecision by burying ourselves in remorse or embalmed melancholy.

Survival is a lonely business. And the Four Horsemen are making it incurably difficult.

But scrappy individualism alone will not accomplish the task, nor will a shelfful of self-help manuals. What it takes, of course, is informed action. And this book has plenty of information.

As a member of the business communications industry, my waking hours are spent with matters relating to the world of commerce, with the price of gold and the price of real estate, with import quotas and with jobs, with stocks that go up and cities that show erosion, with successful people and with failures of all sorts, with the goal of getting rich and the childish credulity of the uncommitted. I feel I am a good judge of the contents of this book. And I believe that this book will help you.

When F. Scott Fitzgerald wrote, "Let me tell you something about the rich. They are different from you and me," he was looking at them through the eyes of the average folks. The difference between the rich and the poor is not so much in the obvious material possessions, but in the attitude towards life. The difference is in the vision. Melancholy may be the private domain of the suicidal, but success is an open territory. Everyone is welcome to it!

Vijay S. Kothare
Editor, FOCUS
Metropolitan Philadelphia's
Business Newsweekly

Introduction

In recent years, our country has experienced significant changes. Perhaps the most important changes have resulted from technological developments. Equally significant, however, are the changes brought about by the dramatic impact of inflation, high taxes, the resultant high-interest rates, and the overall gyrations of the financial markets on the economy.

How To Win The Battle Against Inflation is for people who want to understand what they can do about the conditions caused by the changes taking place. It is specifically for the people who have the urge to be in business for themselves and who want to survive and prosper while building a small business. Because there is no single place to go for detailed instructions (until now), this book endeavors to take much of the guesswork and risk out of giving the entrepreneurial urge a try. It also shows you what to do to increase your protection against inflationary forces.

You will note in the chapters that follow that you needn't start with a large investment. A modest amount will suffice in giving you a beginning in certain small business projects, especially after utilizing the reasonable principles fully outlined by the authors.

Opportunity is all around us. It has been with us since the founding of our country, and in some respects, has never been better. Our country has been built by people who seized the opportunity, worked hard, and applied workable principles to accomplish their goals. Many of these people have started with a basic dream and followed their dreams with *effort*. The result has been the reality of accomplishment. It is from the fulfillment of our dreams that satisfaction is derived.

It is a privilege for me to introduce this book. I have been in business for myself virtually since I was a young boy, with just a short period out for military service. I owned my own business while in college, and applied the exact principles of **How To Win The Battle Against Inflation** in achieving satisfaction and reward of being my own boss and being responsible for my own progress. These principles are basic, and they will always stand the test of time. They will also help you protect yourself against inflation.

Each person in life has individual characteristics and ambitions. Each one of us is unique in what "drives" us, in the way in which we react to the conditions we face. I have always firmly believed that the prime requisite to fully appreciate anything is to share it with others. This is the major underlying principle that **How To Win The Battle Against Inflation** makes–the sharing of the knowledge that you can do what you want to do, even during inflationary periods. The book offers the encouragement needed to overcome the many psychological and personal obstacles so that you can go ahead and do it.

In many years of being an investment advisor, I have often counselled others about going into business for themselves. I have found that most people have many "blocks" holding them back. These obstacles usually range from financial considerations to discouraging personal advice (most of it well-meaning) from others. My approach has always been that positive encouragement is proper when the people involved are serious in their quest to be in business for themselves, and have the right entrepreneurial characteristics that need to be satisfied. Naturally, only you can answer questions in these categories.

In the final analysis, we all help each other in this life of ours. Many people have helped me in getting started in business; I have been privileged to help others. I believe this book is of the highest caliber of help. It encourages, shares knowledge, outlines the principles, risks, and rewards involved in small businesses. It also helps you organize your capabilities, background, and desires into a realistic, inflation-beating plan. Each person reading this book who is sincere in the desire to gain valuable knowledge in running a small business and winning the battle against inflation will not be disappointed.

Franklin A. Burke, General Partner
BURKE, LAWTON & CO., Investments

PREDICTIONS OF THE FINANCIAL FUTURES OF 100 PERSONS WHO ARE 25 YEARS OLD AND ARE WORKING TODAY

In the year 2020, when all of these 25-year-olds will reach retirement age of 65, the following analysis finds them as follows:

* Only 4 will have an adequate income!
* 5 of these persons will *still have to work!*
* 36 of this total group of persons will have died!
* 54 of these persons will find themselves *"dead broke"!*
* *Only 1 person* of this entire group will be wealthy!

Source: Social Security Administration

Part One:

Where We Are Today

Where We Are Today

As the 1980's unfold ahead of us, the small business entrepreneur, along with the endangered salaried worker, is witnessing a rapidly-changing America in terms of lifestyles, economy, values, and its relation to the rest of the tumultuous world. Every small business owner must now chart a course through uncertain, hazardous shoals which lie all around us. Inflation, which has been dogging both the consumer and the business person, has now grown into a full-blown storm.

The initial government efforts to halt the ravages of inflation have failed miserably. Only now does the Administration realize that increasing the money supply is like a volatile fuel that spreads inflation's damaging blaze more disasterously. Paralleling this dangerous condition is another serious economic "noose"– the recession.

Workers in the automotive industry, the steel industry, residential construction, and in various "luxury" product areas, have already felt the sting of the high credit rate crunch by way of layoff notices. They, unfortunately, are in the forefront of other widespread industry layoffs that will occur during the coming years.

How will the small business operator, the salaried worker, or the recently retired person survive financially in this vicious economic cross-fire?

This book, HOW TO WIN THE INFLATION BATTLE WITH A SMALL BUSINESS, has been specifically structured to answer this question positively. It has been written to help you beat back the financial erosion of inflation, and the debilitating effects of recessions.

In these pages is a documented and startling record of the U.S. economy racked by inflation. It points out Administration sources responsible for our present financial morass. It reports how uncontrolled inflation will affect you as a consumer and as a small business owner. In these pages you will find practical, tested ideas and programs which will help you establish a small business so that you will be able to survive the crippling impact of inflation in the years ahead.

This book presents and "blueprints" business opportunities which, if implemented by you, could make you financially independent over the next few years.

There are no empty, academic theories here. Everything you will read is based on actual case histories of successful business entrepreneurs who have been innovative, and not afraid to buck the trend. Many of these people are "loners," well-disciplined individuals able to move out through proper motivation, without the need to lean on dozens of other people for support or decision making.

You will find a number of business opportunities in these pages which you can start *without costing you one cent!* And you will discover new business areas never reported before in any book or business article. Many proposed entrepreneurial operations will require only a modest investment, or, depending upon your circumstances, a substantial amount of funding for the launching of a larger enterprise.

Chapter subjects range from the purchase of farmland as an investment, to involvement in franchises, and careers in chimney sweeping and blacksmithing.

This book will warn you about the "herd" instinct–the urge to rush into investments which, though well-publicized, are sometimes actually unprofitable, even fraudulent. This includes the field of collectibles from coins and stamps to artwork. It warns about the highly-touted gem investment "game," and the error of getting into investment situations you know little about.

Want to beat the high cost of home building? You can start by reading the chapter devoted to every aspect of home building, covering conventional housing costs compared to reduced costs of "kit" houses. There are names, sources, and actual costs detailed for your use.

Do you know how to *barter* as a business owner and conserve cash? Do you know where to go to raise capital to start a part-time or full-time business operation? You will find these answers and hundreds more in these pages.

As a small business owner, you will want to know what economic conditions and lifestyles will be like over the next five, ten, or fifteen years, so that you can plan your strategic moves. And the chapter on comput-

ers and their influence on you, your family, and your business may change your views about the future. It might possibly enhance your chances to build profits.

You will read about some startling and shocking predictions made by nationally-known economists, analysts, designers, computer experts, builders, entrepreneurs, executives. Some coming events may shake your world, and in the process wipe out entire industries dramatically. You will discover that within the next twenty years, life in the United States will be *totally different* from what it is today, from our economy to our lifestyles.

But if you use this book as a guide and establish your own business, you will survive the painful, economic shakeout which awaits all of us in the months ahead!

1 Investment Opportunities For You Today

There are numerous opportunities for successful investments all around us.

Investment counsellors, economists, bankers, and financial managers of huge investment funds are puzzled about the future of the U.S. economy. And most are groping for an answer to the "safe" investments of the future. No one really knows exactly what will happen in this fiscal crisis which is now upon us. This is why it is crucial to re-think all of your financial decisions.

Reasons For The Uncertainty

There are two basic factors for this growing uncertainty in financial circles: insidious, rising inflation and periodic recessions. Both of these conditions are causing unprecedented havoc with investment strategy, conservative financial planning, and the direction financial fund managers should take in the months ahead. Yesterday's financial standards have gone by the board and are irrelevant in today's unpredictable marketplace. The devaluation of the U.S. dollar in foreign countries is another symptom of the U.S. monetary crisis.

Alfred E. Sindlinger, Chairman of Sindlinger & Co., a marketing and opinion research company, said recently in reference to inflation, "People are scared about what might happen."

You need to understand the significance of inflation in order to protect yourself. Inflation is an economic condition which began in the United States in 1965 as a "single digit" annual price rise percentage. It has since climbed to what economists and bankers now refer to as "double digit" inflation in terms of annual price rise increases. Its disasterous effects have been experienced in a wide range of areas ranging from food to fuel. The following chart illustrates the rise fairly graphically:

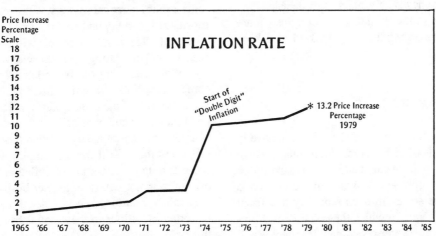

*Compiled by Franz Serdahely from gov't. and financial sources.

We should, at the outset, understand *what* inflation is, and *what caused it to occur,* before we move into a discussion of investments.

Inflation Defined

Inflation is a period when the purchasing power of the dollar is falling because of the government's *increase of the money supply* to cover its own *deficit spending.*

Henry Hazlitt, noted economic scholar, reports:

> "The politicians have concluded that they can continue to hold office as long as they *spend more than they tax;* as long as they redistribute income; as long as they 'soak the rich'; as long as they hand out subsidies to a score of pressure groups under the plea of 'relieving poverty' and showing compassion.
>
> "In this climate, more and more individuals abandon hope of ending inflation by political argument of action, and decide to devote all of their energies to trying to save themselves from being ruined by inflation."

Our present government has created an illusion of prosperity. Administrative aides point to the millions now working at jobs despite the inflation. However, the "drubbing" of the U.S. dollar overseas is a prime example of the U.S. government's misguided policy of excessive distribution of its dollars to U.S. industry, business, and foreign exchange. Since the quantity of the nation's currency is only an arbitrary decision now at the discretion of the President and Congress, more and more dollars are printed in the U.S. Mint to keep up with increased prices!

Supply and Demand As The Remedy

Apparently, our government does not believe in the Austrian School of Economic Philosophy, which states: The only objective regulator of the marketplace is the law of supply and demand. Basic economic problems can be solved through monetary and fiscal *restraints* (a situation in which the dollar demand increases too rapidly). Some economists fear people will be prone to spending their money quickly to avoid rapidly rising costs.

Bankers, investment experts, and pension fund managers aware of the consequences, are seeking "hedges" to avoid fiscal chaos.

Germany experienced a serious and devastating period of hyperinflation after World War I, when prices for products and services rose daily *by thousands of marcs* until the monetary system was wiped out through devaluation.

Many segments of our society making demands for more money for services and products keep "heating up" the economy. The tremendous welfare budget and the large civil service employee roles of government contribute nothing to our Gross National Product and intensify inflation.

When you place all this information in its proper perspective in order to evaluate it intelligently, you should relate your investment plans to inflation as a present factor. This means, in order to survive, you must look for a "hedge" to combat the damage inflation may cause you financially.

Inflation Hedge

"Hedge" is defined as a means employing any method which will *minimize* risks of losses as a result of possible changes in prices and values.

Those who begin to prepare for these economic conditions are obviously better off at this initial stage than those people who *ignore* effects of inflation on their income or investments, and who shrug off implications of a recession. When financial disaster hits this latter group, personal savings, some investments, and mortgaged property will be torn loose to fill the breach. The total effect for these people will be traumatic and soul-wrenching during their financial wipe-outs.

Who, then, will *survive* inflation? What jobs will come through this unsettled fiscal period unscathed? What sections of the United States will be better equipped financially and physically to withstand the shocks of financial "earthquakes"? What businesses will be inflation-proof? Will the self-employed entrepreneur come through this combined inflation/recession still owning a major equity in his/her business, with savings safely guarded? We will detail answers to these important questions in these and subsequent pages of this book.

Who Will Survive

One fact many financial experts do agree upon is this: the *self-employed will survive inflation* if they place "all of their ducks" in the business waters carefully; if they invest intelligently; if they move quickly with price changes; if they anticipate cyclical conditions of the market. Because they are a different breed of cat than corporate or company business people, they will be able to maneuver freely, making a small or large profit opportunely.

Characteristics of Entrepreneurs

Bankers characterize entrepreneurs thusly: they possess the tenacity to dig into a situation; they have the will to work hard; they spend countless hours at their activities; they are motivated to take unusual financial risks. Entrepreneurs will have boundless faith in their ideas, programs, or products, and will go to extreme lengths to achieve their goals. Even when "experts" scoff, they will be relentless in their search for capital to finance their ventures. And when they succeed, they will savor the fruits of their toil!

Unfortunately, there are some segments of our society here in the United States that may not be able to survive the present and future financial crises unless something is done to halt inflation's erosion of personal savings. Millions of retired people with fixed incomes, professional people, and countless workers, have discovered to their dismay that weekly paychecks and monthly income will not weather the storms of inflation in this decade. The tug of war between prices and income is predictably a losing one.

What then are the "bedstones" of security today? How do you *survive* in these turbulent times which inflation has created?

You (and others) who establish your own privately-owned businesses or services will not only establish a good hedge against inflation, curbing its financial onslaught, but will also create a new source of income for yourself. Recommended steps in planning investments will be covered in basic degrees here.

Your Own Resources

Starting at "Square One," your own training, ability, and interest in specific areas–your innova-tiveness–are your keys to security. Hard to believe? Not if you learn about the successful operations of many small and large entrepreneurs who are pioneering new paths with their investments, despite inflation.

During the past several years, four entrepreneurs on the West Coast, unknown to each other, have become *millionaires,* building their personal fortunes from scratch. This is despite inflation. The most important observation to be made about their individual financial successes is that each was *knowledgeable in his own field*. These fields included aeronautics and aircraft, electronics, athletic equipment, and health foods. Each surmounted heavy odds against achieving success, and worked doggedly toward his goal. Thus, it is still possible for a motivated, dedicated individual with an idea which *fills a need* to become financially successful in his/her own business.

Today's investments for the individual must be measured against *today's* economic conditions–inflation and recession–and lifestyles in the United States and elsewhere.

The Effects of Technology

For example, technology has changed the very nature of some industries and businesses. Modern advancements in electronics produced the computer, which is capable of processing information from numeric equations at high speed to storage and organization of statistical data on millions of Americans. The computer has changed accounting methods and financial records. Its impact on the business, industrial, and professional communities has been dramatic. It has revised the concepts of accounting, taking it from a painstaking, step-by-step method of recording financial data to a speedy, accurate transaction.

In the field of medicine, another example, tremendous strides are being made almost daily in the areas of diagnosis because of the computer's use in medicine.

A wide range of activities in the medical field is now possible, thanks to specially-designed computers used in diagnostic work. This involves record keeping, blood analysis, cell comparison, brain and organ scanning, and storage of pertinent medical facts and figures. Here is computer hardware at work around the clock, without a coffee break!

The Effects of Our Changing Lifestyle

Our present modes of living, or what are fashionably called our "lifestyles," are changing rapidly in terms of diet, family activities, entertainment, the type of homes in which we live, the cars and trucks we drive, our clothing, and even our work habits. All of these are *totally different* from previous generations.

These significant lifestyle changes, and related factors have obviously affected marketing and business planning in many areas. These changes will continue to set new trends in the years ahead, creating a different environment for millions of people. Human efficiency has been increased one hundred-fold. It has, quite suddenly, created more free time than was even thought possible a decade ago!

As a result, we now have these areas and conditions which influence investments:

1. Hedonism
2. Travel
3. Creative abilities (developed as a result of more free time)
4. Social activities
5. Boredom and our need to *do something* which has resulted in spin-off areas of activity. Theme parks such as Disneyworld, Four Flags, King's Dominion, and Great Adventure are examples.
6. Large, aging population
7. Mobile society
8. "Fast foods."
9. The growing "singles" society
10. Facilities assisting in the rehabilitation of people abusing themselves with alcohol and drugs
11. Condominium living

Basically, these are factors which have already established wholly new businesses, *filling existing needs,* and providing good investment opportunities for the entrepreneur. Although you need to evaluate each area in terms of present-day inflation, bear these factors in mind.

Effects of Our Mobile Society

Changes in shoppers' needs and desires in this mobile society have brought about radically new shopping concepts. If you don't believe this, look about your own commercial neighborhood areas. Where are the old "Mom and Pop" grocery stores, the barber shops, the meat butchers' stores, small hardware stores, the candy shops, the filling stations, and diners? Most of them have disappeared from the scene, or have been converted into something totally different. Even yesterday's delicatessen is now a "mini-market," offering everything from hot sandwiches and coffee to magazines and paperback books. And outside, you see the self-service gas pumps!

In the major population areas of the United States today, we have huge, attractive shopping malls; facilities that are complete with interior fountains, skating rinks, and growing trees and gardens. Actually, these are miniature shopping cities, built for the express convenience of the mobile shopper. Here you can cash a check at a bank, get a hairdo, enjoy a five-course meal, and purchase an expensive wardrobe in a few hours' time–and in any type of weather. What inflation's effect will be on many of these retail establishments is a conjectural factor. Some small businesses will flourish, while others of the high-priced, luxury product-type, will not survive.

The Benefits of Being Small

Businesses which provide necessities and services, rather than recreation or luxuries, will do *better* during rampant inflation. The small, privately-owned retail operation will be able to ride out the peaks and valleys of erratic sales cycles because there will be lower overheads. They will have fewer employees with fringe benefit costs than the financially-structured massive retail chains with locked-in operating expenses. Sears & Roebuck is experiencing losses on high-priced merchandise which is not selling, coupled with the lack of "low end" or lower-cost merchandise. In the new passenger car market, the luxury cars are not selling well because customer preferences have switched to the smaller, lower-costing models.

The mobile American society has created the shopping malls of the suburbs, and now more recently, those in center cities. It will influence shopping patterns in the future, which may again be totally different. As an entrepreneur, a shopping mall enterprise may hold some investment opportunity for you.

You and Your Financial Situation

Let us begin with the *basics of investments:* you and your financial situation. You have a position, or job, which produces enough money to meet your daily needs and your monthly bills. Perhaps there is a little left over for a few, discreet "extras." You may elect to put some of this into a savings account at the normal passbook interest rates. You may treat yourself or your spouse to an occasional recreational break. But if you have the feelings and the motivation of a true entrepreneur, this isn't enough for you! You have a determined desire to generate more income through other sources.

Maybe you are a small, successful business person looking for other fields in which to invest some of your income or profits. But you tell yourself you are not content with the conservative stock/savings bond/certificate choices open to you. Realistically, you are motivated to try for a higher return because inflation is eating up your profits.

Perhaps you are a senior citizen, now retired, or semi-retired, with enough income to care for your needs (whether they be regular or emergency needs). But you are unhappy with the 8% or 9% bond dividend returns, which because of inflation, do not keep up with the inflation rate. This is true also of savings accounts where the passbook holder really ends up the year with a loss in the value of savings of 8% or more. And the sad part of it all is that there is no end in sight to the dilution of savings!

Then you pose the question: "How do I start? How can I get a rapid return on my invested capital? What are the steps to take to begin an investment program?"

Where To Begin

FIRST: You need to take a long, critical look at yourself and your own circumstances. How well-motivated are you in terms of taking necessary financial risks? What are your *ultimate* financial goals? What do you *want* in terms of lifestyle in five years, ten years, or the next twenty years?

Are you able to live within your present income for a year, perhaps longer? Do you meet all of your financial obligations on time with no indebtedness "dogging" you? Can you get by on a fixed rate of expenditures to get started on a program which will

bring you a high rate of investment return in a few years hence? Living on a tight financial budget for several years while funds invested in several projects are working is not uncommon. Beginning investors–dedicated entrepreneurs–usually live on a modest scale, keeping a lid on everything from food to transportation, in order to save the necessary funds for investment purposes.

Are you willing to spend a considerable amount of time and effort in searching out new opportunities; talking to numerous individuals; gathering information and reports; speaking to bankers and real estate brokers; digging into various publications in your area to obtain *information?* A determined entrepreneur will probe and investigate every opportunity carefully *before* making the first move! If you agree that you are willing to devote a lot of research time under these conditions, then you are on the first step of your investment program.

How much money can you *safely* invest without requiring this amount for emergency use? Can you spare $1,000, $5,000, or even $10,000? Can you afford to let that amount remain in an investment situation for one year, two, or longer, if need be? If you can do this, then you are ready to organize your first business investment venture.

Inventory Your Interests

To begin with your personal financial analysis (which you should detail carefully on paper), list your immediate interests in terms of business, specific fields, hobbies about which you have some first-hand knowledge.

Inventory Your Personality Traits

Then analyze your *temperament* and your disposition. What does this have to do with investing? A great deal, as a matter of fact. Are you a quiet, introverted person, or are you outgoing, gregarious, a person who needs people around you? Do reports and financial details annoy or bore you? On the other hand, do you like reading financial reports, tabulated figures, and related data? Can you make a decision and stick with it? Can you be firm with people even under trying circumstances? Do you trust people, or do you have a basic mistrust?

These personal traits have much to do with the type of investment you will make. Let's examine how these traits match up with financial investment in various projects.

If your temperment is too easy-going, you probably shouldn't get into a landlord situation. This means you may be unsuited to handle rentals from your income property (a small apartment venture, or a modest motel operation). At times, the role of the landlord requires a certain inbred toughness and discipline. The easy-going temperament may be best suited for certain sales-oriented ventures, retail operations where tolerance is mandatory, small repair installations, banking positions, guiding people at various buildings and functions, certain jobs supervising children, or child-oriented activites, listening to buyer complaints, ticket collections, and other activities where mental flexibility in dealing with people's demands is necessary.

Misdirected compassion on the part of a landlord usually ends up in financial and emotional entanglements, and eventually to wiping out the investment.

Quiet, introverted people are probably more effective with investments in certain types of businesses, such as: mail-order operations, clock repair and rebuilding, handicrafts and hobbies, income tax report work, research, rental library activities, radio and electronics work, computer-oriented work, record and music filing. This type of personal trait lends itself well to projects involved with financial detail recording and evaluation.

The gregarious individual does well with such opportunities as dance school instructing, demonstrations of equipment and products, lecturing, sales work which requires contacts with large groups of people, telephone relations activities, and retail ventures where numerous individuals appear constantly.

Most small investment entrepreneurs will not be propelled into public focus by virtue of their investment if this is a concern to you. In many cases, even where investments are massive, there are "silent partners" who seek anonymity for various reasons.

What $1,000 Can Do For You

Now let's see exactly what can be done with the various amounts of money you will set aside for investment. But again, in view of the pressure of inflation, you must evaluate your initial investment in these terms.

A $1,000 investment could purchase an interest for you in a small, successful mail-order operation. Will it survive in a period of recession? Is it service-oriented? Does it involve sales of food products, tea, herbs–things people *want and need* even in slack business cycles? If it is geared to luxury products, watch your step financially! You could also purchase part interest in a small retail venture: bike rental agencies and repairs, photo developing (but *not* a photo studio), a computer "jitney" service, or a small print shop operation. Remember, you are only an *investor* in any of these enterprises–not an operator or an owner.

Generally, these small, cooperative ventures earn a good rate of profit, and any of these could be a "starter" investment effort for you. You can also investigate other business activities through the U.S. Commerce Department, local Chamber of Commerce directories and files, and local business publications.

What $5,000 Can Do For You

What can you do with a $5,000 investment? With this amount of money, you can begin to move into real estate purchases: property, farmland, small buildings, storage structures, leasing operations, or a partnership with others in a small housing development. This activity would give you quick leverage in dealing with banks, or real estate brokers, when you require additional financing.

The $5,000 nest egg for your entrepreneurial venture could also be applied against a share of a retail operation; an office supply and copier equipment repair shop; a picture framing shop; or a mobile lunch wagon service.

Your rate of return on your investment in any of the above ventures could well be at a 10% or 15% level or more annually.

Based on the experiences of many successful entrepreneurs, look for investment opportunities which *are not obvious* to other people. Most of us are attracted to the glamor and highly-advertised franchise offers in WALL STREET JOURNAL, the NEW YORK TIMES, BUSINESS WEEK, MODERN MECHANICS, and other publications and daily newspapers. Remember, the vast number of investors who are attracted to the areas of fast foods, quick printing, the newsletter field, automatic transmission repair, real estate area licensee, home exterminating, and others can quickly diminish the investor's rate of return because *saturation*. There are competitive traps to be avoided here.

The U.S. Federal Trade Commission warns potential investors to check out every aspect of a proposal from a national franchise operator. Many people have lost considerable amounts of money on bogus or phony franchise deals.

Unless you are fully prepared to devote *all* of your time to a business venture (in addition to investing a significant amount of money), you should seek opportunities which will not take up your full time. This is a decision you will have to make.

Real estate investments, for example, do not require full time activity on the part of the investor. Land can be rented for raising crops; leased to an individual; or sub-divided into building parcels. Buildings can be sold, rented, or moved. But all of these are one-time transactions.

What $10,000 Can Do For You

If you have $10,000 to invest in a worthwhile venture, you should again be aware of the effects of inflation on the business activity. This amount of money can (with the joint help of partners) provide for the purchase of a motel operation, farms, farmland, a large warehouse and storage facility, a truck rental agency, a small hotel, or a medium-sized apartment facility, a food processing operation, a retail store, or a mail order company.

Advantages of Getting A Partner

A partnership venture may be the most desirable since your resulting financial return will obviously be greater. If the investment lies in the "recession-proof" business activity (service, food, transportation, institutional feeding, daycare centers), you will be in a good financial situation.

I have participated in several partnership ventures from institutional feeding to the operation of a summer camp.

It is important, however, that *one* of the partners be knowledgeable in the specific area in which the investment is being made. He should also be able to devote all of his/her time to supervision of the operation. There is too much at stake to leave day-to-day control of the enterprise to employees. Absentee ownership is very risky.

As you extend your investment investigations, you discover that people will respond to you. Increasingly, you will be asking questions about certain business activities, and you will get a liberal education in how various businesses operate.

Along the way, you will realize the amount of time, effort, and money that is required to make each enterprise function at a profit. Without committing yourself financially to any specific area, or program, you will find yourself filling folders with notes and reports.

You will also make a startling discovery: many people are unwilling to commit themselves to a good, profitable business proposition even when it is *offered* to them! We mean *legitimate* business proposals. The reason for the reluctance is that very few people out of one hundred are entrepreneurially inclined. The majority are afraid to take a chance on something new, or are overly conservative because of their family traditions, or personality traits.

When I purchased real estate (a house and a lot) at an auction a number of years ago, making a bid of $10,000, there were many other people in the throng. But these people did not bid. Almost immediatley after the auction, I was approached by a man who offered me several thousand dollars over my purchase bid! When asked why he did not bid at the auction, his answer was: "I guess I just didn't *feel right* bidding."

While we should always look at situations in a positive light, we must also be realistic. Follow the old axiom, "Don't bite off more than you can chew." You may wind up with an expensive, disasterous case of financial indigestion! Recognize your limits and your goals, balanced by your needs. Don't be lured into investing in a venture based on a fantasy in your mind, or based on whimsy. Take all the time you need, withing reasonable limits. Consult experts. Find out everything you can. When all conditions meet your criteria, move forward without hesitation!

Below is a worksheet on which you might work out the items discussed in this chapter.

PERSONAL FINANCIAL ANALYSIS

Cash in savings accounts $_____

Life Insurance cash value   _____

Stocks, bonds, certificates of deposit   _____

Cash on hand   _____

Miscellaneous income   _____

Equity in home   _____

Cash value of auto, van, or trucks   _____

Total $_____

*****

PERSONAL INTEREST IN TYPES OF BUSINESSES AND HOBBIES

Business: (list such interests as: construction, aviation, machinery repair, food processing, etc.)

_____

_____

_____

_____

Hobbies: (list such hobbies as: flying private aircraft, soaring, gourmet cooking, collecting old glassware, antique car restoration, etc.)

_____

_____

_____

_____

Personal Analysis of Temperament

_____

_____

_____

_____

2 Starting With New Ideas; How To Make Your Own Opportunities

In planning for an entrepreneurial investment of the risk/reward concept covered in the preceding chapter, we must always take into consideration the risks of raging inflation and its effect on the decision made.

While economists are trying to grapple with their predictions of what lies ahead for the United States in terms of the economy, you need to seek out those enterprises which will not be adversely affected by a recession that inevitably occurs periodically, along with inflation. (See the chart below, which illustrates how recessions have increased since World War II.)

A Prediction

Investment specialists and pension plan managers point to a sobering assessment of the future: *if the present rate of inflation continues* over the next forty years, a twenty-five year old worker will have a difficult time trying to reach his/her retirement goal! They point out that at an annual inflation rate of 11%, it will cost the twenty-five year old about $650,000 to buy daily necessities in the future years. This includes groceries, clothing, housing, and transportation–as compared to purchasing the same items on the average retirement income of $10,000 today. And further, the forecast states that if the twenty-five year old retires at the age of sixty-five in the year 2019, it will cost him/her *about $70,000* just to live each year![1]

Other monetary experts argue that deflationary forces will have knocked out price increases by the year 2025, and altered the U.S. economy to the point of devaluation, where *barter* will become the prime means of obtaining products and services!

[1]*FOCUS Business Newsweekly*, December, 1978. Attributed to a spokesperson for the Social Security Administration.

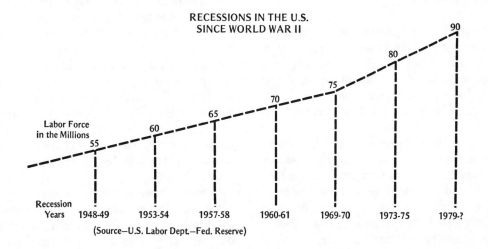

RECESSIONS IN THE U.S.
SINCE WORLD WAR II

Labor Force
in the Millions

55   60   65   70   75   80   90

Recession
Years 1948-49   1953-54   1957-58   1960-61   1969-70   1973-75   1979-?

(Source—U.S. Labor Dept.—Fed. Reserve)

But despite all of the dire predictions and observations, new enterprises will be established by courageous individuals. Fortunes will be made by some, while others will not make fortunes. Risks will be taken to attain financial goals because that is the way of life for enterprising Americans.

Investments To Avoid

Financial scholars with an eye on inflation and recession, caution would-be entrepreneurs to stay away from investing in businesses or ventures in the so-called luxury field. This includes jewelry; power boats; mountain lodge resorts; high-cost clothing or apparel; luxury cars; aircraft; high-cost entertainment or recreation facilities; and confectionery, to name a few.

The small, flexible, self-owned enterprise which is self-supporting, particularly if it is in a service-oriented field, should do well, despite severe economic dislocations.

Going back to your own "Personal Evaluation Sheet" on which you listed your financial assets and net worth, you also included your personal likes in terms of hobbies and special interests in business areas. Now, project from this point into specific categories—manufacturing, construction, transportation, wholesale and retail trades, finance or banking, medical activities, fishing, and sports. Begin to narrow these into a few specific selections.

Beating Competition

Obviously, if you are going to establish an operation on a national or regional basis, you are going to be concerned about competition. Before investing in a business operation, you do not want to run into a stone wall of established, well-financed competitors, dominating a specific market. It could be financially disasterous!

Those who have launched "fad" or "trend" products (skateboards, disco dancing, etc.) report they were successful because they were *first* in the marketplace. They could establish prices and sell their products quickly, *before* imitating competitors began to move in. They would attempt to preempt the market.

The lone entrepreneur had the "edge" because he/she has the ability to work on a small budget, if required, and can move quickly and expediently.

Another way for you to prepare an investment strategy is to approach the area from a perverse point of view. The buzz words here are: *conserve cash*–guard your money against the happy overtures made by the con artists. First, take a good look at the areas in which you should *not* invest. Inflation will take its toll from your income, without squandering it on schemes prepared by the Freddie Fraud artists.

How To Spot Investment Con Games

Be careful about high-powered sales pitches made by representatives totally unknown to you, whether the offers are made by telephone or by mail. They will cover a wide variety of items and programs you will be asked to purchase, or to "make a token investment" to earn "enormous profits." These will involve investing in commodity futures; oil exploration deals; consumer product syndicates; franchises; high-profit exporting and importing; dubious mail order operations; Canadian and Mexican securities; "Beefalo" raising; Bahamanian or Haitian investments; and other types of programs pushed at you.

Be warned! If these salespeople assure that you will be able to *make* thousands of dollars in a short time, *why are they sharing this knowledge with you?* Why, indeed? People who make spectacular profits from ventures *never* share that information with total strangers among the general public. The only people who will make money from these rip-off schemes will be the sales representatives themselves.

The horror stories of people who have invested in precious stone propositions, involving rubies and diamonds, which were *synthetic* in many instances, are numerous and shocking. The age of gullibility, unfortunately, has not yet vanished.

Never invest in anything which you cannot check carefully or thoroughly with bankers, attorneys, or authorities in the field. The proposition must obviously be legitimate before you invest one cent of your money. Your knowledge about business areas, or your hobbies, will be important when looking for an investment opportunity.

For example, if you know something about artwork, including painting in oil and watercolor, sketches, prints, and sculpture, you then have an advantage over others if you are thinking of investing in this area.

If you still want to invest in artwork for a profit return, but lack the knowledge of basic art differences, techniques, and mediums, you need to consult a professional artist, art teacher, or dealer beforehand.

It will become quickly apparent to you that people who take risks of a financial nature (like you and me) are a different breed than the average investor. We are the "fringe minority," seeking new and unexplored investment areas. Certainly, you would not be reading this book if your only objective was to purchase Money Market Certificates, or short-term Notes.

There are many diverse opportunities for both the small and large entrepreneurial investor. But there is a sharp distinction between the *collector* who may be a dealer in specific articles (or a serious hobbyist specializing in one vertical area, and selling when the occasion demands), and the individual who may shift from one investment area to another, depending upon the profit opportunities.

Using Your Innovativeness To Spot Opportunities

There is a classic story circulating among advertising agencies in Chicago. It concerns the novel entrepreneurial experiences of a well-known art director. This ad executive was trying to find twelve weathered old boards from a barn to use as "props" in a photography session for a client's advertisement. The product was a can of well-known motor oil which was to be shown against the backdrop of the weathered barn boards.

The art director toured suburban areas, and outlying rural farm areas, looking for an old abandoned barn from which he could get the dozen boards. After three days of hunting, he located an abandoned hay barn which was in a state of near collapse. It was located on the premises of a retired, aging farmer who lived nearby. The art director offered to buy the boards and remove them himself. However, after some shrewd trading, the farmer offered the entire barn to him for $200. The ad executive accepted the proposal quickly and closed the deal. He not only got his twelve boards, but a lot more!

When the word got around later that he had a storage area filled with hundreds of aging, weathered barn boards, he got offers from set designers, photographers, department store decorators, and others for the purchase of numerous boards. The price per board

started at $3.50 each. He sold out the entire contents of the storage area for almost $3,000! Since he had found a product that was in great demand with *no competition*, he decided to look for more barn board sources in the area.

The art director now has a profitable entrepreneurial avocation. He employs two part-time people to dismantle large farm sheds, barns, and old buildings which he purchases after location trips. He also now owns a large metal storage building on his suburban five-acre plot, which is a miniature "old lumber" supply outlet. Its sales net him thousands of dollars annually, more, perhaps, then he could make with conservative investments. It is an important supplementary source of income during these inflationary times. Moreover, this example points to the *innovativeness* found in successful, low-cost investments.

Turning Your Hobby Into An Inflation-Proof Business

A retired insurance sales representative, who had been a private pilot over a period of twenty-five years, was intrigued by aircraft of World War I vintage. He had collected photos, art prints, and scale models of Curtiss "Jenny"; period aircraft; the American "Eagle"; and other early aircraft designs.

On a western trip several years ago, he spent a few weeks at a dude ranch in Arizona. While inspecting the interiors of several barns on the property during his spare time, he saw part of a ragged, fabric-covered fuselage of an airplane hanging from the cables in the dimly lit loft.

He quickly climbed to the loft and examined the dusty, but sturdy, fuselage framework of an aircraft in awed silence. He also discovered the torn, time-ravaged wings stacked in a corner, covered with layers of dusty hay. He recognized the find as the skeleton of a Curtiss "Jenny"–a prize antique aircraft!

Within hours he had arranged for its purchase from the ranch owner. Curiously enough, the ranch owner had inherited the Jenny from the previous owner. The original owner had discovered the abandoned aircraft in his field years before, and had towed it into the barn for safe-keeping. The retired insurance representative offered the owner $500 for all of the aircraft components, and it was accepted on the spot. While it seemed a bit high at the time for tattered parts, his entrepreneurial mind was thinking ahead.

A year later, the rebuilt, refurbished antique aircraft sold for $10,000 *twenty times* the original investment.

The former insurance representative is now a full-time antique aircraft "finder" who has, over the past several years, located about nine old aircraft. Seven of these were sold for high prices. Two prize antiques are on display at his home hangar. His spare-time income as an entrepreneur is immpressive and welcome during inflation. At the same time, his experience illustrates the use to which knowledge and hobbies can be put.

Are you intrigued by classic antique cars, gourmet foods, herb farming, old railway cars, or Christmas tree farming? You may want to check out investment opportunities in these and related areas.

What about new ideas? How can you put these to work successfully with a minimum investment to bring a profitable return despite inflationary pressure? To illustrate the diversity of new ideas and programs inspired by entrepreneurs, we have presented a few case histories of people who developed their new ideas into profitable ventures. Here are two novel and unique experiences.

The "Borrowed" Idea That Built A Fortune

Toy industry publications have, over the years, periodically featured an unusual story of a financially-frustrated homemaker who lived in a modest income neighborhood in Philadelphia. She single-handedly (and against great odds), put her entrepreneurial idea into operation. Her dogged, persistent plan flourished into a successful sales program which in later years brought her into national prominence as a business executive in the toy industry.

The enterprising mother of four children, and wife of a hard-working (but struggling) plant electrician found she could not seem to stretch her weekly budget. This was twenty-three years ago. She dreamed of making extra money–enough somehow–to be able to purchase new wardrobes for her children, her husband, and herself. She also wanted to refurbish the clean but rather drab house in which they lived. She could not take a daytime job because of her small children. And part-time work at that time was not plentiful.

One night, she was invited to a beauty products "party" at which a young woman demonstrated applying and using beauty creams and products. Later, over coffee, the young woman passed out order blanks and descriptive brochures. Thinking about this experience later at home, the young homemaker became intrigued with the idea of presenting doll and toy "demonstrations." She thought that with a minimum of money, she could purchase a supply of dolls, toys, and other items in a low price range, which she could sell directly to low-income families.

She felt she could demonstrate features of the dolls, toys, and recreational items to other homemakers over coffee and cake in her home, and in theirs. She could also prepare order blanks which she would later leave with the women. Then, in a day or two, she would collect these with cash, and prepare to deliver the merchandise.

One night she outlined her idea to her husband. He listened patiently, then gave her $50 he had been saving secretly for her birthday gift. He advised her that once the money had been spent to *forget* the whole idea. But she would not forget it. In spite of the dire warnings and predictions of failure from professional toy salespeople she had contacted, the young homemaker persisted in the implementation of her plan.

She located a toy wholesaler who sold her five cartons of new toys and dolls, doll clothing, and toy shovels for her $50. Impressed by her demonstrated interest and determination, he told her if she sold these items, he would extend her credit on future sales.

The woman's first "toy demonstration" amounted to about $75 in new orders. Three more toy parties that month brought the sales totals past $450. Now she was more than convinced that she was on the right track.

Months later, there was more than enough money to buy a number of things for her family. Despite her neglected housework, she continued her unique sales programs; this resulted in her business mushrooming during the next two years. She was forced to move her toy demonstration business to a small warehouse several miles away. This was because the family was unable to move about the house now crammed with cartons of toys, bags filled with new doll clothing, and hundreds of dolls in paper wrappings!

Her husband, who had been doing all of her accounting and administrative work in his spare time, finally quit his job and joined her as a partner and business manager.

Today, the toy distribution business, which this bright young entrepreneur founded is a $12 million enterprise. Operating out of a $1 million office building, there is a 75,000 square foot warehouse nearby.

This is all situated on a fifteen acre-tract of land. The company of which she is now Chairman of the Board, employs about 800 people at peak seasons, and has a full-time staff of about seventy-five. The street on which the operation is located was named appropriately enough, "Dream Lane." And its enterprising executive has been honored numerous times for her inspirational techniques.

This is one classic example of two of the traits helpful in becoming a success: *recognizing an opportunity* and *having the determination to take the risk and see it through.*

Can a janitorial service return an impressive profit to enterprising workers? Yes, indeed! This type of service can be handled without too much difficulty at night or on weekends. Sex or age is almost immaterial, and the business can be started without much capital or equipment.

Guts and Determination

One case history on this: Two young women in a small Pennsylvania community near several industrial parks wanted to open a dress shop in which each could share needed time for sales work. Upon extensive investigations of a few retail dress operations nearby, however, they found store hours were long, and customer demands were quite frustrating. Inventories, they learned, could cost thousands in cash and credit, and were climbing because of growing inflation. Rents and employee salaries also took an appreciable part of the gross income of those stores. Competition, too, trimmed volume of sales. Their original idea was discarded after some intense soul-searching.

Later, one of the women learned (quite by accident) of a janitorial service being offered for sale by a retiring couple. They had owned it for more than twenty years. At first examination, the business seemed about as "unglamorous" as it could get. Yet more research revealed it to be *well-established, profitable, and non-competitive.*

A meeting with the couple who owned the business resulted in discovering that the operation could be purchased for less than $10,000. The purchase price included a small pickup truck. Without consulting anyone, the women quickly put down a deposit of $100 in cash, and signed a letter of intent to purchase.

One week later, after lengthy family conferences, the two women returned with a check for the full amount of the sales figure. The following week, dressed in old pants, tops, gloves, and carrying brooms, mops, and pushing vacuum cleaners, the entrepreneurs were introduced to the various buildings which were the small cleaning firm's responsibilities.

Three years later, after countless hours of hard work and with little time off for relaxation, the two women sold the janitorial business. It had been expanded, the selling price was $80,000, *eight times the purchase price!* The buyer was a large maintenance firm. It netted the pair an excellent profit, to say the least. Since one of the families was moving out of the area, they decided to liquidate the operation. The parting was made easier by being able to savor the fruits of their successful entrepreneurial effort.

This case history illustrates another important trait for those planning to be in business for themselves: *hard work pays off handsomely.*

Inventions As Opportunities

What about *new* products you may have developed for the marketplace, or *inventions* you feel may make you a great deal of money? Have you also asked yourself, "How will these do in this inflationary period?" If you examine your idea or invention, your new product, which had been inspired in this perspective, you can think about the planning needed to get your "brainchild" to the market.

In the case of new products you have originated (a new type of lamp or, perhaps, work gloves), you must obviously interest a manufacturer in its purchase.

Realistically, these new product samples would be extremely difficult to patent since there are dozens of glove and lamp patents now on file. But you instruct your patent attorney to begin a search, and make an application so technically involved that your invention can be offered on the basis of "Patent Applied For."

When you present your product to a few lamp manufacturers showing the unique "adhesive holder" feature, you find mild interest displayed. But you are told, "We can't gamble on an *unknown, untried* product. It would cost us thousands of dollars just to tool up!"

As an entrepreneur, you have the option of doing one of several things. You can contact a reputable marketing specialist for recommendations on selling the product to the consumer; getting the product made by a small company, and then selling it yourself through mail order advertising in national or regional magazines and newspapers. Your final choice is to forget about it altogether, and investigate another opportunity.

A marketing specialist will charge you an hourly rate for consultation which could run from $50 to $100. The specialist might give you a list of sales companies through which you could market the product. These would include distributors, sales representatives, and dealers.

You could also contact one of the several advertising agencies in your area which markets consumer products for clients by means of individually created advertising campaigns. There is no cost involved when you meet with these advertising experts the first time, because they are usually receptive to prospective advertising clients.

If your product has "inflation-proof" marketing characteristics, or is related to an area of business or industry that can resist the ravages of inflation and actually prosper during this period, you have an excellent advantage.

The Inflation-Proof Industries

What are the "inflation-proof" business or industrial areas? Economists such as Lacy Hunt, Senior Economist, Fidelity Bank, Philadelphia, who is nationally known for his knowledgeable observations of the U.S. economy, states that the food industry (from processing to packaging) is inflation-proof. Other areas include the tobacco industry (from manufacturing to sales); liquor and beverages; automotive and machine rebuilding; and service-oriented industries.

Others report that computer manufacturing, and computer-oriented industries which assist in increasing plant productivity, will be inflation-proof. But there is some disagreement on this. A few have pointed out that computer-oriented industries are "cyclical" in nature and may not be able to stand the rising inflation pressures.

The experts also point to private schools, vocational schools, and various areas of the medical field, institutional feeding, janitorial services, truck gardening, and dairy farming as offering opportunities in periods of severe inflation. Tailoring will see a sudden emergence, because people will repair clothing rather than buy new apparel.

We will expand upon these specific fields in later chapters in terms of establishing businesses.

Economist Hunt also adds that new technologies (lasar beam oriented; high vacuum processing; solar energy areas) will flourish in spite of inflationary forces.

Again in terms of launching a new product, you may want to consider starting a mail-order operation. By inserting advertisements in national magazines, you can reach thousands of potential customers directly without going through conventional distribution channels.

A Mail Order Business As An Inflation Hedge

A former eastern advertising executive who liked sports (and frequently worked as an official during semi-professional football seasons), had a difficult time keeping track of play scores while on the field. This was due to the fact that no scoreboards were in operation. He devised a simple, ruled, plastic-laminated card, measuring about 2½"x3". By using a short grease pencil, he could note scoring easily, then quickly stuff the small score card into his pocket. When completed, he could wipe away the figures in seconds.

When the product was not accepted by sports products manufacturers, he decided to have the card produced at his own expense, then market it himself. He placed an order with his printer for 3,000 units, wrote his own advertisements, and placed these in various sports magazines and selected newspapers. The response the first year was excellent. He received more than 800 orders at $3.00 each, plus postage. The product has sold well for the past six years. He has also added a second product to this line, which is also moving well.

If you are interested in this type of distribution, there are numerous mail-order publications, books, and direct mail associations to help the novice mail order operator. Magazines such as "Modern Mechanic," "Popular Science," and others will send rate cards and mail order advertising information when you write and request it.

Unless you are experienced in dealing with printers, artists, and with the purchasing of materials (paperstock, plastic sheets, etc.) in bulk quantities, let someone more experienced handle this for you. An art director or free-lance advertising specialist can assist you in this area.

Let's consider the marketing aspects of a new game idea, and later the new invention.

Inventing New Games

Ever since the success of the game "Monopoly"™, millions of people have felt that they, too, had a "winner" in terms of a new board game. This is most likely due to the tremendous amount of publicity regarding the sweeping success of Monopoly™.

A check with the editors of various toy industry publications, representatives of the Toy Council of America, and research and development directors of various game manufacturers, however, has revealed that the *unsolicited* game idea has little or no chance of being accepted by this group today. In fact, even the smaller game manufacturers refuse to look at new game ideas, or three-dimensional models, sent to them by novice game developers.

As a potential game developer, if you are one, you probably won't take "no" for an answer. Listen, however, to what these game companies say:

MILTON BRADLEY: "We *never* purchase new game ideas from amateur game developers, or from the 'outside'."

SELCHOW-RICHTER: "We develop our own games in-house through our own R & D people. We *never* look at unsolicited game ideas."

DAYSTAR COMPANY: "We *do not* purchase new game ideas from people we do not know; nor do we have contracts with anyone but *professional* developers. There is too much legal hassle involved when you work with amateurs."

The industry representatives did suggest that if you feel your idea for a new game is outstanding (and *no* board games are recommended), then you should contact a professional game designer. And where do you find such a person? His/her name and corporate firms involved in game design and development are listed in directories published by "Playthings," "Toy and Hobby World," and similar trade papers. Designers do occasionally purchase new ideas from the outside, but must work out all legal details with you in advance of submitting new game ideas. The trend in new games now is in the molded plastic, three-dimen-sional expensive variety which usually incorporate electronic sound and action.

The subject of inventions and the entrepreneur's role in this area is a controversial one, depending upon the authority contacted. Also, the picture in terms of making a great deal of money, is not a bright one. For example, it is reliably estimated that about 100,000 various types of patents are granted each year to individuals, companies, corporations, educational institutions, foreigners, research organizations, and government agencies.

However, according to such authoritative groups as the American Society of Inventors, Narbeth, Pa.; Inventor's Club of America, Springfield, Maine; and noted patent attorneys, only *one percent* of the patents granted annully ever get marketed profitably! With inflation, that figure could drop further.

The large manufacturing corporations such as General Motors, Sperry Corporation, Boeing Aircraft, and others (including government agencies), turn down thousands of unsolicited patent ideas for products because they have their own research and development teams working for them. As a result, when a new invention or product is developed by these corporations and governmental groups, it is assigned to that body. Therefore no royalties or cash payments need ever be made to any individuals! Millions of dollars are saved through this legal structure.

Yes, lightening does strike occasionally. Some fortunate inventor will be rewarded handsomely for years of effort. But too many will have spent their $2,000 in legal fees, patent searches, disclosures, drawings and documents, for an impressive piece of paper with a government seal and little else. The basic reason for not getting new inventions into the market place is: *lack of marketing knowledge*. It is one thing to develop a new idea, and quite another to sell it successfully to a manufacturer. The "closed door" policy of corporations is a part of this invention syndrome.

Beware of Invention Promoters

Too many novice inventors have been ripped off tragically by certain invention promoters who pretend to do an intensive marketing job for the individual, for a fee. Their ads pop up in all of the popular "mechanics" magazines and in some daily newspapers. But the truth of the matter is, these promoters *cannot do anything more* than you can in circulating copies of your patent to companies! There may be legitimate promoters, of which I am not aware, but these individuals charge a steep fee for sending photocopied versions or reproductions to a list of corporations. The corporate recipients more often than not, throw the material into the waste basket! Some of these promoters charge inventors an additional consultation fee which is a fraud! Stay away from these predators!

Again, you are probably determined to find a way to market your invention. You have made an investment and now you want a return. You may be interested to know that both small and large investors are responsible for financing and manufacturing more than one-half of all inventions and new products getting into the marketplace.

How To Determine If Your Invention Will Make Money

Will your invention *save money, time or labor* for someone else? Will it still be useful and helpful during a recession? Will people find the price attractive in spite of rising prices? Can it be sold in mass quantity, or is it limited to a special group of people? Consultation with an accredited marketing specialist might be in order here. Also suggested are talks with small manufacturers who specialize in building equipment, tool, or products for consumers. Listen to what they tell you.

Send copies of your patent together with a written news release (a detailed explanation in the form of a news story) to editors of trade magazines in the field you want to reach. Also include a sharp, black and white glossy photograph for reproduction. You may attract the attention of the buyers of big retail chain stores such as J.C. Penney, Woolco, K-Mart, Western Auto Stores, and other firms. A number of successful inventors have done just that.

The tips and suggestions presented here are among those which some inventors have used to market their inventions backed by carefully-planned and executed advertising/promotional efforts by professional marketing specialists in the field. Other inventors have gone through the sales distribution routes of large wholesale distributors after the product was manufactured. These are the only ways to make any money out of an invention. Funds for this effort must obviously be budgeted and spent prudently.

It is vital for you to explore every avenue of marketing for a way to earn a profitable return on your investment. If your funds have been committed to costs of obtaining the patent, then it is mandatory that you expend additional money to get it into the marketplace. But do it wisely, professionally, and do not get taken in by the rip off artists!

Part Two:

The Best Investments For The 80's

3 Purchasing Land And Buildings At Auction

One of the best ways to earn income from real estate is to buy land, farms, houses, small apartments, and homes at auctions. Despite the growing inflation rate, income from real estate can net you a 15% to 20% and higher return annually, according to experienced real estate investment specialists.

Advantages Of Buying At Auctions

A distinct advantage in purchasing real estate at auctions is that you are directly involved with determining a sales price. You will be bidding against others, however, who also recognize a value in the property. But there will be times when you may turn out to be the *lone bidder* and you will have bought the property at your bid price! Auctions are perhaps the most basic form of selling.

If you have never attended a real estate auction either in the country, in a city, or in a small town, there are a number of things you need to be aware of if you intend to participate as a bidder and potential buyer. Before I relate several of my auction-buying experiences at land and farm auctions, I would like to point out two distinct differences in real estate auctions.

Types of Auctions

1. *Absolute Auctions*
You will see this definitive announcement at the top of a notice at an auction sale which is usually advertised from thirty to sixty days in advance of the sales date. In the case of the absolute auction, if you are the highest bidder at the final bidding, you will have bought the property *regardless* of the level of the price.

It will be "knocked down" (sold) to you if your bid is the final one.

You then give the auctioneer's representatives a check for 15% of the price you have bid, which is accepted for the seller. The balance of the payment will be made at settlement at their offices within a period of sixty days.

In addition, at absolute real estate auctions, there are *no minimum* or "starting" price bids. This is a decided advantage for the bidder.

2. *Regular Auction*
There is a marked difference in this type of real estate auction as opposed to the absolute sale. To begin with, there is generally a "floor price." That is, the auctioneer will announce to the gathered group of bidders, "The bidding on this property by agreed terms will start at $25,000!" That is known as a "floor bid."

At the conclusion of the bidding, when the highest possible bid has been obtained from the proposed buyer, the auctioneer or a representative will approach the seller. There will be a short conference. If the owner decides that the "knocked down" bid was too low, the seller can exercise an option to reject the bid-in price. This happens a lot of the time and the time spent by would-be buyers is fruitless in such circumstances.

How To Bargain For The Best Price

On the other hand, there are occasions when a determined, experienced real estate auctioneer will bring the highest bidder and the seller together at the site for a "horse-trading" session. And if the auctioneer is persuasive enough, the seller will be advised that the price is as much as he/she could hope to receive. If convinced (and a number are), the seller will then accept a deposit check from the buyer, extend a handshake, and will usually sign an "Agreement of Sale" on the spot.

How To Prepare For The Auction

You will see some strange things at a farm auction, and at other real estate auctions in terms of emotions and frustrations of those who are outbid. But first of all, you should always inspect the site–land, buildings, or the property–prior to the actual sales date. Posted or advertised notices will indicate an inspection date.

Some professional buyer/investors will get an appraisal, or check the tax records at the township office or county seat. They will visit the tax assessor's office, if possible, to check the estimated value of the property, and its present assessment.

Where To Get Information About Forthcoming Auctions

Most real estate buyers will get notices of future auctions by mail from several auction houses, or from well-known auctioneers. You can get your name on various lists to note future sales of apartments, small hotels, plants, warehouses, farms, suburban property, and other real estate. This gives you time to make a decision on attending the event, or in your case, to add to your future knowledge.

Notices of real estate auctions can also be found in many small town weekly newspapers, farm publications, on posters in stores and service stations in various communities, and on the properties themselves being advertised for sale.

A First-Time Experience

My first real estate venture came about quite accidentally while attending an auction in a small community. After reading the advertisement in a newspaper, I found there would be a quantity of furniture offered, with some antiques and numerous chairs. I was interested in the purchase of several old chairs. I arrived at the site in the morning of the appointed day. The property being offered at auction was a large stone residence with an historical background. It was said to have been used as an Officer's headquarters building during the Revolutionary War, but had been rebuilt extensively over the intervening years.

I listened to the auctioneer's detailed announcements of all the items which were being put up for sale. I realized I would be at the site for many hours before the auctioneer would get to the household items.

As the auctioneer opened the bidding for the main house and lot, I suddenly shouted a bid of $10,000, thinking I might expedite the bidding and move things along! I did this despite the fact that I had no investment funds set aside!

Strangely enough, *no one else* in the throng made another bid over mine! I was somewhat apprehensive as I heard the auctioneer calling out my bid for the second time without any response from a soul. Then he announced, "Sold to this gentleman for $10,000!" He had "knocked down" the house to me–*sold it at the price I had bid!*

To say the least, I was quite surprised, and shortly after wrote a check to the auctioneer as a deposit. His assistant took my name, address, and other details, telling me an Agreement of Sale would be mailed to me within a few days, confirming the sale. I forgot completely about purchasing any chairs.

As I walked toward the car, following an inspection of the property, I felt I had got a bargain. As I opened my car door, I was approached by a gentleman who had been standing several feet from me during my bidding. He had not participated in the bidding for some unknown reason. He asked me quickly if I would accept $2,500 from him in return for signing over the right to purchase the property for $10,000! I could have made $2,500 on the spot! But I refused politely, since I now felt certain the property was worth more than I had bid.

Another gentleman who had been at the property auction had not bid, he explained, because he could not communicate with his wife properly to get her views on the possible purchase. He had obtained my address from the auctioneer. During our conversation, he offered me $5,000 for my Agreement of Sale on the old stone building! He, too, was politely refused.

Obtaining Financing

That same day, I visited a local savings and loan institution not too far from my home. I posed the question, "What amount of mortgage could I get for the property, assuming I owned it free and clear of any encumbrances?" The president of the institution replied, "We would give you a $20,000 mortgage any time on that basis."

Next, I privately borrowed $10,000 from a good friend for a few days. This made it possible for me to own the recently acquired stone building outright with no debt. I obtained the $20,000 mortgage funds, then repaid the $10,000 quickly to my friend. I spent $4,000 from the remaining $10,000 to remodel the building, and also improved the appearance of the overgrown weeded lot. I pocketed the remaining $6,000. I then rented the property to a family for a period of six years. At the end of the period, I sold the stone building and lot for $39,000, paying off the $20,000 mortgage. This left me wtih a balance of $19,000, a very good profit return for a $10,000 investment made as a result of my auction bid.

I have purchsed numerous farms, land, and buildings since that time at absolute auctions. I do not attend regular real estate auction sales unless there is something exceptional offered.

Becoming An Expert

The thing to remember if you are planning to purchase real estate at auction for investment purposes, is to attend one or two different auctions (or perhaps more) depending upon the amount of time you have. Get to different auctions to see how bidding is carried out. Become familiar with bidding procedures–bidding in mulitple sums as bidders move up their bids to get a top offer established.

Then you ought to make a list of real estate auctioneers in a loose-leaf notebook, with some history on each firm, and where they are located. You might even want to check with your local banker, and some real estate brokers in your area, to find out about the credentials and experience of the real estate auction firms. Below is a worksheet form you might want to adapt to your purposes.

Real Estate Auction Data Summary

1. Name of auctioneer _____

2. Address _____

3. City and State _____

4. Telephone number_____

5. Credentials/Affiliations_____

_____

_____

_____

6. Type of real estate sold _____

_____

7. My purchase of real estate with this firm:

Date: _____

Price: $_____

Property description: _____

_____

_____

Present income value: $_____

Get your name posted on mailing lists for notices of future real estate auctions in your county or in neighboring counties. Look at the literature you receive–the physical description of the properties being offered by the auction firms for the owners.

Beware Of Unlicensed Auctioneers

In most states, auctioneers handling real estate sales are licensed and bonded for obvious reasons. Occasionally, someone who is not licensed or bonded will conduct a real estate auction sale and will, unfortunately, have "shills," or accomplices in the bidding crowd. These people will try to boost the bids artificially high by making heavy bids–those that are considerably higher than the previous bid made. And the unsuspecting bidder, naively believing the property is worth more than he previously thought, will be suckered into purchasing an overinflated piece of property.

These incidents are rare in most states since auctions are monitored carefully by real estate brokers, authorities, tax representatives, and township officials. Incidents like the one described above happened in two southwestern states in remote village areas because of the lack of proper supervision by authorities. Again, you should always know with whom you are dealing in any real estate transaction. Know the reputation of the firm, and be fully informed on the situation.

Things To Look For At Auctions

When you are serious about the possibility of-making a purchase at a real estate auction, here are a few tips:

Get close to the auctioneer. Let him/her know you are bidding by holding up your hand on each bid. You can also use a gloved hand, a folded piece of paper, but make certain he has you in his gaze. Listen to the multiple sum being asked for from bidders. Be decisive in your bidding. Remember the amount of money you can afford to invest or spend on the sale. Don't get in over your head by over-bidding, or because you think the property is a bargain. It won't be if you over-bid!

You're A Land Owner!

Like any other large purchase, once your bid has been accepted by the auctioneer on the "knocked down" as the best offer on price, you will be committed to a deposit of 15% of the total amount of your bid price. Then you will be legally bound by the Agreement of Sale to complete the final purchase.

There are other sources of information on real estate auctions. These include city, county, and township tax offices where delinquent tax properties (including homes and farms) have been abandoned or foreclosed. They are posted every month. These are "tax recovery" sales or "Sheriff's sales" auctions which bring in revenue to the county or township handling the sale. By searching and studying the offered properties carefully, you may be able to purchase an income-producing property that will repay its original price over several times.

Using Real Estate As A Financial Lever

Remeber this. Real estate is excellent as a "lever" in financing, particularly during periods of inflation, and is often an inflation hedge. And when you own several properties, and perhaps an appreciable amount of land acreage, you will be in a good position to obtain substantial bank financing by mortgaging your combined equity.

Renting Your Property To Tenants

Once you have purchased a small farm, for example, and you survey the buildings which still remain on the propery, you may be able to think of several ways to have these facilities begin to build an immediate return for you. The risk/reward principle should be put to work moving cash into your bank account.

I have remodeled old farm buildings remaining on several of the farms purchased at auctions over the years. If the farm is located near a village, a small town, or is on the edge of a suburban community, you have an excellent chance of renting out the buildings. Do people want to rent a farmhouse for a residence? You bet they do! If the price is right on the rental, you will not have a problem.

Be sure to protect your lease against inflation by having a clause included which states that the rent will be reviewed annually and adjusted if the Consumer Price Index rises.

If you are not mechanically inclined, have a carpenter or a small contractor survey the buildings with you to determine what work will be needed. Even if you pay these people for their time, it will be worth that small sum of money to you to know how much much must be done to put the building into first-class condition for rental. The house rental will bring you the most monthly return, next to leasing the land to a farmer for crop cultivation.

I have had farms rebuilt and have replaced both plumbing and heating systems with good success. These houses were immediate income-builders and imporved the value of the property for later resale. When someone lives on the property, using the house and small buildings nearby, it enhances the value of that parcel of land. A rundown, abandoned dwelling and support buildings have a negative effect on the farm and land value to neighbors and potential buyers, who feel most of the value of the property has slipped away due to neglect.

Your Strategy Plan

When you get to a real estate auction, have a fairly well-established plan of strategy developed in your mind. If you go there with the idea that the property you hope to buy is an investment opportunity for you for the short-term or long-term, you will then be able to bid intelligently. You will also know within a few hundred dollars, what you can afford to invest in the land or property being auctioned.

If you are attending a farm sale at which dairy cattle and other animals and farm machinery are up for auction, I would not pass up any bidding in this area unless you are planning to actively farm, or have plans to re-sell.

"High Stakes" Auctions

Some auction sales at farm sites can be startling in terms of the high bids offered. For example, Pennsylvania has some of the finest farming soil in the United States situated in one county: Lancaster, a south central locality. Here, top soil runs almost four to five feet deep! Most of the county is dotted with hundreds of large, excellent farms with modern barns and huge dairy herds. Farm acreage here is normally sold by real estate brokers for about $8,000 to $10,000 per acre!

Many of the farm families located in Lancaster county are of a religious-oriented group known as the Amish. They are hard-working, thrifty people who are largely self-sufficient. They use mules and horses for field work rather than tractors, which their religious beliefs prohibit. During the past five years, as older Amish farmers have retired, or whose family members have died, their 200- to 400-acre farms have been auctioned to high bidders. I attended several of these Amish farm auctions to check land prices being bid by hopeful buyers, and got the shock of my life at the amount of each bid!

Many of the families have lived in Lancaster County for the past 100 years, with their grandparents having farmed the same plots of ground. They are reluctant to see land sold off at auction to real estate buyers. They know the land will be sub-divided in some cases, and sold at huge profits at homesites. As a result, many Amish farmers have developed a bidding strategy at these Lancaster County farm auctions.

It is not surprising to see as many as 100 farmers and their families all in black hats and bonnets gathered near the auctioneer. Also gathered in most crowds are numerous real estate brokers, out-of-state syndicate buyers, private investors, and farm association representatives. They are on hand as observers to see what happens to the farm.

The auctioneer (one of several who live in the county, or in nearby communities, and who are well-known to these farm people and have their trust) will begin by auctioning all dairy cattle, mules, wagons, and household goods.

Then, usually after a short luncheon period where food has been prepared and sold by local church-women, the sale of the property (land and buildings) will begin in earnest.

The auctioneer will normally set a "floor price" for bidding, because in many instances these are not absolute auctions. But there is no doubt in his mind that the farm will be sold at the top dollar value because of the tremendous demand for Lancaster County farm land.

The bidding will generally start at $5,000 an acre, and "asked" at the rate of $1,500 per bid upward. The bidding will be spirited. The auctioneer has learned to study faces and moves closely at these auctions because each bid is a serious one. Then you will hear two or three farmers move each bid higher above those being bid by "outsiders"–the real estate brokers or private buyers.

The farm being sold at this particular auction was a fifty-acre tobacco, corn, and grain tract with large pasture land for cattle. It was here I listened in amazement to a lone Amish farmer in faded denim overalls and shirt, black hat and beard, keeping pace in the bidding at $10,000 per acre with two real estate brokers. Then one dropped, leaving a lone outside buyer paired with the farmer in the final sessions of the auction. At the final bid, the farmer, looking cool and unperturbed, eyed the auctioneer closely. To his left, a perspiring, nervous man in a Stetson, grey jacket and trousers, waited for the next bid. The bid from the farmer was now at $12,000 per acre.

The auctioneer was hammering his gavel, repeating the bid of $12,000 he had received. Would the "outside" buyer go higher? There was a long pause, then the "outsider" dropped his gaze. He had given up because he had been outbid. There was a look of resignation on his face. He would not go any higher.

The auctioneer then "knocked down" the farm to the Amish man for a final price of $12,000 per acre, or a total of $600,000! A high price indeed, but the Amish farmer knew the price was worth the investment. There were cries of approval from the mingled farmers and their families. This was a strategic victory for them.

There was no fear on the auctioneer's part that the money due for the final sale would be forthcoming. I had seen these thrifty farmers reach into their jacket pockets and pull out worn leather pouches. Then they would begin to count stacks of $100 bills for deposit, and pick up the Agreement of Sale with their left hand. They were prudent farmers and had ample funds. The outbidded private investor walked away slowly, shaking his head. He was no match for this group. The Amish could pool as much as *one million dollars* for a farm purchase among them, if that was necessary!

They would leave the "outsiders" to purchase the five- and ten-acre chicken and small truck farms at the fringes of the county because this was not the prime farmland all sought to protect and preserve.

The Moral Of The Story

I think there is a valuable lesson to be learned in the experience narrated here, if you are interested in acquiring property at auction. Time and again, the real estate brokers and outside buyers will get their heads "bloodied" when they attempt to outbid Amish farmers in their own backyard. There is an unwritten agreement among these neighboring farmers to protect each farm offered for sale from getting into outside hands and thus reducing available acreage for farming.

Auctions In Big Cities

If you attend an auction of real estate property in center cities, particularly large cities in the East, where buildings on fair-sized lots are being offered to bidders, you will find intense competition from professional buyers representing real estate syndicates or trusts. And if you note that the auction announcement reads: "Terms: $25,000 deposit by cash, or certified check accompanied by bank letter of guaranteed payment," you can be certain the "big leaguers" (professional buyers) will be on hand. This is because the potential and actual value of the property is apparent. The tip here is to listen. Do not bid. Simply observe and take notes. Use this as a learning experience. The same thing holds true in the case of small manufacturing plants being auctioned, and large apartment developments, motels, hotels, and retail stores.

If you are starting out as a real estate investment entrepreneur pursuing the auction route, stay out of the heavy bid areas described above. You will find many other opportunities in smaller cities, communities, or towns–such as old farm buildings, small farms, small shops, and similar properties. These are generally not of interest to the real estate syndicates because these groups are oriented to the investments in large city projects brought at auctions.

The Best Areas Of Real Estate Investment

Small town real estate investments are recommended over investments in property in cities during rampant inflationary periods. There is much more stability inherent in this kind of property, because there is less chance of civil disorder, crime, and other problems associated with a big city.

Becoming more aware of the size and scope of real estate auctions is a part of your strategy covered in detail earlier. You must know your limitations in terms of your risk/reward objectives, amount of capital available or which you are able to secure, and the amount of time you can devote to acquiring property. Then you must plan to develop the investment into a profit center.

Here are some background tips to add to your knowledge, prior to attending an auction:

Things To Know Before Attending An Auction

1. If you are attending a "Sheriff's sale" auction, and have decided after inspecting the property being auctioned, to buy it, make certain you bring along a certified check for at least $1,500 for use as deposit money, in the event you are the high bidder. City tax bureaus, and township and county tax revenue departments normally specify deposit checks be certified.

2. Have a detailed list of the properties being auctioned in your hand prior to the time of bidding. Check these and prices offered in the bidding, along with your own, if you participate. Keep a record of prices accepted.

3. Listen to the auctioneer carefully. It is not the "patter" he/she is uttering that is important–it is the *multiple sum* being asked for, or the proposed price level he is looking for as he calls out a figure. Keep a mental track of the bids, or note them on a pad, so you know where the bidded price is pegged.

4. When you have made your successful "buy" bid, and the one that has been accepted by the auction as "final," make your deposit quickly. Get your receipt for your down payment, plus a copy of the Agreement of Sale. Make certain that all of the Agreement terms are spelled out so there will be no surprises at the time of final settlement.

5. Now that you have made your down payment on the real estate, what are your plans for financing? Can you cover the balance of money due with cash? Will you mortgage the remaining balance? Will you go to private sources, seek bank mortgages, go to a financial institution, find an insurance company, use equity in some other property? Remember, commercial banks can charge higher mortgage interest rates than formal financial institutions, so check this first carefully. It's all a part of your inflation hedge strategy.

The Payoff

It has been my experience after purchasing buildings or a tract of land at an auction, that plans for developing profitable payout follow quickly. But I also include a tabulation of tax costs, and any maintenance charges that will be involved. In several cases, where I purchased farms with substantial acreage, I rented all available ground to a neighboring farmer. They are always looking to expand cash crop acreage. This is an additional inflation hedge you will want. Then I inspect all of the buildings carefully for the second and third times. I look at the barns, sheds, and the farm house itself. Barns can be rented easily to neighboring farmers who never seem to have capacity for hay or grain storage. If the lower portion is built of concrete and has good drainage, it can be rented as an additional cattle barn for use during winter months.

As I explained earlier, farm houses can be rented without much difficulty once all improvements have been made–new wiring, plumbing, and modern heating facilities. Sheds are ideal for monthly storage rentals.

You can readily see from this that you can earn an immediate monthly return of several hundred dollars on your investment, with a few dollars and time expended. Certainly this is significant in terms of diminished returns from other sources during these severe inflation cycles. Also, don't forget to establish a "tax account" to cover real estate taxes on the property.

Other Income Sources From Auctioned Property

Other immediate income return from purchased property can be generated if you purchase a small hotel, motel, small retail store, or small rental property. The cash flow to you would begin weekly or monthly, depending upon your terms. Thus, you have capital for future investments, or have added to your regular income as a hedge.

I have had friends tell me about a number of auctions held in rural areas with final bidded prices coming in at surprisingly low levels, and they weren't there to do any bidding! The reason: lack of information. They had no advance knowledge of these auctions because they were not advertised widely.

Entrepreneurs don't wait for an opportunity to fall into their laps. They go out and discover investment opportunities, making efforts to obtain information on a situation which interests them. I advised my friends to take the time and make a regular habit of visiting small towns and communities out beyond the city limits. They should stop at the local newspaper office, rather than a city hall or township building.

You will find that most small town newspapers carry all of the area news, ranging from farm sales, cattle and farm animal sales, to news about residents, and auctions being scheduled. These will be either carried as news items (since they are of great interest to the residents), or there will be "display ads" announcing future real estate auctions.

Like my friends, you should ask questions about these future real estate auctions in the immediate area. You will discover quite pleasantly that rural newspaper people are considerably more friendly than large city newspaper employees. They do not see many "strangers" in their course of employment, and when they do, they are helpful and courteous.

A polite query from you about an auction and you will have the newspaper person thumbing through a file quickly. He/she will tell you where and when the auction will be held. And for a small price, you can purchase a copy of the newspaper with the name of the auctioneer and other details.

If you can make several stops in a twenty-five mile radius, visiting these small newspaper offices, you can easily gather a considerable amount of information about rural auctions being scheduled. This will give you an even chance with local bidders who will show up at the appointed time. And a call to the auctioneer may give you additional details, including a history of the property for sale.

The Need For Quick Action

Now that you know, among other things, the difference between an absolute auction and a regular auction, relating to real estate sales, and you see an opportunity in this area to expand your investments, get your planning started at the earliest possible time. The obvious need for expediency here is our serious, climbing rate of inflation. Values are affected in these times. And you need to be a bit sharper and more flexible in an effort to acquire land being sold at auction. You build a hedge through acquisition.

The right buy at the right price requires a bit more effort now than in years past. But as an investment, this is just another challenge to be faced and met intelligently and successfully.

4 Converting Acreage Investments Into Cash

Reasons For The Rise In The Cost Of Land

At the present time, farm acreage has been appreciating at the rate of about 25% annually. Since many investors regard ownership of land as an excellent inflation hedge, prices have been driven upwards sharply in some areas of the nation. For example, some farms in California's Imperial Valley, regarded as the finest vegetable soil in the country, have been sold for as high as $1 million! And the U.S. Agriculture Department, together with the General Accounting Office, has been investigating the sudden buying of farmland by foreign corporations and individuals during the past several years. This activity alone has caused prices of land in the West and Southwest to accelerate.

The states where farmland is in great demand by investors include Pennsylvania, California, Texas, Georgia, Illinois, Kansas, Iowa, Montana, and Washington.

Since food (corn, grains, vegetables, livestock, chickens, hogs, pigs, and turkeys) is produced in staggering quantities to meet today's domestic and foreign needs, land values will continue to increase for at least the next decade. Despite the fact that periodic recessions will dampen food prices with some significant reductions in meat and package goods, the agri-business industry will continue to grow, but at a smaller rate of annual profit.

New Method Of Land Use

We have covered the utilization of farm buildings and the rental of available farmhouses and sheds. But we have not explored new methods of land use by entrepreneurs.

The Sub-division

Perhaps one of the quickest and most profitable forms of return on investments in land is the sub-division and sale of building lots. I have purchased farms and later sub-divided a considerable portion of the acreage into half-acre building lots, which were sold for prices ranging from $2,000 to $6,500 each. Since these lots were beyond water and sewer lines of developed areas, this cost was borne by the purchasers–drilling of wells and building of cesspools and related sewage facilities.

Certainly all proposed housing development efforts must be approved first by your local township planning boards and utility authorities, in addition to complying with county and state regulations.

Let us assume you have purchased a fifty-acre farm a few miles off a main road, or a state or county highway. You have arranged for the rental of the farm buildings, but you have held out a fifteen-acre tract for future development. The thirty-five-acre section has been leased to a neighboring farmer for cultivation. This will bring you a very nice monthly income which will not only pay your annual property taxes, but will give you a nice profit.

Your Attorney's Role

A visit to a local attorney will not only be beneficial, but will also be profitable to you. He/she will assist in clearing any legal hurdles you may encounter securing approval for residential development on the land you own. A formal application will have to be made to the township zoning board, and your tax structure will obviously be altered on the land, following its approval for sale as building lots. Unless you receive written approval, you cannot proceed with sub-division planning.

Developing A Written Plan

As an entrepreneur, you have spent many hours thinking and planning about this land conversion, and you should have several detailed folders with portions of the plan developed in written form. A calendar of proposed steps in your program should also be included.

Folder #1: Record of land purchase, and date of purchase, together with sketch of dimensions of land owned from local tax assessor, or collector.

Folder #2: Proposed plan spelling out size of lots to be "cut out" of the fifteen-acre tract. Also include details on well-drilling and self-contained sewage facilities. Then include proposed selling price, *subject to change* after you consult with local builder.

Folder #3: Plan for advertising building lots, including proposed price; name of builder to be recommended to buyers; details on sales; names of buyers, and types of houses to be built on the lots. Include photos of sub-division, and views of completed homes for permanent file.

On the financial side, keep a detailed record of all your transactions; monies received, costs of preparation, and estimate of your state and federal taxes based on your profits.

The Surveyor's Role

Some words of advice: have an engineer/surveyor plot all of the lots so that titles and deeds to the unencumbered lots can be presented to purchasers at the time of settlement. And during the period prior to the actual survey and plotting of the land proposed to be sold as lots, the engineer should assist you in a topographical study of the land. Obviously, you are not going to sell lots at the bottom of a dry bed creek that could become flooded during a cloudburst and cause misery to some unsuspecting homeowner! The engineer will be able to assist you in these matters.

Making The Most Attractive Building Lots

Building lots are attractive only when they are *not too far* away from a highway; when they are on higher ground; and when they are located near trees in a pleasant setting.

In my own case, in one sub-divided development, I shared the cost of road construction with the contractor who built the homes.

Like any plan, you must follow-up each phase of your program. If you are doing work on the project in your spare time away from your regular job, it will mean a lot of hours in meetings, telephone calls, and trips to the local tax assessor and county planning departments. But it is all part of your investment strategy.

When To Use A Real Estate Broker

If you do not have the time to market or to meet prospective lot buyers, then place the project into a real estate brokers' hands at an agreed-upon commission on actual sales. You may even make a better profit.

City-bred people tend to think of modern farms in terms of dairy cattle, hay barns, yards filled with chickens, turkeys and ducks, while corn and pumpkins are grown in adjacent fields. This is not true any more, since modern highways now connect rural and urban communities. Millions of small truck farms, and large acreage farmers, make profitable incomes from direct marketing–roadside stands–at which everything, from milk to home-grown pork sausage, hams, and cider, is sold!

The Roadside Stand Venture

One eastern farmer who owned a large farm on which he grew sweet corn, melons, potatoes, cabbage, carrots, lettuce, numerous varieties of squash, and fruits grown in a small orchard, joined with a former food market owner to establish a small stand on his farm, next to a busy highway. The farmer was too busy working his farm to manage the roadside stand. But the partner devoted all of his time to the marketing task.

He spent several thousands of dollars constructing an attractive building complete with counters, cases, and a cold storage cabinet for cider. Following the opening, the roadside stand was a regular stop for tourists, residents of nearby communities, and commuters. The first season's gross topped $75,000! Five years later, a 40,000 square foot "roadside store" staffed with almost fifteen people with check-out counters now stands on the spot of the original market! Entrepreneurs should give this idea consideration.

The Meat Packing Venture

Another eastern farmer, who felt he was not getting a profitable return on his herd of twenty-five dairy cows, decided to raise Aberdeen Angus cattle, a quality beef animal, and several Hereford cattle, and sell the animals to a local meat packer at maturity. Later, he kept two of the steers for himself and his family and "dressed them" out for his own freezer locker. Word got out on his project, and he received five requests for large-quantity beef purchases.

The farmer prepared five more steers, then sold all of the meat for a profit of several thousands of dollars! And the following year, he devoted five acres of his farm to a "drive-in" meat market. He built a large retail meat market, and hired a full-time butcher and a helper.

While the market is several miles from the nearest community, his parking lot is crowded with cars five days a week! Beef, pork, poultry, and lamb are sold from the market in small and large quantities at excellent profits.

He has completed plans with a contractor who is going to build a frozen food locker on an adjoining acre of land owned by the farmer. The lockers in the building will be rented to people who purchase large quantities of meat. The building will be leased back to the contractor at an excellent fee.

The Advantages Of Being Out In The Sticks

The landowner estimates that if he had constructed his market, the food locker, and parking area at a suburban location, his cost would have reached about $750,000. But since he is in a rural-zoned area, his costs were one-tenth of this. While he is in full compliance with local and state health regulations, and zoning laws, he has escaped the burden of heavy taxes usually faced by suburban business people. Converting acreage to a business enterprise has proved profitable for this entrepreneur.

Several eastern farmers supply veal and poultry to New York markets from their own processing plants built on their farms.

One business person purchased a fifteen-acre tract of land in a New Jersey area which was undesirable crop cultivation because the land was extremely irregular and somewhat hilly. Farmers in the area greeted the new landowner with sympathy. But the entrepreneur, a wine fancier, had plans of his own.

The Vineyard Venture

Analyzing the soil prior to the purchase, he found it was ideal for the growing of a certain type of grape used in the making of a variety of wines. And within a period of three years, he was growing a grape for the making of wine in the winery which was established on the site. In addition, several truckloads of picked grapes were sold to a chain of supermarkets at top price.

The value of this person's fifteen-acre vineyard and winery facilities has increased more than *eight times*. And with his growing annual business volume, now extremely profitable, he will be quite able to weather the effects of inflation.

Stone Quarry Opportunities

I saw a unique conversion of land to a profitable enterprise by two individuals, about five years ago in a neighboring eastern county. The men, one a small building contractor and the other a real estate broker, purchased an eighteen-acre tract of hilly, rocky land which had been literally "sliced off" as a result of road construction which ran through a farm property. The retiring farmer who owned the original fifty-five-acre tract had received money from state highway authorities for road and right-of-way property which split his land into two separate sections.

The farmer, in his late seventies, had sold both the eighteen-acre tract, and a twenty-five-acre remaining portion, to a nearby farmer and was leaving the area for retirement.

The two entrepreneurs had bought the eighteen-acre portion for approximately $22,000 and were particularly interested in a secion of cropped stone strata. It had become exposed when the ground had been scooped away by bulldozers to make way for the road level below the hillside. One of the partners recognized the shading and texture of a native stone. He believed this stone was being used in residential construction throughout the state.

After a thorough study of the terrain and the exposed rock, the two called in a friend who owned a stone quarry located about twenty-five miles from the present site. For more than two hours, the quarry owner chipped and dug away at the stone cropping and surrounding soil. He made several observations to the new owners.

He told the two that he would be interested in a lease arrangement for at least five years or more. He would quarry the building limestone which was in ample supply, and he would construct a rock crusher to manufacture crushed stone for road and construction work. The lease would be contingent upon the construction of a gravel road into the tract, and the availability of the new concrete highway for use by his trucks.

A deal was struck that afternoon. By the latter part of the year, the highway was opened to traffic, along with a newly-constructed gravel road leading into the proposed quarry area.

The two men have been receiving an excellent monthly and annual return on their land investment, regarding it as a formidable inflation hedge.

Inflation Effect On Land Investments

When analyzing the benefits of investment in raw land, several things become apparent. These observations are based, however, on the effects of inflation.

(a) Land value usually parallels or exceeds inflation's rate of climb.

(b) Taxes often lag behind during inflationary periods.

(c) People are more inclined to invest in quantities of land (acreage) during inflation, because their devaluating dollar will never buy more than at present. As a result, these people are willing to assume higher debts on mortgages for land purchase, because they feel they will be able to pay off this obligation in the future with "cheaper dollars."

Survivors Of The Great Depression

A study was made several years ago by a Midwest group of economists. These people had studied those who had survived the Great Depression, which started in 1929 in the United States and lasted until the early 1930's. It also included a summary of those who did not survive.

The report concluded that Americans who lived on large farms, small farms, and on large lots in rural areas, were almost self-sufficient during the Depression. Virtually all grew their own food, raised livestock, poultry, and even provided themselves with sources of fuel. Larger farm families who owned dairy herds were able to earn a source of cash income through dairy sales of milk purchased by dairy processing plants, and through sales of grain, corn, and other staples. Despite the fact that prices were low, these farm families could pay utility bills and taxes and save some of the cash for other purposes. Their standard of living, when compared to urban families at that time, was quite high–particularly in the area of food and physical comforts.

Smaller farmers, truck farmers, and entrepreneurs who lived in small towns not only kept their own families in food and fuel, but were able to barter where cash was unavailable.

The Ones Who Were Hardest Hit

The hardest hit groups were the millions living in small and large cities whose incomes, now cut off, were linked with closed plants and factories. By virtue of their environment, they were not self-sufficient, and had no other means of earning an income. The only funds came from public aid sources, along with state-supported food deliveries. It was a meager existence for millions, but it was the only alternative. In many cases, people abandoned their homes and moved into the country, or migrated in search of jobs, food, and shelter.

Ironically, there were thousands of Americans who were able to live on a modest scale, thanks to dividends from utility companies and a few firms such as A.T.& T.!

The Best Inflation Hedge Of All Time: Land

Today, there are a number of economists, business people, agri-business representatives, entrepreneurs, and the authors of this book, who contend that an investment in land (ranging from five to twenty-five acres) could eventually be the greatest inflation hedge, next to a significant holding in gold coins!

There have been numerous income-producing plans ranging from conversion of land lying fallow to profitable, full-time or part-time supplementary ventures.

Tree Farming Opportunities

Farmers and landowners in southern states, the Northeast, and the far Northeast, have discovered over the past ten years that the growing of trees for harvest, by logging mills and lumber interests, is a profitable sideline. It is reported that 60% of all lumber manufactured for housing, cabinet and furniture building is purchased from farmers as a crop! Mill buyers constantly scout areas for new sources, these farmers report, and will pay immediately for good growths of trees. People who own substantial tracts of land in these areas take note, as this is another good inflation hedge.

On a smaller scale is the increased cultivation of evergreen trees (commonly known as "Christmas trees") by thousands of small and large landowners in the Northeast, Midwest, and a few selected Southern states.

If you own at least five acres of open land in a hilly or irregular terrain, which are not necessarily fertile, you can grow and cultivate crops of evergreen trees for the market. There are two markets for evergreens: wholesale Christmas tree sources, and wholesale nursery buyers. The nurseries, specifically those located in or near large suburban areas where housing is being built, will purchase hundreds of evergreen trees in three to six foot heights for use in landscaping work.

Growers of evergreen trees on both small and large tracts will purchase seedlings from large nurseries in the East at a few dollars per thousand. These will be planted by hand in cultivated rows, irrigated and fed several times per year. Following their second and third year of growth, these evergreens need only sparse attention. The two main problems encountered with growing evergreen trees as a crop, according to growers, are intense cold and droughts. In some northern states, hay is used as an insulation during cold weather months, and the trees are irrigated during dry spells. Some seasons will produce a crop of mites (insects) which, if not sprayed will cause damage to branches.

Good inflation-hedging incomes have been reported by these growers, who in many cases, need not deliver their stock. Buyers come into their fields with their own trucks! And it is a "cash-on-delivery" enterprise.

Sod Farming Opportunities

A farmer who decided to seek an easier way to earn a good income, other than milking cows and cultivating corn crops, and who owned about 500 acres of New Jersey farmland, become an entrepreneurial sod grower!

Beginning his operation about ten years ago, he is today regarded as one of the largest sod growers in the state, employing about fifteen regular workers who also deliver sod to building sites, residential tracts, and government buildings in the area. He had developed and patented special "lawn rollers" or "sod cutters" and loading equipment. He purchases top quality lawn seed, growing and harvesting several cuttings during each season. The tons of rolled sod sold from this location are said to be valued in the hundreds of thousands of dollars!

There are smaller operations in the sod growing field today which are also successful. Since the growing and harvesting season extends from six to seven months in northern climates, it is not a part-time venture. One person who recognized a secondary value in his "table top" acreage, rents out his 150-acre tract after each frost to several aircraft flying clubs for use as a base for their activities!

Trout Farming Opportunities

Another operation which is netting incomes for participants, depending upon the amount and location of acreage involved, is the "trout farm" venture. The raising of various types of trout for restaurant and home consumption began in the Northeast by farmers who were fresh-water fishermen

Landowners who had small streams running through their property, screened off portions of the water course, stocking these with "fingerling" trout purchased from state hatcheries. Larger size fish were also added. Fishermen paid for the privilege of fishing in these private streams, and took home baskets full of their catches.

For the past fifteen years, large trout farm operations have been established in the Midwest and in the East on former farm properties. Trout are raised from a tiny size to twelve-inch lengths in special concrete tanks. Water temperatures are monitored closely and tanks are carefully filtered. Feeding of trout is a regularly scheduled event.

In other operations, earthen dikes are built that will hold thousands of trout. The bottom surfaces are covered with plastic sheets and the water temperatures are controlled. The operation, like many other commercial trout-raising enterprises, is a full-time project, involving many people.

It is not uncommon for one of these midwestern trout farms to ship as many as 5,000 trout to wholesale outlets each month! They in turn sell to restaurants in both fresh and frozen form. It is regarded as an excellent profit-making venture.

Trout raising has become so popular that the U.S. Government Printing Office now publishes a guide on procedures and related information. Numerous farm publications have also published supplementary sections on this income-producing venture. It is another example of converting land acreage into profitable use, and creating a hedge against inflation.

Fishing Preserves

In another area of creating private fishing preserves, many land owners and farmers in the Midwest have built small farm ponds and miniature lakes in which fish have been stocked. In most cases, the poorest land was used to create the fishing sites.

Farmers and owners of land charge their customers varying rates (from $2.00 to $5.00 per day) to fish in these ponds for bass, perch, and other fresh water varieties. One pond owner reported that while it had cost him about $200 for the excavation work which he completed later himself, he grossed about $5,000 for the season!

People who own land unsuitable for farming or the growing of trees, might consider converting it into "fishing grounds" for producing needed income.

Camping Grounds

Many farms in the East which contain soil unsuitable for high-profit farm crops because of its physical composition, have been converted successfully into camp grounds by their owners. These range in size from twenty to one hundred acres. Some are sparsely wooded, while others are wooded with rocky terrain and are located near natural streams containing fish.

With a modest investment, acreage can be successfully converted into camping areas and camp sites, complete with outdoor toilets and fireplaces. At the present time, there are several national franchised camp ground organizations which have developed all of the phases required in establishing and operating a publicly-used but private camp grounds. Their popularity has increased in the past decade. Whether these private camp ground organizations will be affected adversely because of the energy shortage and gasoline costs, is a question the future will answer. But camping is gaining in popularity because of the high cost of vacations, particularly lodging, for the average family.

Entrepreneurs cannot be faulted for lack of ingenuity, particularly when it comes to converting acreage investment for use as an inflation hedge.

A farm magazine editor, whose publication includes readers in the state of West Virginia, related this experience:

A Unique Farming Venture

A young man, a graduate of an agricultural college in the East, and his wife, returned to West Virginia after two years in the Midwest. He had been selling farm tractors and equipment, and had managed to save a considerable amount of money from his sales commissions. His wife had inherited money from her father's small estate.

They found a thirty-five-acre farm in the foothills of the Allegheny Mountains that had been priced ridiculously low. The reason: the farmhouse had collapsed into a shamble of lumber, and the front portion of the acreage was covered with massive growth of weeds and brush. The overgrowth covered part of the gravel road leading into the place. Only the skeleton remained of the large barn and nearby sheds.

The young entrepreneur, who saw an excellent bargain in land in disguise, played down his interest for the benefit of the real estate broker. His wife uttered a stifled scream at the sight of the farmhouse. Within a few hours of discussion with the broker, it was agreed that a $5,000 down payment with a mortgage for the balance of $15,000 would make the couple owners of the neglected farm property.

Two weeks after the final settlement on the property, the young couple drove up in a new farm truck pulling a house trailer. The trailer would become their home for the coming year.

Clearing The Land

Neighboring farmers who heard of the sale smiled in amusement, shaking their heads. Having a healthy reserve of cash however, the young couple now brought in a small flock of sheep. This again piqued the interest of their neighbors, but the reason for the sheep was soon discovered. Within a month, the herd of sheep had cleared by grazing all of the undergrowth and brambles from several acres of front land.

Rebuilding The Barn

Next, they completed the rebuilding of the barn with the aid of a hired carpenter. They re-fenced several acres for the sheep, and constructed a barn/shelter for them.

Fertilizing The Soil

Several days later, a huge truck arrived at the site, carrying hundreds of White Holland turkeys. The wife had planted a small garden in a cleared area where the soil appeared to be excellent. Then she watched as all of the young turkeys–a $500 load of birds–were unloaded.

The turkeys were penned into a five-acre tract by wire mesh fencing and guarded by dogs the couple had brought with them. The dogs also guarded the new tractor, plows, and harrowing equipment.

Within the next six months, all of the land which had been cleared by the sheep, was now being *fertilized* by the massive turkey flock. And shortly before the second week in November, all but a dozen turkeys were sold for a total of $3,000! A new well had been drilled, and electric power had been brought to the farm.

Planting The Crops

The following year, the young farmer/entrepreneur planted prize corn, grain, and hay crops on his own land and land he had leased. He also planted dwarf trees and purchased five Hereford calves. Farmers were aghast at his corn and grain harvests. They learned about his agricultural knowledge later as a County Agent related figures on his harvest.

Building The Farmhouse

Today, several years later, the farm is a showplace. The farmhouse is a striking, prefabricated structure with baked enamel siding, incorporating all modern conveniences from kitchen to bathrooms, and meeting the needs of the now-increased family of five. Evergreens and shrubs in decorative plantings highlight the house.

The young entrepreneur has been offered $175,000 for the *farm alone,* but refuses to sell. In addition to a herd of beef and dairy cattle, he now has prize hogs and turkeys which he raises for the wholesale market. He also employs two full-time workers in his apple processing plant built on the site. He supplies two large bakeries with sliced, pared apples of several varieties, that are delivered in special waxed cartons to the customers.

Diversification Is The Key

His diversification has positioned him profitably against the ravages of inflation, generating several areas of cash income which will serve him well.

This classic example of converting acreage investment–increasing its value tremendously through entrepreneurial *planning* and *work,* buttressed by adequate *funding*–is a case history that bears careful study for the ability to visualize a risk/reward payoff!

5 Build Your Own Home On Your Own Land

Perhaps the largest investment the average individual takes during his/her lifetime in terms of dollars, is the purchase of the home in which the owner and family will live. In normal times, it will take most people about twenty to thirty years to pay off their mortgages, and clear this investment of any obligation other than annual taxes.

However, with inflation dogging Americans mercilessly, millions of home buyers may not be able to pay off excessively high mortgages in the event their jobs are wiped out because of the eroding economy.

With the average single home now reported to be selling for about $65,000 nationally (with the exception of the West Coast where the average single home now costs about $100,000), inflation is pushing housing costs higher every month! It has in fact eliminated millions of families from the new home market.

Home Building Alternatives During Inflation

Then what are the alternatives in this inflationary period for the "Young Marrieds" with a family, or middle-aged couples who want housing, and if they are entrepreneurially inclined? Some may have cash savings, stocks, or bonds, or may have been fortunate enough to have purchased several acres of land, a large lot, or several small lots in a rural area or the suburbs a few years back.

Can the average family afford to build a modestly-priced home despite "sky high" construction prices? Yes. It is not only possible, but many people are doing just that *today*.

The First Step: Buying The Land

Part of the strategy of the entrepreneur/builder is to own the land first. If you do not own a lot or a section of farmland, go out at your earliest opportunity and buy a location for your future house. Ah, but the present prices of land, you say, are too expensive. True, but there are modestly-priced land "buys" still around—if you *look for them!*

Doing Your Own Footwork

Obviously, if you want to purchase building land through a real estate broker, you are essentially "buying off the shelf," and will be forced to pay top price. Look around beyond your immediate area. Stop at farms near the edge of your city and talk to the farm owner. He may just be thinking about selling some of his farm. Okay, some of the land may be back off the main highway. If that is the case, you can negotiate the sales price. Besides, there are no development cost to cover—sewer or water lines, or curb pavement costs.

If the area is somewhat hilly or irregular, don't be discouraged if the price is right for a few acres. Incidentally, the terrain will dictate the type of home to be built. A hilly, irregular tract lends itself toward the construction of a "tri-level," "split-level," or modern "step-slab" house. Flat land is ideal for a "ranch," "Colonial," "Cape Cod," or any other style with one-level entrances and garage entry.

You might also check with your local banker if you live in a smaller community. Inquire about available building land. There may be lots available through foreclosures which can be purchased at a fair price.

Saving In Building Costs

The entrepreneur has one objective in mind once he/she has a tract of land which is owned: to build a new house which can be constructed for *one-half to two-thirds* of the average $65,000 price. Can this be done? Thousands of people have built (and are building) homes at substantial savings, based on programs they have initiated.

There are several avenues open to you today, to build the type of house that will meet the many future needs of your family–with a choice of design and materials. Here are the choices open to you:

Types Of Homes Available:

The Pre-fabricated Home

1. Purchase of a *pre-fabricated, factory-built home,* available in about fifteen to twenty different designs, types, and sizes. All components are delivered to your building site by tractor-trailer. You assemble all sections from blueprints. Cost range: $10,000 to $25,000. Time to complete: three to five months.

The Modular Home

2. Purchase of a *Modular Structure,* a factory-built, steel, aluminum, or wood building with five to six rooms. Completely built and assembled into finished rooms at the plant, two halves of the module are delivered by trucks to your building site. The halves are joined together from the peak to base like two sections of a triangle. Labor is required for this, and connecting plumbing, heating unit, water, and electricity. These homes can be put together by three people in two or three days, if the foundation has been completed. All utilities are installed in the house including showers, kitchen sinks, and range. Carpeting, paneling, and all windows have been installed. Cost: $18,500 to $28,500 on your lot.

The Kit Home

3. *"Kit" Houses.* There are a number of these kit houses available on the market today in a wide range of designs, sizes, and prices. The difference between this type of house and a "pre-fab" is that the kit house has every board, trim piece, frame, and bit of hardware *numbered and keyed* to match each sheet of the assembly blueprint! Each piece has been cut and fitted in advance, and only needs to be nailed or joined as directed. Kit homes feature lumber structures from Canadian Western logs which are peeled and sanded, or Red Cedar lumber and Northern Pine, which is stained. You can construct a house of notched, fitted logs, an "A frame" structure, or a massive two-and-a-half story mountain lodge house from kits.

How it looks when it arrives.

The team at work.

How the joints are fitted.

The finished product.

Photographs by Charles Stevenson. The "Beauti-Log" home under construction in northern Pennsylvania.

The kit packaged homes which are delivered in plastic-covered packages, can be ordered through *"Shelter"* magazines, *"Better Homes & Gardens,"* *"House & Garden,"* *"Handyman,"* *"Popular Mechanic,"* and selected farm magazines. All packaged components are delivered by truck to your building site. Cost: $15,000 to $30,000. Time to build: Six months to one year.

Building Your Own Home

4. *Build your own house* from scratch by purchasing all materials and building supplies needed from local dealers. You would have to contact lumber yards, plumbing wholesale houses, electrical supply dealers, hardware firms, cabinet, tile, and paint dealers. This method, obviously, takes considerably longer than assembly of the previous choices described. It can take as long as three years to complete a house from digging out the basement until completion!

"The Stick House" is a custom-built house as builders refer to it, and contains all components cut and fitted, mortared and cemented on the site. It is all manual effort, built to conform to specifications indicated in the blueprints you have. Cost: a seven-room one-story house built by you might range between $10,000 and $20,000.

Sub-contracting

5. *Sub-contract* the construction of your house. You act as general contractor. Since general contractors get about 25% of the profit on a house for their efforts, you could pocket these savings yourself in an inflation-fighting effort. You can also get "bids" from competing contractors and take the lowest bids for their portion of the work. These "portions" include carpentry, masonry, plumbing, etc. The house is custom-built to your blueprint specifications. And you pay each contractor at the conclusion of his/her part of the construction. I will relate some of my experiences in the building of my own house, later in this chapter.

Any of the above proposed house-building programs will not only help you fight back against outrageously high housing cost, but you will stand to gain a handsome profit return on your investment in the next several years!

Reasons For High Building Costs

Why are housing costs so high? Several things are responsible: *labor costs* which amount to as much as 50% of the total cost of the use, and less profit mark-up, because wages have escalated as a result of inflation. *Raw materials:* lumber, concrete products, plumbing supplies, plaster board, wiring, and electrical supplies, hardware, wallpaper, paint, and other items have gone through successive price increases over the past eight years. Added to these is the inflated *cost of developed land* on which to build residential houses. Then add *profit margins* of each contractor, general contractor, real estate broker, banks, and financial institution profits and you have your answer.

Let us examine some building cost figures. Conventional housing in most parts of the country costs about $30 to $40 per square foot for construction. For example, an 1,800 square foot ranch houser would cost you about $72,000 at today's construction prices. However, if you built that same 1,800 square foot home *yourself,* either by using a "kit" package of construction, or by building from raw materials to completed house, it would cost approximately $10 per square foot to build the same house! You are talking about a *savings of about $20 per square foot,* or a total cash savings of about $36,000!

Being Your Own General Contractor

If you act as general contractor on your new house, and sub-contract all of the work to be done to separate contractors, the same 1,800 square foot ranch house would cost you about $25 per square foot, or about $45,000. You could reduce this price if you stuck closely to the lowest possible bids. But the net savings are still a significant amount.

Where To Learn How To Build Your Own House

The number of Americans who are building their "dream " houses today to escape inflated costs, number in the thousands in virtually all sections of the United States. As a matter of fact, there are "House-building Schools" now in existence for people who know nothing about residential construction, but want to learn.

One such school is called "Shelter Institute," founded several years ago by a couple who successfully built their own house. The school is located in Bath, Maine. The founders and instructors of this "How-to-Build-Your-Own-Home" course charge a tuition rate of $300 per individual, or $450 per couple.

More than 3,500 individuals have graduated from the course taught by fifteen part-time and full-time instructors. And there is a six-month waiting list! More than 600 graduates of this course are now building their own houses. Subjects taught range from reading blueprints, bricklaying, carpentry, and electrical work, to surveying a site, and related tasks.

There are also thousands of vocational and trade schools across the country where house-building courses are taught. A number of evening schools also feature courses in carpentry, wiring, bricklaying, and the use of power tools, in addition to the reading of blueprints and drawings.

Necessary Skills

I should point out here, that unless you are mechanically inclined, or have taken a course in building construction, can read blueprints, or know how to use power tools safely, plus have some familiarity with building terminology, building products, and techniques, do not attempt house-building on your own.

The true entrepreneur, while assuming risks, does not attempt to undertake projects about which he knows little. If he does, he is courting financial disaster.

Since I did not have the time to build my present home by myself, or with people who would have helped me, because of my busy medical practice, I elected to act as general contractor on my proposed house construction. There were several reasons: I knew the type of house I wanted to build, and I expected to keep costs to a minimum; and the house could conform to the land surrounding it.

A Case History Of Building My Own House

In 1961, I purchased eighteen acres of farmland at a cost of about $200 per acre. It was not too far away from the small community which was the center of my medical activity. Then I decided I would build my house on a selected two-acre site which had some pin oak trees and a few maples. It was high enough for drainage, and close enough to the main blacktop road. I would need to have a road built for access to the house.

I had sketches made for use by sub-contractors in making their individual bids on everything from plumbing to roofing work. With a growing family, I required at least 2,000 square feet of space, four bedrooms with two and a half baths, laundry, kitchen, dining area, study and library, two-car garage, workshop, and other support facilities. A basement was also indicated. Materials would include brick, stone, clapboard siding and an asphalt shingle roof.

At that time, residential costs per square foot were around $15.00. Remember, I felt I could bring the cost lower, perhaps in the $7.50 to $10.00 per square foot range. I also owned the land which meant a savings of at least $4,000 to $5,000.

Because I had been working with a variety of contractors on other projects, including renovation of farm homes and buildings, road building and grading, I was knowledgeable in the area of sub-contracting building jobs.

However, I would need funds with which to pay each sub-contractor at the conclusion of each phase of construction. This is important because, as general contractor, you must obtain a "waiver of lien" from each contractor when the job is completed. This means he/she has been fully paid by the general contractor for the owner. If not, the sub-contractor *can put a claim against the property*. This means the owner cannot get a clear title to the house which would complicate securing a deed, by blocking occupancy, or causing problems in the future sale of the house.

I visited a local bank with which I had dealt in the past on real estate transactions, and secured a loan on the land. This gave me enough money to move ahead with the entire construction project.

What I Saved By Doing It Myself

I sub-contracted the entire project to individuals supervising all of the phases of work carefully, and making necessary changes when needed. Some doorways and window areas needed modification, but posed no problem. Where expensive items were offered, more modest substitutes were made. With only slight delays for weather, and some changes in sewer and water line excavations, all work on the house was completed within a seven-month period. My price estimate was correct. The house was built at the $10.00 per square foot level!

The General Contractor's Role

If you were to purchase a custom-built house from a building contractor specializing in the building of residential structures, you would only be paying *the general contractor*–rather than paying individual subcontractors. In this case, the general contractor who is building your house, would receive payments in a three-step contract agreement: 10% on completion of the "framed-in" house, completed fireplace and chimney, and all sewer lines and "rough" plumbing lines installed; 33% on all interior work completed up to painting and wallpaper and finish cabinet work. The remaining money due would only be paid *after* final inspection by you, together with lien wavers, issuance of a certificate of occupancy, and a written agreement to guarantee any defects discovered in products installed, or workmanship within a six-month period.

I recently watched an entrepreneur erect and assemble a unique and novel prefabricated house, called a "Topsider." This is an octagonal-shaped house with massive window and panel areas, on a *sixty-degree* slope of ground. The 1,000 square foot house is perched on a fifteen-foot circular first level foundation, which is also the entry and utility rooms. Supplementary steel piers are also employed.

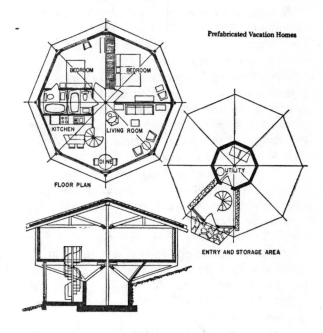

Prefabricated Vacation Homes

The octagonal house costs approximately $19,000 delivered to the site, in packages in two separate loads by truck from the factory in North Carolina.

It took the owner and four carpenter/helpers about three weeks to complete the assembly and all sewage and water "hook-ups," plus connect power for electrical units.

The novel house contains two bedrooms, two bathrooms, a kitchen and living room, all with magnificent views, and the lower utility room. A sundeck has been added, connecting the house with the hillside.

The lot on which the structure is built was totally unsatisfactory for conventional housing, and the 100' x 250' tract, hilly and somewhat stony, with several trees, was purchased for $1,200!

The owner liked the steel-truss design which gives the house central support to the roof panels. His investment of approximately $22,000 compares favorably with a conventional house that would sell for about $75,000!

Converting Barns

A number of house builders in the New England area have purchased old barns with one to two acres of ground, along with the structure. These, in every case, were purchased at reasonable prices because few people want to live in barns! But in virtually every case, the entrepreneurs stripped away all of the barn siding down to the bare timber frames.

After getting foundations rebuilt with additional concrete piers poured, and replacement flooring with new joists and subfloors, the frames were treated with penetrating wood preservative chemicals to remove any danger of termites. (Foundations and subfloors were also sprayed and treated.) Individual floor plans, fireplaces, or woodstove areas, were prepared. In one case, the owners built a three-level structure within the original timber framework, providing them with a *ten room house!* There was a bathroom built on each level.

All stock window frames, exterior and interior paneling, were purchased–some of it used, but in excellent condition. Both metal foil and Fiberglas™ insulation were used. All new plumbing and wiring was added, along with sewer lines and piping to cesspools and septic tank installations.

The completed "Barn Houses," which ranged in cost from $12,000 to $18,500, now resemble huge Colonial structures. The third resembles an attractive Swiss chalet, right down to its window boxes. Their present values are estimated to be as much as *five times* the purchase price and reconstruction costs!

Perhaps the obvious lesson to be learned here from these entrepreneurs, is that each *was not satisfied* with the conventional types of house designs on the market, nor were their high prices acceptable. One does not fight inflation effectively by purchasing an expensive home at its top price, and then battling to meet staggering monthly mortgage and utility costs! An investment at soaring prices will not pay off a decade later if recession batters the market.

Your Program Of Action

You need to detail your house-building plans and program as carefully and diligently as in making a significant investment.

1. Purchase your home, or house-building plans or skeletons, to meet your family's *needs*.

2. *Review your financial inventory of assets*. How much money have you saved in terms of investing it in housing? How much can you raise to make a commitment?

3. *Purchase the land or a large lot*. If this has not already been accomplished, start looking now.

4. *Develop a timetable*. When do you want to move forward on the construction phase of your new house? How much "lead time" do you require to raise cash, purchase land, buy your prefabricated house, your "kit" house, or building materials?

5. *Obtain financing*. Have you talked with officers at a financial institution, a commercial bank, or people who would loan you a substantial sum of money, about mortgage funds?

6. *Think about being your own general contractor*. Are you knowledgeable enough in all phases of building to handle your entire house construction program? Can you tell the differences between high and low bids in terms of deliberately low-bidding? Can you prepare the building specifications in detail so that contractors who bid can estimate properly? Can you get all contracts prepared legally and properly, plus lien waivers? Can you get the funds required to pay each sub-contractor when he/she completed the particular phase of work? Are you skilled and experienced enough to check carpentry framing, rough plumbing, and masonry work? Can you tell the difference between "cheap" or poor-grade lumber, and quality

materials? If you can't answer "yes" to all of these questions, investigate a few "house-building" courses or schools in your area.

7. *Consider remodeling an old structure into a new home*. Have you considered the possibility of purchasing a fine old house and remodeling it completely to your own design? Would a well-built barn on a choice section of land be suitable for your family if it were converted into an attractive house with sufficient room?

The choices are numerous and your options almost unlimited. When you regard your house as an investment, you begin to think in various levels of financial return. It is one way of building an ample fund of capital for future activities. Millions of people have sold homes at good profits, providing them with enough money to purchase an additional new home–and money to invest for profitable return!

It has been reported by the National Board of Realtors that most families move about five times in their lives. Fifty years ago, the "first" house usually turned out to be the "final" house for many couples, even after the children left home and were married. Not so today. First houses are now regarded by millions of people as "starter homes."

Remember That Your Home Is A Capital Investment

The entrepreneur, by and large, will regard his/her home as a substantial investment, but will not let any good opportunity pass by. His/her house represents *capital* which can be utilized for many purposes. There are numerous successful business people who now live in luxurious homes, reporting that their "starter" homes were the origin of their ultimate wealth!

Opportunities in real estate (homes) exist, but you need to seek these out and have the imagination and motivation to get something accomplished. Here is an interesting case history which illustrates this point.

Moving An Existing House

A new state highway to be built in central Pennsylvania was plotted through the center of a small residential community of about ten stone and brick, single story ranch houses. Owners were given the options of either moving the house at state expense to a new site, or accepting a demolition fee. All but two house owners opted for demolition, and plans went forward.

A young electrical contractor became familiar with the entire program by discussing it with two homeowners in the area. He had also read about the project in the newspapers, and had spoken with workers on the highway crews. Spending an entire weekend inspecting the houses in the area, he consulted with his wife and decided to make the demolition contractor an offer on one of the houses to be demolished.

He knew the houses were worth about $35,000 each, despite the fact that they were at least fifteen years old. He made an offer of $1,500 to the demolition contractor, contending that the house would be a total loss once it was destroyed. He also told him he would have the house moved at his expense.

His offer was accepted by the contractor, since it enabled him to move ahead by two days on his contract. Meanwhile, the young man contracted with the house-moving contractor already in the area, and had the house transported about three miles distant. The cost for doing this totaled $5,000 and would take an entire day of moving time. A signed agreement was completed on the site of the proposed highway. A week elapsed.

Owning a 100-foot lot several miles west of the site along uncluttered roadways, the young man arranged for a building contractor he knew with rigging experience (underpinning and the movement of massive objects) to build temporary footing piers to support the future house.

A week later, the stone and brick ranch house, cabled and cradled in a protective timber framework on a massive flatbed truck, arrived at the site of the entrepreneur's lot. Within a few hours, the single story home, measuring about 50 feet in length, was carefully lowered to the temporary support piers. It had made the three-mile journey with only one framed window cracked!

Several days later, he had a masonry contractor building and pouring concrete footings, and block piers for permanent support installed. With an additional expense of about $3,500, the young man would have masonry work, sewer and water connections installed, and electric power lines brought into the house.

Thus, for a total of $10,000, the young couple had an "instant house" on their lot, completely built with an increased value already assured because of its location.

Looking For Similiar Opportunities

Is there a similiar opportunity in your immediate area? Are homes slated for demolition because of new highways, shopping center development, or industrial park building? Investigate. With some planning, you may be in for a pleasant, and profitable surprise in terms of getting a house and getting a "leg up" on inflated housing prices!

6 The Computer And How You Can Benefit From It

How The Computer Has Changed The World

Historians credit the passenger car and the airplane with having the greatest impact on American life, customs, and habits in this century. However, an innovative, scientific electronic development introduced in Philadelphia in 1947 by Mauchley Associates, shook the world. It affected the worlds of industry, commerce, academia, and medicine. It was the first computer system able to take stored information and very rapidly perform complex calculations. It could also correlate, select, and compile mathematical and scientific data.

The massive electronic structure, with literally thousands of vacuum tubes, semi-conductors, and miles of wiring and related component hardware, could be compared now with the early Wright Brothers aircraft in mode and design. In the ensuing three decades, on science, industry, business, the Armed Forces, the government, and even the world of sports, its effect has been devastating!

Mini-Computers And Giants

With the advent of the microprocessor chip the size of a fingernail, on which thousands of electronic circuits are printed, is today the microscopic "mini-computer," which is being fitted into glass eyes to create artificial sight for the blind, bypassing optic nerves, using tiny electrodes such as those used in the Pentagon and by NASA. This is "hardware" which costs *millions* of dollars.

Personal Computers

In between these two extremes are literally thousands of computer systems that sell from $800 "personal" computers to $100,000 systems, able to process information in a series of languages. Some are interconnected to as many as fifty terminal stations across the country to receive "print outs," and for "inputs" into "main hardware." These are third and fourth generation types.

We are not presenting a primer in electronic computer systems or operations here, since there is a wealth of scientific data on this subject in libraries for you to investigate. We are trying to bring you into a related perspective of the fastest-growing industry in the world. The transistorized electronic computer has dated earlier technology.

Earlier, we reviewed my experience with the use of the computer in practicing medicine. The computer is used in this respect for record-keeping, redundant data, invoicing and related matters. Since a computer *automatically processes information* (called: data processing), it can only be as good as the information (called: programming) put into the electronic machine (called: hardware). For the purpose of definition, computer system operation is divided into two categories: "Hardware," which refers to the video terminal, printer, keyboard, cabinet in which electronic components are housed, and any other component which may be used in connection with the system's operation; and "Software," which refers to *programming* which is fed into the computer by means of magnetic tape, "floppy" discs, hard discs, magnetic "cards," and other magnetic media. This information is then coded in the language you direct, to do any of a series of projects, depending upon your specific needs.

The Uses Of Computers

There is a wide, growing group of economists known as "Econometricians" who do financial forecasting with the use of elaborately-programmed computer models. And now we are seeing the advent of the "Supercomputer" such as "Cray-1" and "Cray-2." These are termed by computer programming directors as "*lightening fast* in performing complex calculations — in the flash of a second!" Able to handle thousands of variables in such fields as weather forecasting, defense problems, and laboratory experimental projects, they work at unheard-of high speeds. The "Supercomputers" will next tackle the problems of medical technology; the restoration of hearing, sight, and touch, and the eventual elimination of diseases.

The Problems Computers Have Created

One of the startling problems brought about by modern computer technology is that the human brain cannot absorb information at the rate of speed it is being presented by advanced computer systems. Banks are complaining that their financial records prepared for programming are sometimes *weeks behind* computer printouts using the same basic data!

Another serious problem, which computer system developers were unaware of in refining modes and designs, is the present growing area of *theft of information* and computer abuse. These are interrelated and have brought about an entirely new vertical industry — computer security. Despite computer codes, safeguards, screening of programmers and directors, theft of vital information worth hundreds of thousands of dollars to competitors is occurring every month. This information comes from the F.B.I., since computer information theft is considered a federal crime. Most of the computer abuse problems and theft cases are "in house" actions committed by "authorized" personnel.

Since we must put all of this into its proper context looking at the big picture of the computer system industry, we want you to look at this multi-million dollar data systems industry in terms of what it can do for you.

How Computers Can Help You In Your Business

If you have launched a new business, or are in the final planning stages, you may have asked yourself whether a "minicomputer" or a "microcomputer" system, at a price of about $800, might be right for you. You may have looked at recent models at several electronics equipment dealers. Usually, these systems have a microprocessor, a keyboard a display terminal, and a floppy disc for programming.

The Computer As A Capital Investment

Remember that a computer, like any major piece of equipment in a business operation, is a *capital investment*. You need to ask yourself what the computer will do for you, in a series of serious questions:

Questions To Ask Yourself About The Need For A Computer

1. Why do I need a computer?

2. Specifically, what am I trying to program in terms of information, and what will I retrieve from it?

3. Would I be better off renting computer time elsewhere?

4. How complex is my business operation?

5. Who is actually going to program the information or data to be processed?

6. How will the computer help me during this inflationary period?

7. Can I project costs, profit ratios, and expenses for analysis over a period which is uncertain?

8. How will I store this information when it is procesed?

9. What will it cost to house my computer in terms of protecting it from temperatures, weather conditions, and tampering? Will I have to build an expensive room for this machine?

10. If I maintain efficient financial records and other operational data with an accountant's help, why do I need a computer?

Your frank answers to these questions will give you enough basis for an intelligent decision — on a "go" or "no go" action.

How A Computer Can Help You at Home

What about the personal computer's use in your home for your personal financial records, tax data, insurance payments, mortgage financial information, payments due, stock portfolio, checking account information, household costs, food costs, sales tax information, tuition costs, and auto and homeowner's insurance data? Maybe you will want to buy a mail-order computer hobby kit from any of a half dozen houses, and at a cost of about $250. With this, you can build your own computer system. This might give you a working period in which you can program your household and personal information for proper processing. Then, perhaps, you may want to purchase a larger model from a computer retail store at a later date, if the system proves satisfactory.

Service Considerations

One of the complaints of smaller business owners who have purchased computer systems from small electronics manufacturers, is that there is no service follow-up. There are no service people available from that particular company. If the operation is located in a small city or town, miles from a large metropolis, you have a major problem in getting a repair technician to check your system.

Remember, too, an important part of your system is the software, which should also be obtained from the store where you purchase the "hardware."

Becoming A Computer Service Representative

What about giving some consideration to establishing yourself as a service representative for personal and business computers? You might have a vertical market to begin with, since the national computer systems manufacturers "look after their own" in terms of service. But there are thousands of other small business owners who now own small microcomputers who do not know a "circuit board" from a "data buss." And they obviously need help when their computers break down, just like any other piece of equipment!

How versatile and broad are small business computers in terms of assisting with business operations? Basically, any computer is used to solve a problem.

Consider a moment the problems involved with sending a rocket to the moon. The multitude of mathematical variables was incredible! Literally thousands of factors had to be computed in terms of time, speed, distance, weather, cycles, earth's rotation, human capabilities, and navigation — to name a few. If physicists and mathematical experts were to develop these equations manually, one scientist estimated that it would take from *twenty to thirty years* to come up with written answers!

We know that electronic computers not only solve the tremendously complicated sequences of calculations for NASA, but they are now being used extensively in science, engineering, and business, in areas ranging from inventory control to estimating sales and profits over a span of several years.

Basics Of Computer Programming

The *Binary Principle* is inherent in electronic computer operations, from the most simple type to the highly-sophisticated complex hardware used by NASA and the Armed Forces. And the instructions to "add two numbers" (binary principle) and "compare two numbers to determine whether they are equal," must be prepared in the form of coded instruction.

Different types of computers have different sets of instructions. Even though they do the same thing (such as adding two numbers), they usually have *different formats* to complete programmed projects. This means that the "software" programmed for one computer will not run on another electronic computer. As you advance your equipment toward bigger and better computer system operations, your costs move upward sharply. The reason for this is that you now must program new series of instructions modes for the new computer. Time and expert knowledge can cost significant amounts!

As a result of computer incompatibility in terms of software, the computer industry has developed a software called COBOL, or "Common Business Oriented Language." It was specifically designed by programming experts to solve or ease the problems of program writing, computer compatibility, program testing, and program modification.

With training covering a period of several weeks, a business person with a logical mind can prepare a moderately-complex program for use in his/her computer with the help of a COBOL system. Later, the programmer can check the programming (called: "debugging") for errors which will yield incorrect results if not detected.

By now, you are probably saying to yourself, *"What has all of this computer talk got to do with hedging against inflation? What can it do for me in terms of earning additional income to help my deflated bank account?"*

Using The Computer On Inflation Hedge

Plenty! You don't fight a raging fire with a bucket of water! You use the most modern, most effective means of fighting a blaze threatening you. In this case, it is the modern electronic computer which may help you earn a higher spare time or full time income in a business operation. It may, if handled accurately and properly, solve many of your business and personal problems!

Here is an actual case history of a business person who was anxious to find a full time business operation to earn a good income. He was in his late fifties and knew it would be almost impossible to re-locate with another firm. His previous field had been in advertising and promotion, at a high salary. His previous firm had been acquired by a large corporation. The operation had been moved to the West Coast. Since his wife had been ill, he decided not to move to another area. He did, however, plan to establish his own business. If properly managed, he expected his business could earn him a good income over the next ten years until retirement. This meant, of course, that he would have to find and purchase an income-producing operation, as opposed to starting from scratch. He had saved about $25,000 in cash, and had a small portfolio of stock and bond investments.

After weeks of investigation and search, he discovered a small printing plant, doing commercial work. It was located at the edge of his city and was scheduled for auction. The owner had died suddenly, and his widow was anxious to sell. She did not wish to "haggle" with interested buyers, which could take months in a normal sales transaction pattern. She had opted for a *regular* auction, subject to her confirmation and acceptance of the price.

The advertising man recalled a friend who owned a business computer in his real estate brokerage business. Since his background knowledge included extensive experience in graphic arts, he checked the firm's sales estimates with sales personnel familiar with the operation. He inspected all of the equipment and facilities with the auctioneer's representative, and also found the firm had several small, but profitable, accounts on its books. He had one month to develop a basis for a decision.

Using The Computer To Validate A Business

Being an electronics "buff," and with some basic knowledge of the computer environment, the advertising man rented computer time from his friend. He programmed all of the facts he had developed on the small printing operation into the computer. These included estimated costs, salaries, types of printing jobs, time required, net worth of presses and related equipment, margin of profits, printing capacity needed, and, finally, costs of purchasing the operation.

When the print out of cost figures, profit margins, and an estimated worth of the business operation fell into his hands, he knew he would have an excellent opportunity to earn a good income for himself.

Armed with his data, the advertising man attended the auction on its scheduled day, and actively took part in the bidding. Since most of the bidders were only interested in the presses and related equipment, he was able to outbid them with his knowledge gained from the computer calculations. His final bid of $200,000 (which was $15,000 over the competing bidder) cinched the sale of the business. He had his deposit check with him and, filling in the fifteen percent required, signed the Agreement of Sale with the auctioneer.

One month later, following confirmation of the sale, the entrepreneur was able to arrange for bank loans to cover the balance of the purchase. The computer print outs aided greatly in his loan request at the bank. Within a period of fourteen months, he had increased his firm's printing volume to more than $800,000. Today, this graphic arts firm is located in a new building which is five times the original size, and its gross business volume has reached $2.4 million!

Could this business operation have been handled as well without the aid of computerized data? Perhaps. But it would not have provided this entrepreneur with the same business opportunity. With the help of the computer, he was able to recognize and go after the business offering with processed business data, which removed much of the speculation inherent in purchase considerations.

Can you apply the same investigative techniques for computerization in terms of narrowing down a business opportunity? Yes, indeed! You can contract for computer time required through a number of facilities. Okay, then what about projecting futures on a new venture you think has excellent profit possibilities?

Using The Computer To Investigate A New Venture

Planning for computer programming on a new venture must be well thought-out, with financial data input developed accurately. There isn't any room for "blue sky" speculation of profits here! If your new product is a revolutionary golf ball, for example, with remarkable strength features and balanced so well that it moves like an accurately-aimed bullet, your basic objectives would be to determing: (a) cost of materials, (b) cost of manufacturing, (c) margin between costs of manufacturing and sales costs, and (d) advertising and promotional costs. Knowing these, you could arrive at your profit figures, or your estimated profit return.

Almost every type of business, from farming to real estate brokerage, can benefit from the use of electronic computers.

Practical Computer Applications On A Farm

We recently visited a modern, 1,000-acre farm and were amazed to find the owners busy in an office complete with computer system. This particular system had two Z-80 microprocessors, one for the video terminal and the other for the computer. This data processing system had been installed three years before.

"We raise beef cattle, calves for veal, operate three dairy herds on nearby leased farms, grow grain and corn crops, and also have four turkey flocks for the market," explained the farm owner. "Our computer calculates feed required for our stock, advises us when to stop feeding, and when to process. It gives us data on purchasing grain, seed, and fertilizers — what prices are best for us. It indicates margin of profits to be expected on sales, costs involved, and handles all of the other accounting and tax data invovled in the operation. And it gives us a chance to make comparative studies from season to season to change our marketing strategy! It is worth *five times* its cost to us!"

This is a far cry from the average farm owner some forty years ago who labored seemingly without direction. Back then, a farmer was known to put in eighty hours a week for 365 days a year, simply to earn a daily living from his small section of land.

Here are a few more examples of computer application in a wide variety of entrepreneurial operations today:

Five Small Business Computer Applications

Real Estate Broker

* A ten-office real estate brokerage form utilizes its computer to locate a *specific* type of house, in a specific neighborhood, with comparative sales prices. All of this is provided with mortgage cost details, taxes, and related data; it is available within three minutes. Each office has its own terminal connected to the main office computer. The computer can also be programmed for all of the administrative and financial details for each sales transaction and settlement, establishing dates, times, and places.

Construction Company

* A small construction company found that it could save up to $100,000 in materials each year through precise calculations by its computer when plotting each job as it was planned.

Restaurant

* An eastern restaurant has a library of software of its 100 different meal menus. This enables purchasing of food products weeks in advance of scheduling, saving the firm money through quantity buying. The computer also indicates profit margins, and various overhead costs.

Detective Agency

* A private detective Agency has programmed all of its clients' activities in terms of business functions, all physical plant descriptions, types of employees, work schedules, holidays, records of losses through thefts, risk characteristics, man-hours needed to protect each establishment, all polygraphed employees of clients, and other data. Were this information not available within minutes to the detective firm, massive files would need to be maintained, and the margin for error would be much higher.

Employment Agency

* An employment agency furnishing 150 personnel managers with skilled talent in the engineering field, can retrieve data on individuals within minutes, to match specific needs of clients and experience criteria.

Since computers are able to increase productivity of individuals, departments, and entire manufacturing companies, this field will not only survive the brutal financial impacts of inflation, but will give companies with computer systems, a wide edge of profit margin over firms without computers!

As a lone entrepreneur starting a business, consider the possibility of adding a small computer system to your operation. For less than the cost of a good used car, you will be able to hire an electronic "brain" which will not be continually asking for a "cost of living increase," fringe benefits, and double pay for holiday work!

Priceless Information
From The Computer

Consider this, too: a computerized analysis of the venture you may think will make you a millionaire in five years' time, may prove to you that you would make more money selling pretzels on some convenient corner! The savings involved in discovering this kind of information is priceless.

Whatever path you may elect to take during this decade, you may be certain that somewhere, somehow, an electronic computer or its processed data, has already been probing into the future. And in some remote way, you will undoubtedly benefit from this data evaluation.

7 Barter Can Save You Thousands of Dollars

Barter, which is the oldest form of exchange of commodities, products, and services, will perhaps become the most important factor in the act of inflation survival for millions of American families during the next five years! If you or your family have never bartered or exchanged any household goods, it would be beneficial for you to learn some basic rudiments about this type of transaction. It could prove to be a most important step in getting the things you and your family may need in the future, *without benefit of cash!*

Beginnings of Barter

Since the early Stone Age, when tribal members exchanged animal hides for stone axes, and later during biblical times, when wheat was bartered for camels and tools, the basic "swapping" of goods and services has continued over the centuries. Barter is in full operation today, (in such remote countries as Tibet and Central Africa, and even in the United States) despite the use of dinars, rubles, shillings, dollars, and piasters.

Modern Barter Organizations

Financial authorities recently revealed that twelve hundred "Trade Exchanges" (barter organizations) exist in the United States today, and the number is growing. Together, these organizations reported a total national volume of *$18 billion* in bartering of products and services!

What was bartered by these thousands of exchange members? It included automotive products, clothing, meat, water beds, motel lodging, printing, office machines and equipment, legal services, and job counselling, among the five hundred products and services on the lists.

There are two general areas of bartering for review: first, *business and commercial*, as outlined briefly above; and second, the *personal bartering* for family use and needs.

Business and Commercial Bartering

On the business side, there has been a proliferation of trade exchanges because of the tightness of the national economy with inflation as the major vehicle. The Mutual Credit Buying organization in Los Angeles is the nation's largest formal barter operation, representing thousands of individuals and companies. Then there are the Philadelphia Trade Exchange and the Delaware Valley Trade Exchange in the East, along with the Butcher Trade Exchange in Fort Washington, Pennsylvania. There is also the International Trade Exchange, Washington, D.C.; Portland Trade Exchange, Portland, Oregon; and others in Milwaukee, Chicago, and Boston.

Somers K. Butcher, former investment banking firm member and now president of Butcher Trade Exchange, said in an interview, "the quickening flow of goods and services in replacing cash transactions had important limitations–but it has also shown significant advantages."

Butcher said his trade exchange is not "consumer-oriented." A prospective member of the exchange *must have a specific service or product to offer on the market* to qualify for membership. Whether the prospective member is a beginning entrepreneur with a special service, or a giant corporation, either or both will gain attractive advantages, including improved cash flow, increased sales, and a better net profit.

Cash is conserved when products and services are "swapped." To protect members who offer the same services or products, these are restricted by geographic area and the type of product offered.

Trade exchange members pay an annual membership fee of $100, which includes an annual directory of members and a monthly newsletter for use in marketing planning. There is also a one-time entry fee. Members must call a central office for the "uncoded" name and number of the exchange member with whom they wish to conduct business.

In the case of trade exchange transactions, here is a view of the system in operation:

An Overview of How It Works

"Green Up" Landscaping Services, a ten-store chain, ordered a fork-lift truck for its warehouse, which cost $5,000 from another exchange member. When the fork-lift truck was delivered, an authorized supervisor signed a charge slip for the vehicle. The fork-lift firm then received a credit on the exchange of $5,000. The "Green Up" company was debited $5,000. The fork-lift dealer member received a credit of 5,000 *trade units*. "Green Up" company pays no interest or commission to the trade exchange *until* it exchanges some of its products or services.

On the "selling" side, there is a five-percent service charge on the total price of goods or services sold which goes to the exchange. The commission paid to the exchange is "payment for bringing in a new customer" to the seller. Members receive a "credit line" from the exchange of $1,000 to $150,000. It is predicted that numerous new exchange offices will be opening in American cities within the next two to three years.

Eliminating Accounts Receivable

Butcher states, "Within our system, there aren't any *accounts receivable*. If someone needs your product, they simply call the exchange, and we record the account number of the buyer and seller. We also send out statements every month. And we are broadening the range of products and services every month to combat inflation's effect on our economy."

The View From The IRS

What does the Internal Revenue Service think of barter? Here is what an IRS official told us during an interview on the subject, relating primarily to the Trade Exchange: "In bartering, or exchanging services or products, the *fair market value* of your services or products must be included in individual tax returns as *gross income*. In these transactions, the medium of exchange–goods, products, or services–is being *substituted* for money. But the value of each still remains financially representative."

Personal Bartering

The second general area of barter is, of course, the exchange of used items, products, raw materials, and personal services.

"Swap Shops" have been in existence for many years in the United States featuring everything from used clothing to furniture. In many cases, where a person has nothing to swap or trade, he/she will purchase the item needed for a small sum. This money goes into the shop's general fund for a variety of expenses.

In many neighborhood newspapers over the past several years, columns have appeared in the advertising section which offer items for barter. These include baby carriages, bicycles, electric appliances, childrens' furniture, clothing, passenger cars, trailers, boats, heaters, snow removal equipment, tires, reading lamps, rubber boots, raincoats, books, typewriters, rugs, bunk beds, and numerous other items.

Used Clothing

There are a number of "Tots-to-Teens" used clothing stores and shops appearing everywhere. In a few cases, the parent looking for clothing for a pre-teen youngster, brings along various clothing items the child wore in early years. If the clothing is in good condition, it is appraised in value and credit is applied toward cleaned, used pre-teen clothing. A small fee is sometimes charged for cleaning, or because of lack of sufficient "credits."

Many large supermarket stores in small towns and larger communities now post "Swap Sheets" on bulletin boards at their entrances, as a public service. Only household products and "family use" items are permitted to be bartered here. One family swapped a riding lawn mower for a complete set of kitchen furniture. Another family bartered luggage for lawn furniture. One store reported that virtually all of the barter items posted in a month's time were traded.

Hard Goods

Flea market operators have "swap shop" dealers who work on a "no-cash-involved" basis if items are in demand. Some examples of typical swaps: chairs for cut glassware; paperback books for old fountain pens; bushels of vegetables for cordwood; and costume jewelry for walking canes. One dealer offered five ball-point pens for a clean, corrugated box! Another dealer swapped fishing gear for a canoe and boat paddles.

Food

One retired mechanic in Maryland gets a four-month supply of vegetables, chickens, and a pig in trade for plowing one-acre and five-acre garden plots in the spring for people in his community. He accepts no cash in payment, but barters for his tractor service by taking bushels of vegetables at harvest time, along with chickens, and a fair-sized pig.

Home Sewing Equipment

A fabric shop in Chicago distributes a monthly bulletin for its customers, in which items such as used sewing machines, fitting forms, cabinets, and lamps are offered for barter.

How A Retirement Community Uses Barter

A retirement community in New Jersey, where people must live on modest pension incomes (primarily from Social Security) launched a successful barter program three years ago. There are more than two hundred people living in the mobile home site who began to feel the pressure of inflated food costs. The barter program here began with the basics: food. There were four large vegetable gardens in which some twenty-five people were involved. From early spring, when lettuce, tomatoes, early plantings, and other garden crops began to flourish, the barter program moved into action. "Shares" of harvested crops were exchanged for meat — chickens, ground beef, stewing meat — which had also been divided into "shares." As the season progressed, there were many bushels of green and wax beans which were picked by the gardeners. Since this crop was so large, it was exchanged at a small supermarket for chickens and turkeys.

Shares of tomatoes were also swapped. Now the supermarket owner bartered canned goods — corn, peas, fruit juices — for this crop, which was a pickup load of tomatoes!

More than fifteen of the male residents of the retirement community were excellent deep sea fishermen. Since the site was located less than fifteen miles from the ocean fishing areas, there was a serious motive involved in their fishing trips. Boats were loaned to the group for fuel costs only. Almost to a man, their catches were good, and well-packed plastic bags of sea bass, whiting, and other fish were "harvested" and brought back to the settlement.

About fifty of the residents made a joint purchase of two used freezer chests into which the cleaned, dressed fresh fish were placed. After, barter for meat and baked goods was completed.

While the retirement community is not wholly self-sufficient when viewing a total food program, it has been able to cope with outrageously high food prices through this system of barter. There are barter programs involving books, furniture, and tools at the community. A plan is now underway to manufacture doll houses to be sold in order to purchase a community van. If the program is successful, reports its committee, furniture will be built for bartering to outfit the community recreation center.

Barter for Owners of Luxuries

Barter is not confined to any specific economic level of the American population. For more than thirty years, a tri-monthly aircraft publication has carried a "Swap or Trade" section. Ads in "TRADE-A-PLANE" offer everything from choice waterfront land to heavy construction equipment for barter on used aircraft! One advertisement offered a complete 4,000-KW diesel-powered electrical plant, located in the Panama Canal zone area *at a value of $180,000,* for an aircraft of comparable value!

Another advertisement offered a houseboat in "sunny Florida" that is forty-eight feet with twin Chrysler engines, complete with furnishing and air-conditioning units, for trade on an airplane "up or down" in value. An interesting ad appeared in the publication offering for barter a "$60,000 position in a $1 million Texas real estate venture for a high-performance single engine aircraft." You see, just about anything can be bartered in one way or another.

Radio and Television Advertising Time

A marketing technique widely used in radio and television station programming and scheduling is the barter of air and viewing time for products. There are numerous time barter brokers in areas of the United States who accept products for purchases of air time. Normally, specific mail order houses selling records, tapes, kitchen cutlery, dishes, utensils, jewelry, and automotive products (specifically automotive polishes and cleansers) will exchange these products for advertising exposure. Brokers who buy the time sell these products to third parties for cash.

Some small stations will in fact accept products ranging from new tires, new cars, gasoline supplies, to furniture and other products, directly in barter for air time. As the owner of a small radio station told us, "You will see a lot more barter going on in the next few years if the recession deepens. Network contestant programs, offering consumer products, swap time for products. These range from color T.V. sets to freezers. When money becomes a scarce commodity, this may be a way of life for smaller stations like ours!"

A recently-retired woman executive had been instrumental in establishing barter stores in an eastern city for women's organizations, churches, and fraternal groups as a spare-time venture. She pointed out that barter may ease brutal financial pressure caused by inflation, for millions of Americans.

The Future Of Barter

"I believe that barter will be the only way many families will be able to acquire children's clothing, toys, furniture, and other household items over the next several years," she reported. "The present financial squeeze has only begun for many–and may get worse–narrowing the financial budget down to food-buying only and payment of vital bills.

"And it will not only involve poor families in cities, but many so-called 'middle-class' families as well, when the 'second-job' lay-offs take place!

"If women look hard enough, they will find barter shops already in operation in many communities. These are operated by church and women's groups, offering a variety of cleaned, used clothing for children and women, shoes, boots, rainwear, lamps, and some furniture. And if you bring in your 'swap' items, they will exchange these for things you may be able to use now. Sometimes they ask for a small cash donation to defray store expenses. Many times they do not.

"I really believe you will see *hundreds* of new barter stores come into existence in the next year and perhaps after that."

Clothing

A company publication in Florida carried a news story concerning a retired clothing manufacturer. He is planning to open three new clothing "recycling stores" to be manned by part-time retirees, who will be earning a small weekly income.

Customers who come into these stores to purchase clothing for pre-teen and teenage children will do so on a "buy-back" agreement. They will agree to re-sell the pre-teen clothing back to the store. The customer will then purchase clothing for 60% discount on the teen suits which will be used, but clean and fashionable. On another trade-up, the discount will be 30% until the transactions drop to a ten-percent "off the top" price of the last recycled price.

Vehicles

Barter extends to passenger cars, trucks, and vans in these turbulent inflationary times. There are numerous "auto clubs" emerging on both coasts where members bring their cars and pickup trucks. Even exchanges are transacted by owners. One club executive reported that pickup trucks are now in great demand because of their versatility in terms of "earning their keep" through short haul jobs. One automotive rental dealer traded a new truck for five older used passenger cars! These ranged in age from five to ten years. The member who now owns the cars will use them in a "used" car rental agency operation.

Books

There are many paperback book barter stores in existence. In a number of cases, three used paperbacks in good condition are accepted in trade for a new paperback with slight imperfections. In other stores, paperbacks are swapped on a one-for-one basis, then are re-sold by the owner to vacation and campground libraries.

Toys And Games

According to an area business publication, two entrepreneurs are planning to open a toy and game barter store in the East. The two business people, who have had extensive experience in retail hobby and game sales, plan to stock stores with games purchased from bankrupt manufacturers, "close-out" or discontinued items, and with "recycled" games accepted in trade from customers. They will also add electric trains, cars, and toys in good condition to the inventory.

The barters of used games for new models of games is a novel one, but the entrepreneurs point out that they will sell the used train sets and more expensive games to collectors who look for certain items.

Furniture

A furniture retailer, refinisher, and rebuilder in the Northeast, who advertises his business as "The Trading Post," has for the past twenty-five years, bartered furniture with customers. The firm has profited over the years because it has bartered customer's old-fashioned furniture in worn condition, for its own refinished modern furniture. But in a number of cases, the old oak-finished pieces have, on close inspection, proved to be antiques! Young people trading in old furniture are happy to take newly-refinished furniture in trade, including chairs, tables, bed frames, and chests.

One old cherry dresser was severly water-damaged after remaining in an old leaky farmhouse for years. This was taken in trade for a newly-refinished maple dresser. After a considerable amount of work, involving refitting drawers, re-gluing, and total surface refinishing, the dresser was discovered to be an early Colonial piece and was sold for a premium to a collector!

Where To Look
For "Swaps"

While there are numerous mimeographed "barter bulletins" published by organizations, church groups, and private individuals, the only recognized national barter publication is "BARTER COMMUNIQUE" published by Full Circle Marketing Corporation, Sarasota, Florida.

Several trade publications have "swap" departments, or products for barter. Real estate publications feature sections where homes in various parts of the nation are offered on a "house-for-house" trade basis. Boating publications have for many years had columns listing boat trades for sea water and fresh water enthusiasts.

With college tuition rates climbing as fast as the inflation rate, college newspapers feature barter columns which offer everything from clothing, bikes, furniture, and books, to dishes, clocks, T.V. sets, and utensils. In additon, periodic transportation is offered in return for a suitable "swap," ranging from meals to purchase of the fuel for the trip.

Attorneys, electricians, carpenters, and dentists have all made "cashless exchanges" for their services. Cars, motorcycles, lumber, shrubbery, and T.V. sets were exchanged for the specialized services of these professionals. In addition, there have been barters in connection with funeral services, eyeglasses, surgery, and hair-dressing services!

When queried as to thoughts on barter, a secretary for a Pennsylvania farm association reported that farmers in her group have exchanged horses, cattle, and hay for fencing materials. They would be willing to barter with businesses in the areas of fuel, tractor repairs, construction work, appliances, automotive repairs, and equipment.

Would farmers in her group barter with consumers for food — apples, vegetables, chickens, pigs, and corn? "It would depend greatly on the barter offer," she replied. "Does the consumer have artwork — paintings, sketches? Can the consumer teach French or another foreign language? We might consider sets of encyclopedias. Can a consumer set up an electrical generator? We would advertise these in our monthly bulletin which we circulate, and the response would determine whether a barter arrangement could be made."

Collectibles

Hundreds of hobby groups have built their activities around barter, from beer cans and coins to comic books. Circular resin records, which feature thirty and forty-year old orchestra recordings, are now in great demand by these hobbyists who offer small stereo systems in exchange for particular records!

Wood For Fuel

The present fuel shortage offers numerous opportunities for the homeowner who can split wood with either hydraulic equipment, mechanical power, or some other source. One large woodlot owner in the East offers a cord of wood valued at around $85 to anyone who contracts to split eight cords of wood for him.

Various business people report that a homeowner who needs a wood stove can barter, if he/she gets out to a small community where some services and products are scarce and needed by the stove dealer.

The same method of barter can be developed with storm window and door dealers, in smaller cities and communities. It does not work with national retail store chains, however, you will not generally even discuss the possibility of barter. It's best to stick to small towns.

Bartering Your Way To Financial Security

A former shop mechanic who retired fifteen years ago was disturbed because he was idle when not caring for his one-acre plot and house. He picked up a rundown fifty-year old fire truck and rebuilt it into a gleaming, well-running vehicle. The fire truck attracted a lot of attention from the local news media. Following an inspection of the truck, a visitor to the area offered a twenty-foot Fiberglas boat with a virtually-new engine, a trailer, and a garden tractor in exchange for the fire truck.

The barter offer was accepted and the retiree then went on to barter these items for a sail boat with an inboard engine. He traded the boat for two pieces of construction equipment a few months later. In succeeding barter transaction, he obtained a bulldozer, a small truck, six wheelbarrows, twenty fuel drums, two garden tractors, and a hay wagon!

Three years later, the bartering mechanic had a five-acre tract on a main highway, displaying fifteen massive construction equipment vehicles, three dump trucks, a building filled with compressed air equipment, tools, bicycles, and new truck tires! He had sold about $50,000 worth of equipment the previous year, and was planning to purchase *three more* fire trucks from an auto wrecking yard for restoration.

He explained his bartering philosophy this way: "I really believe you can barter just about anything that is in serviceable or working condition — something *someone can use.* You must let people know that you have something to trade, and you do that through ads in *all kinds* of newspapers and publications. Maybe you don't get the product you want the first time around —but you will if you stay with it! And the nice part of it is that somewhere along the line *you get money offered* to you in place of a trade. Sometimes the offer is pretty profitable!"

"What about food bartering?" we asked.

"Yes, that's possible, but you must deal with people on a regular basis — like some kind of farm co-op outside the city. Unless you know a farmer personally — one who raises beef cattle, hogs, corn — you may have a tough time. I think if several people formed a trade group and approached a farm co-op outlet and laid out a plan, it could work. I would also advertise on a regular basis, to farm groups in small town weeklies in a twenty- or thirty-mile radius of the area in which I — or the group—lived. You have to work at it. It won't come easy right away — but you will find barter *does* work!''

Part Three:

Considerations Along The Way

8 Evaluate Your Objectives

There are numerous ways to evaluate your personal investment objectives. Earlier in this book, we recommended the preparation of a detailed financial accounting of your income, assets, and fields of interest. Presumably, you have selected various potential areas of investment which you feel are hedges against inflation.

Mapping Your Financial Future

You have tallied the various figures, and, depending upon your individual circumstances (a salaried worker, small business owner, government employee, or a retired person), you need to begin to map your entrepreneurial financial future. Even if you are a retired person, you can still list your various sources of income in addition to your Social Security checks. The difference between the risk/reward venture routes will be the ages of each entrepreneur and the amount of money required for each individual's lifestyle — now and when younger people reach retirement age.

For those of you who are still many years from retirement, the thing to do now is to establish an *arbitrary income level* at which you would like to be able to retire. Under pressure of 12% and 13% annual increases in inflation, we realize this is difficult to do. Someone making a $30,000 annual salary would appear to be earning a good income. But begin to deduct taxes and Social Security contributions, and the net return would be reduced considerably. In terms of our 46-cents-dollars, the present cost of food, housing, clothing, and transportation for a family of four or five could whittle that amount down further. But a 10%

portion of the $30,000 should (and must!) be set aside for the future. Obviously, this percentage moves up in proportion to income above this amount.

Determining How Much You Will Need

How much will you need in the year 2020 to live comfortably if you are now twenty-five years old? What kind of lifestyle do you want? Will you be married, remain single, own your own home, live in an apartment or condominium? Will you have owned a business? What effect will the inflation and recession in the '80's have had on the U.S. economy?

Franklin Burke, of Burke, Lawton & Company, nationally-known investment specialists, says:

> "One basic fact that is easily overlooked by millions of people is this: our economy, like life, moves in cycles. Note the unpredictability of the stock market movements over the past decade. Note, too, the introduction and passing of many popular fads in music, lifestyle, and the films, books, and television programming. And as a result, the U.S. economy in 2020 — or 2025 — will be totally different — perhaps considerably improved over that being experienced today."

For the young person trying to establish an arbitrary income level for retirement, we suggest factoring in a minimum of 15% for the next five years, accounting for inflation increases.

One Theory: The Economy Will Slow Down

A slowdown in the U.S. economy could cause "stagflation," a period where inflation and recession have mired the economy with lack of movement. Unemployment would rise, and sales of goods would drop at a slow rate each month. The annual inflation rate would then taper off to about 9%, according to qualified bankers.

The Other Theory: Prices Will Double

This same group of bankers make the bold observation that in 2025, prices will only have *doubled*! They see two periods of recession, a deflationary period in the 1990's, which will flatten prices of every kind.

Unlike previous generations, young people of today earn higher incomes, own larger homes and more expensive property, own high-grade stocks and bonds, and are well-insured. Many are placing money into pension funds and programs such as I.R.A. and Keogh plans, and have invested in annuities. It is a safe bet, say investment specialists, that millions of young people will probably be able to retire at a better level of income from diversified sources than their parents did.

What To Do If You Are Retired

Ironically, the retired person has already arrived at that stage in life (all things being equal) when he/she should be able to live quite comfortably on Social Security income, savings, stock dividends, and other income. Unfortunately, the ruinous effect of these inflationary times have upset this planning. Two decades ago, Social Security income would cover most needs of the elderly. We all know this is no more.

Everyday we hear and read about older Americans in the '60's and '70's who are forced to go back to some type of employment on a part-time basis, ranging from teaching to stockroom supply work. Many simply cannot meet their increased monthly obligations on their inflation-eroded incomes. Added to these woes is the fact that many are forced to move from apartments because these are being converted to condominiums which they cannot afford to purchase.

A Business Of Your Own

If they cannot locate part-time employment, retired people must become entrepreneurs. Some of them launch profit-making ventures. Others invest in high-risk activities to earn a quick, profitable return in the 10% to 15% range.

Make Personal Loans

Some fortunate retired people have even loaned money on a high-interest, personal note basis to people of high integrity, or to family friends able to furnish excellent collateral. Monthly repayments to the lender in these cases provide excellent interest return.

Sub-Lease Property

Other retired people in Florida, for example, have sub-leased condominiums to employed people with high incomes, and have themselves opted to take smaller and more modest apartments. The financial difference has proved to be a substantial source of extra entrepreneurial income.

Lease Equipment

In one unusual and quite novel case, a former corporate executive has sub-let his twin-engine aircraft to a highly successful computer firm for a significant monthly fee. His Mercedes sedan has also been sub-let to a firm under another satisfactory financial arrangement.

Become A Consultant

Numerous retired engineers have gone back to consulting work to bolster their incomes. In Minneapolis, eighteen full-time retired agri-business experts are grossing about $2 million annually as consultants on a national and worldwide basis. They advise corporations and individuals on everything from the use of proper farm chemicals to the raising of new breeds of chickens.

What To Do If You Are Young

Let us shift our perspective for a bit and look at some hypothetical examples for young people planning their financial futures at this time.

A twenty-year-old with $1,000 who thinks he/she will need an additional $5,000 each year, can try to convert the $1,000 into $50,000 in forty-five years with a 10% return, or into $100,000 in forty-five years with a 15% return.

A 15% growth rate *doubles* your money *every five years* (four times every ten years); *sixteen times* every twenty years; *sixty-four times* in thirty years; *128 times* in thirty-five years; and *512 times* in forty-five years. On the other hand, a 7½% growth rate will be half of these amounts.

Since $1,000 can grow to over $50,000 in forty-five years at an annual growth of 10%, there is no reason then to gamble on high risk/reward ventures unless you enjoy gambling, or have some compulsion to lose! That is not to say that the 15% annual growth is always there, but it is not pie-in-the-sky thinking.

The hard advice is: *stay with your growth program*. In the words of an experienced entrepreneur, "Don't pick any of the apples until they are ready to be harvested." To be blunt, don't dig into your growth fund until it has reached the point at which it has achieved the objective you established earlier.

Here's an example of a high rate of return:

You purchase a "Systems Engineering" 12% Bond. This is a $1,000 bond, which earns $120 per year.

You borrow $2,000 from the bank at 10.5% interest to purchase two more bonds.

Total interest for three $1,000 bonds at 12%	$360.00
Interest to the bank	210.00
Balance on your $1,000 investment	$150.00
	(or 15%)

Protecting Your Income From Taxes

Unfortunately, like a fact of life, the government does not reward you for accumulating savings or making money from investments. You are taxed on your interest and dividends. Your "silent partner," the Internal Revenue Service, wants his share every year! The more financially successful you become, the greater the percentage the IRS will have coming. Hence, many people are constantly searching for tax hedges, or tax shelters, and deferral programs such as:

1. Mutual funds
2. REITS (Real Estate Investment Trusts)
3. Tax-sheltered investments

If we are going to "coin" an axiom in investing, it would go something like this: If any investment program were perfect, everyone would participate in it, and then, obviously, it would no longer be a perfect program.

Diminishing returns result from a number of factors, with the basic reason being *too many people* desire the same return from the same investment when it is numerically impossible to achieve this. During an inflationary period like the present one, however, normal investors are cautious and their plans have been tempered by fear. In the past, there have been many examples of the "Lemming Syndrome" where common stock value in the market has been diluted due to overbuying.

An extreme example of this action is the "chain letter" scheme. This curious phenomenon is illegal because it violates U.S. Postal Service regulations, and is classified as a fraud. The postal inspectors point out that chain letter scams are fraudulent because after only a few cycles, nearly every person on earth would need to participate in the stunt in order to receive a return!

Casino gambling is another example of diminishing returns on "investments" of which you should be aware. In casinos, house odds are as high as *40 to 1* against your chances of earning back your wager. Informed sources state that some casino slot machines are set to pay out only *once in seventeen to eighteen tries!* A well-known banker remarked recently, "If you want to make some money in gambling casinos, then buy gambling casino stocks! It's a lot better than gambling several hundred dollars away on a roulette wheel!"

All of this is being presented within the framework of evaluating investment opportunities designed as inflation hedges that are open to you.

Earlier in this book, we discussed the importance of determining your personality and how this is related to potential entrepreneurial investments. Have you listed all of your areas on a second sheet attached to your financial profile?

Your Personality
As An Asset

Your personality can be a help, or a hindrance, in terms of entrepreneurial activities. We discussed the landlord role of the individual who owns rental property of any kind, and the type of personality required to cope with tenant problems.

A personality trait desirable is that of being able to remain satisfied with a seemingly monotonous program of setting aside a specific sum each month for future financial returns. Once a program is launched, the individual must be consistent in carrying the plan forward for months.

Are you inquisitive about how people earn their money? Do you seriously want to know how some individuals amass fortunes; or are able to put together business propositions which will eventually make money for all participants?

Information Is The Key

Information is *the key to building wealth*. Did you know, for example, the rich and super-rich (along with principals in huge corporations) pay as much as $50,000 per year for day-to-day financial information and political news so that they can plan their investment strategies?

Your Valuable
Spare Time

Is your spare time spent loafing, relaxing, or playing at some sport, hobby, or other past-time more important to you than sacrificing this extra time in "hustling" to find additional sources of revenue? Will many hours of spare time effort keep you content in the knowledge that what you are doing will ultimately bring you a considerable amount of money?

It is in this realm of questions where we begin to separate the entrepreneur from the merely curious individual who is afraid, or unwilling, to go the risk/reward route because of the contributions of time involved.

Your Locality
As An Asset

We arrive at the next stage of evaluation — your immediate environment and how it relates to your future entrepreneurial activities.

Where do you live, and why? Are you located in a major city in the Northeast, a suburban community in the Midwest, a small town in the deep South, a remote eastern farming area, or in a foreign country? Are you in the armed forces, or in a retirement community in Florida, California, or Texas? The reason your location is so important as an investor is that it imposes certain conditions which will govern your ability to control the operation. In many cases, you must be able to observe, participate in, travel to and from the point at which your risk funds are at work. And certain economic forces in *your particular geographic area* can help or dampen your chances for success.

Where Survivors Of Inflation
Will Be Located

A group of eastern economists who have been studying the inflation closely, predict that entrepreneurs will do better in the "Sunbelt" states for a number of economic, phsychological, and physical conditions during the next five years. They point out that the states or regions of southern California, Arizona, New Mexico, Texas, Louisiana, Florida, Alabama, and Georgia offer the best opportunities for new ventures. They add that these states are highly diversified in terms of business and industry, are high on the personal income levels, have growing populations, and have better natural resource bases. They observe that more new ventures and new industries have been created by entrepreneurs in southern California than in most other areas! It is their claim that this "Sunbelt" area will weather inflation better than other areas of the nation.

Yet all economists do not agree on even the basic subjects. Did you know, for example, that the National

Bureau of Economic Research, a private group of economists, has *not yet* declared a recession?

Vijay Kothare, editor of FOCUS Business Newsweekly, a financially-oriented business publication circulated in several eastern states, believes that entrepreneurial fortunes will be made in the so-called Northeast Industrial states, and in the heavy manufacturing areas of the Midwest. He contends that new business ventures will supplant those which will disappear as a result of crushing inflationary forces.

Psychological View of Entrepreneurial Investing

Like star athletes, entrepreneurs find they must "psyche" themselves into achieving their goals. It is one thing to write a check for a stock or bond purchase and send it to your broker, then sit back and go about your daily activities. It will be quite another thing to invest several thousands of dollars in a small business venture five miles from your home, and be unable to see how that business activity is developing day-by-day.

In an effort to understand the changes the future will bring about for the small business owner, it is necessary to trace the past for clues.

How We've Changed

A number of generations ago, before the advent of the passenger car, people lived near their places of employment. Their job bases were most likely factories, mines, ocean docks, quarries, canning plants, and other product manufacturing activities. This meant that their lives were largely uncomplicated because they could walk from their homes to their jobs within minutes, and could also return to their homes with a minimum of delay. People generally stayed with their jobs for their entire working lives. The cost of living at that time was very moderate because financial needs were more structured and quite simple.

At the end of World War II, however, a new era of population mobility emerged, inspired by the modern passenger car and the expansive growth of highways. Millions of peple moved away from the large cities into suburbs and to small communities, disrupting the established structure of American life and business. Plants and factories followed the migration of people, deserting the cities for open land and small communities.

Part of this phenomenon was based on the desire to escape crime, vandalism, and high city taxes. In the new industrial parks, firms located complete industries because of attractive tax rates, space for future expansion, and because of proximity to major highways and waterways for greater distribution potential.

Today, we find people do not live near their place of employment, but they are close enough to the roads and highways that can take them to their jobs quickly.

Let us say you live in a small community and you commute by car daily to your place of employment. You may, perhaps, live as far as twenty to thirty miles from the job. As you drive, do you notice the area around you carefully?

Are there numerous self-service stores along the route? Are there service stations, shops, apartments, or is the land unoccupied? People going to work usually need such products and services as lunches, work clothing, newspapers, minor car repairs, or a place where they can launder clothes. They may even want to cash a check, or pay a utility bill.

How To Spot Opportunities In Your Area

As an entrepreneur, you must be a keen observer of the opportunities to *fill people's needs*.

Here is a case history which illustrates this point completely. An accountant for a large TV manufacturer and a friend who was an unemployed hosiery plant superintendent, would drive by a small community every Saturday on their way to play golf. They would usually stop at a small cross-roads to purchase gas for the car, and to buy snacks for lunch. It was the only store operating in this rural area.

They observed that the small store was quite busy on Saturdays, keeping the owners (an elderly couple) moving between the small counters and the lone gas pump. Since the product inventory was usually low, some customers would walk out without purchasing anything.

The accountant remarked to his friend that perhaps by expanding the store, sprucing it up a bit, and adding more groceries and other consumable products, business could be increased considerably. Two pumps, he pointed out, in place of one, could handle more gasoline sales.

They discussed the little store several times that day. Suddenly, the thought occurred to them. If the store could be purchased, it would furnish full-time employment for the unemployed hosiery superintendent. Like others, his plant had moved to the South at the end of World War II. The accountant realized the store purchase could also add to his regular income with only spare-time participation. And both were certain their families would assist in clerking and sales.

Later that night, they stopped at the small store and discussed the possibility of a purchase with the elderly couple. The owners confessed that the store operation was beginning to become a tremendous burden. Then the accountant casually mentioned a "buy out" sum in the low five-figure area. This would be contingent upon a quick sale — within thirty days. The couple chatted among themselves for about fifteen minutes, then agreed to the proposal.

A quick handshake all around, and a written agreement prepared on a sheet of stationery with all parties signing, closed the deal. The accountant gave the owners $50.00 in cash as a deposit on a forthcoming downpayment within a few days. The final settlement would be completed immediately after a full inventory of the store and its facilities had been made.

Later, the two families approved the planned purchase and the cash for the store was obtained. Within a month's time, the unemployed hosiery superintendent (now a small businessman) was operating the store at a regular salary, rebuilding the interior, restocking new merchandise, while the accountant tabulated receipts, paid bills, and kept financial records on weekends when not busy at the gas pumps or assisting at the counters.

In a year's time, the small store had doubled in size. A delicatessen was added, and was fully stocked with food products. Outside, there were two new gas pumps. A small building was stocked with lubricants and other automotive supplies.

The partners formed a corporation with three other family members to obtain operating capital. The store hours were long and tedious, but they persisted in improving their investment. They purchased a five-acre tract of land across the road because they had observed two residential housing tracts being built about a mile from the store location. They decided to construct a newer, larger store which would include several departments: a meat market, bakery department, delicatessen, and a vegetable and produce de-partment. Their plan also included the building of a full-sized service station nearby.

The five entrepreneurs who "knew nothing" about large retail food operations began to ask questions of food wholesalers, and toured other large retail store and supermarkets to obtain information on merchandising.

They had plans drawn for their large store building, presented these to a series of area bankers who *turned them down* on their loan request of $150,000! Finally they obtained their loan from a financial institution only by pledging *all* of their homes as collateral. Within seven months, the new store was constructed and opened for business.

More unemployed hosiery workers were hired and trained as retail clerks to staff the larger store. Business volume grew dramatically as new homes were constructed in the immediate area and the population expanded.

The Payoff

Today, the well-established corporation which now has numerous "built in" inflation hedges, has three of the original principals still involved on a full-time basis. The accountant is now the Chairman of the Board. The firm owns five other supermarket operations and mini-market centers within thirty-five small retail stores. Three other affiliated corporations owned by the same individuals and their families operate apartment projects, own commercial land, and office structures. Stock in the combined venture is valued in the millions of dollars.

The risk/reward principle narrated here in detail to show you how this venture was developed on a step-by-step basis, is a classic example of entrepreneurial intelligence, judgement, and hard work.

What if the original members had decided to forget their evaulation of the purchase of the small store? What if they had decided it was too much trouble to handle in their spare time, and continued playing their Saturday golf games? The answers to these questions are obvious.

The accountant was a vital part of the operation from its beginning. Because he knew the accounting functions, business principles, taxes, cash flow, payroll preparation, financial matters, and bank operations, he utilized all of this information. It was his strong suit. His associate learned quickly, and kept building experience in the retail area. Both sought additional information over the years and obtained it.

Your Knowledge And Experience As An Asset

What is your strong suit? What part of your experience or knowledge can help you as a small business owner? Are you an accountant, attorney, farmer, construction worker, architect, salesperson, computer programmer, pilot, truck driver, mechanic, teacher, retired detective, or real estate broker? Any of these occupations offer a *knowledge base* from which to operate.

Obviously, people who are concerned with daily financial activities such as accountants, investment specialists, banking personnel, stock brokers, real estate brokers, insurance specialists, are closer to the "money scene" than are most others. However, it all comes down to a question of perspective in terms of a financial objective for yourself.

Although the average person finds his/her only exposure to the world of finance is through a bank deposit passbook, checking account transactions, intermittent dealing with stock brokers, or contacts with a bank officer when applying for a personal loan, this poses no great obstacle toward your financial goal.

As a matter of fact, thousands of stock brokers or account executives who deal daily in stocks, bonds, or commodities, *have not made fortunes* (as many would believe), despite the fact that they are "next to" the market. In a goodly number of cases, the only income they have made is from their *sales commissions*!

So, do not let the fact that you have not studied financial reports, don't know a "leverage factor" from an "option," don't fully comprehend financial summaries, do not know various aspects of real estate appraisals, or have not rubbed elbows with bankers, keep you from getting into a good opportunity. You can *learn what you need to know* from your own perspective about financial reports. You can learn to understand the terms of mortgage loans, deeds, sales agreements, tax sale data, and other related information.

Earlier, we covered aspects of your environment, your immediate living area, and the type of occupation in which you are involved on a daily basis. Are there real estate ventures still affordable in these inflation-

marked days available to you in your town or city? If you live in an outlying area, or suburban community, you may be able to find more properties and buildings available than in an urbanized area.

Opportunities In Real Estate In Your Area

Here's a case in point. A construction worker, driving to and from his job site in a suburban area over a period of months, thought he recognized an opportunity. He noticed there were two abandoned service stations near a busy intersection. Both structures, which included service bays and offices, had been boarded up to prevent damage from vandalism. Apparently, each business had closed because of a variety of reasons, ranging from too much competition to poor management.

The construction man noted that there was a considerable amount of commercial development in the immediate area for about one-half mile. There were small stores, apartments, several service stations, fast-food operations, appliance repair and auto supply shop outlets, plus two supermarkets. He noted with interest, that there were no office structures of any kind in the vicinity.

On a Saturday, he took several hours to inspect one of the abandoned service stations, checking the 200 feet of space once occupied by gas pump islands and service parking areas. The building structure itself was approximately 25' x 70' in size, with veneered enamel paneling on its exterior. There were the usual two restroom facilities at one end of the building.

His enterprising mind pondered the possibility of converting the unused building into a small, one-story office building with three partitioned offices. Additional restrooms, a heating system, and air conditioning would have to be installed. But the basic structure was already there, and appeared to be in good condition. There would be adequate space for parking.

When contacted by our construction worker, the owner asked for $75,000 in the sale of the property. After a short bargaining session (when it was pointed out that the site was not drawing any money and was a liability to the owner), the price was reduced to $65,000. Our proposed buyer also pointed out there would be no commission in the transaction, since there wasn't a broker involved. But the construction man learned that a settlement had to be made within sixty days since the owner was planning to retire to Florida with the proceeds.

After some financial planning, the construction worker found he could raise $15,000 on his own, but needed the additional funding. He met with his employer and outlined the entire proposal, offering a partnership arrangement in the proposed project. After a careful inspection, the employer agreed to add $15,000 to the down payment amount. Then both men obtained a mortgage for the balance from an area bank.

Work on converting the building into a three-tenant office structure developed during weekend periods and in the evenings. Within three months, a new building emerged with attractive window areas, a brick-framed entrance, and bright new office areas complete with all required facilities. A real estate broker in the area obtained tenants, who leased for two-year periods, and paid several months' rental in advance.

The Payoff

Over the past three years, the two men have purchased five additional abandoned service station buildings and have converted all of these into attractive, one-story office structures. With rentals from all the buildings totaling about $40,000 annually, these men are now converting former supermarket buildings into "mini-market" specialty shops, home appliance stores, and mini-malls. They have created solid inflation hedges for themselves.

An observation on the experiences of these two investors can be made. The construction man saw a *need* for office structures in a particular area, then *filled the need* with the help of an experienced partner. He evaluated his objective and his opportunity intelligently, then moved, implementing his risk/reward situation.

Look at this experience: We have a young woman who lives in a small town far from large, bustling cities. Married to a man working for a local daily cooperative, she is raising three children, one in high school, and the others coming up quickly through the grades. At one time, she was considered an efficient secretary who worked for the local sewer and water authority. Now, because of inflation's effect, she needs additional income to supplement her husband's deflated, limited salary.

She found she had five free hours every day. By staggering her housework, she could utilize three full days to some income-producing work. She began to investigate the opportunities around her. Were there any opportunities for a "house-bound," but business-knowledgeable homemaker in a small community? You bet there were!

Recognizing Needs In Your Area

She quickly eliminated all the standard part-time sales positions because she was essentially bound to the house and did not have transportation. She understood (from overhearing a conversation at a local bank) that several small business people in town had no secretaries. They spent a good amount of time on sales calls, but had no one to answer the phone while they were away from the office. Neither did they have anyone to answer correspondence, do typing, make copies of documents, or complete reports. Her enterprising mind went to work.

Deciding that a phone-answering service with a live person response, rather than a taped message would appeal to these business people, she decided to offer secretarial services. She called two of these business owners late that afternoon proposing the plan. For a fee, she would take their calls in her home "office" for them during the day. Both were quite interested and said they would pay the phone company to install lines in her home. Also, both business people mentioned their need for her typing and secretarial assistance.

Checking the phone directory, she located other business people and the heads of small firms in the immediate area. Together with calls and letters, she found at least ten people who *needed* and *wanted* her services.

Agreeing to have a spare room converted into an office, her husband added second-hand office furniture, a rented electric typewriter, and supplies. The telephone company installed a special "answering board," linking this outlet with all of her subscribers. She was now in operation — a business venture of her own!

Keeping a daily log of calls, times, and messages, she typed correspondence and reports in slack periods. She found the first checks for her services beginning to make a difference in the amount of cash left in the family "till" every week. It began to build slowly. Always thinking of expansion, she began to investigate additional ways of providing services to her customers. She bought an electric copier for "walk-in" customers and for her clients who needed copies of certain documents. Additional requests for secretarial services began to roll in, and the answering end of the business expanded to a point where she needed to hire a woman from down the street for about three hours a day.

A local woodstove manufacturer asked her to make a series of calls every day for him at a good fee, to be followed up with sales letters. A fuel dealer found she could handle the stuffing of invoices less expensively than his office staff, and offered her 1,800 invoices with addressed envelopes each month, at a profiitable rate.

Now she was able to put her high school-aged daughter to work on both the telephone answering service and the typing of letters. She found her business had expanded to the point where she still needed another part-time person. And she found her income from the operation was making life easier in this inflation-plagued period, offering a hedge against income erosion. She will survive the effects of a recession because of her low overhead and flexibility.

This case history is an actual account of a New Jersey homemaker's profitable secretarial service, including telephone answering facilities. It illustrates how she utilized past experience successfully in pursuing a risk/reward venture. Granted, her original investment was less than $1,000, but it required the same amount of judgement and direction as would an investment of ten times that amount. She achieved her original objective because of good planning, intelligent evaluation of needs, and the fulfilling of the needs. She will maintain a profitable operation despite severe economic dislocations because she is self-employed and because her clients can save money by using her services.

Combining Two Needs In
A Successful Business

Among other records of successful women entrepreneurs is this one of an older woman who started a "house sitting" agency in her western suburban community. She found that older people, many of whom were living on Social Security and had sold their homes, needed additional incomes. They also needed

pleasant surroundings and something to keep them busy. That was the first need. The second need resulted from the vulnerability of numerous expensive homes located in the area. Owners of these homes took frequent, extended vacations and business trips. Theft, burglary, and vandalism resulted from break-ins in these absentee-owned houses. Their very emptiness was literally inviting criminals to enter. Traditional burglar alarm systems proved ineffective. At homes placed under police surveillance at the request of the departing owners, the sight of a cruising police car alerted burglars who were able to leave quickly. The solution to this serious problem was to combine the needs of the homeowners and the retirees, and the formation of the house-sitting agency!

Rather than have her house-sitters merely drive by, collect the mail, water the plants, and feed the pets, this ingenious woman had a different idea. Her house sitters would actually *live in the house* while the owners were away.

Jobs were created for many retired people. They were afforded a constantly changing environment and pleasant surroundings. They also felt their efforts were appreciated because of the responsibility they had assumed. The homeowners were happy, too. They would no longer have to rely on cooperative neighbors to keep a watchful eye on the house; to notify police to make security checks; to notify the Post Office to stop mail deliveries; or to drop pets off at kennels.

Success has made a difference in this house sitting entrepreneur's life. She has now franchised her agency throughout the West Coast area, and is writing a guidebook about the details involved in starting and operating a successful house sitting agency.

Questions To Ask When
Searching For Business
Ideas

* What do people in your area *need* and *want* during these inflationary times?

* What *type* of services would they be purchasing if these were available to them?

* What type of business is *lacking* in this vicinity, and *why*?

* What will these services cost?

* How much profit will there be after all costs have been calculated?

* How much "front money" will you need to get started?

* Will you be covered with enough insurance to give your family a return on your investment in case you should die?

* Will you need licenses, permits, official approval, changes in zoning, extra help, accounting or bookkeeping services?

* Can you get some solid business information on your proposed venture from your local banker, or the area's Chamber of Commerce?

* Should you get into sales, service, consultation, franchised operations, or start a mail order business from your home; do electronic copy work; operate a picture-framing business; cultivate mushrooms; start a one-acre herb farm; clip newspapers for clubs, associations and firms; or convert old houses?

These suggested income-producing ideas are not the "wheeler-dealer" stories you read about in *The Wall Street Journal* or *Fortune*. You know the kind — purchasing gold in Chile and selling it through a broker in London, then investing the profits in the Japanese stock market or in Swiss francs. Nor are these similar to the purchase and sale of power boats to strange types at high profits, while they constantly look back over their shoulders for signs of Federal Agents!

Take a good look at a lot of enterprises, consider many new business ventures and ideas, measuring them against growing inflation pressures and possible profits. Then ask yourself: "What do I *want to do* to earn an additional income to act as a hedge by reason of investment?"

Evaluate your objectives in terms of your own background and experience. Weigh all considerations in terms of the proposed project. Do you have the funds to invest in a venture at this time? Are you equipped to cope with cyclical changes which inflation and recession will bring? Are you motivated to the extent that you will carry out whatever task your venture requires of you?

When you have answered all of these questions on the proper evaluation of your risk/reward opportunity, you are ready to put your planned strategy into action.

9 Risk Capital—What It Is

There are a number of definitions of "risk capital." Basically, it all comes down to this interpretation, which investment authorities, financial analysts, securities market broker/dealers, and bankers agree is accurate:

Definition Of Risk Capital

"Risk capital is money, or funds, *you can afford to lose* without disrupting your daily life, or your family's, in terms of financial needs."

Where We Take Risks

Risks are taken daily, even in these inflation-marked days by investors in the stock market, in commodity purchases, in gold and silver futures, in financial futures, in certain types of real estate operations, and in other cyclical areas which may be adversely affected by an unexpected, sudden situation. This jolting state-of-event can be anything from a national calamity, increased rates of inflation, bank prime rate increases, poor weather, international crises, political decisions, or bad financial reports from major corporations.

We have been relating detailed histories of the experiences of various entrepreneurs who have followed their own risk/reward concepts and principles. Obviously, there are small risks, and there are RISKS of the monumental variety. How you make a risk judgement depends upon your individual circum-

stances: your age, your annual income, your personal lifestyle, and your future objectives.

Determining Where You Are

Quite possibly, you fit into one of these three classes of measurement:

1. *Young married couple/Young single individual with growing income.*
   — *You are able to take risks and deal with long-term investments for profitable returns.*

2. *Middle-age married people with growing children with income fairly well established.*
   — You can take some risks, but need a fairly quick return. You are also looking for some form of tax shelter if in higher income brackets.

3. *Older people of retirement age/Recently retired people/Older widows and widowers, on fixed rate of investment.*
   — You cannot afford to take high risks, or long-term investing. You must get a quick, profitable venture which produces a quick return.

The "Young Marrieds"

The "Young Marrieds" category with growing income (usually two incomes) is most likely to become involved in risk/reward ventures. They can afford to seek risk capital and take certain investment risks because of their flexibility and age.

Individuals of all the classes must exercise good judgement and intelligence in making difficult financial decisions. Information and investigation are the two most important factors in any entrepreneur's life where investments are concerned. If these are ignored, then you may as well visit a gambling casino and bet at the roulette table, because you will lose your money.

Perhaps you are among those in a declining group who still observe daily those common stocks which look like the "growth" variety. You may still feel quite strongly that there is money to be made in the market, and you are going to attempt to get it. If you have probed the securities market records, reviewed all of the daily transactions of the various exchanges, read the *WALL STREET JOURNAL, BARRON'S, DUN'S REVIEW, JOURNAL OF COMMERCE, FORBES, MONEY*, and other publications which monitor the market and financial scene, you must know by now that there are "good" stocks and there are "bad" stocks in terms of investing and return.

The Retired Group And The Elderly

Certainly, the elderly and people on retirement incomes should be with "Blue Chip" stocks and bonds, only where dividends are important. However, young people can adopt the same investment stance if they do not want to take warranted stock risks.

Growth Stocks

Basically, stocks are purchased for either quick return (Blue Chip stocks), or as a gamble for the future growth and higher profit returns — a speculation. The so-called growth (or "hot") stocks usually originate in *new technological areas*. Many people will recall the spectacular growth of Xerox two decades ago. Then came the skyrocketing computer hardware stocks. These were followed by the stocks of firms which were heavily into NASA-oriented industries. The high risk investments are still with us, but must be regarded as extremely speculative for the *average* individual.

Today's Growth Areas

What are today's new technologies? They include lasar beam developments; telecommunications; medicomputer innovations; pharmaceuticals which are termed "wonder drugs"; computerized graphic art techniques; bionic parts industries; sophisticated electronics; nuclear-powered engines for space use; new revolutionary photo camera developments and photography. All of these are among some of the numerous and dramatic developments now being tested in secrecy in corporate laboratories and shops, and in government research and development (R&D) departments.

The growth stocks tied to new technologies seem to burst into public prominence almost overnight, hurtling to record highs in a matter of days. The "trick" is *to know as much as you can* about that specific stock, and to move *decisively and quickly* before the stock is oversubscribed. This is what separates the professional stock investor from the amateur investor. The amateur usually follows the "Greater Fool Theory" of stocks purchasing which is:

> "Sure, I'm a fool to have purchased that stock at such a high price, but there is another fool who will buy my stock at a higher price after I've sold!"

And there is some credence to this philosophy as it relates to stock purchases. But it also applies to the purchase of real estate at inflated prices.

Glamour Stocks

Glamour stocks are tied to the state-of-the-arts in specific fields–electronics, nucleonics, engineering, and energy.

Cyclical Stocks

Cyclical stocks are those associated with companies whose products are linked to spendable income of individuals. These take wide swings as products are purchased in record quantities or levels. These products include passenger cars, clothing, houses, recreation vehicles, furniture, appliances, sporting goods, and other items related to travel or recreation. When the spending stops, you can see an immediate drop in stock value.

In other words, you can see a one-year high at one point, then an average value another year, followed by a poor year over the following twelve months. Financial analysts using charts plot these visual trends scientifically from transaction figures. They use the Sigma Curve technique. Some examples of cyclical stocks are U.S. Steel, General Motors, Winnebago Industries, Sears, United Airlines, Spalding, and others. Blue Chip stocks include A.T.&T., Du Pont, Exxon, General Foods, and others. Growth stocks include IBM, Bio-Gas Colorado, Resorts International, and others.

Most securities broker/dealers advise you today that your returns (including commissions involved in buying and selling the stocks) won't be as much as if you had deposited the money in a savings account. This is true unless you intend to make a substantial investment of $5,000 to $10,000. Strangely enough, there appears to be a fringe group of securities broker/dealers who were once conservative in financial evaluations who now show interest in growth stocks in place of bonds!

Over-The-Counter Stocks

Some stock investment entrepreneurs are still enchanted by the so-called "Cats and Dogs" stocks found in the over-the-counter market (OTC). Some people believe it is these stocks, where perhaps 50¢-per-share stock of a small corporation will either blaze into national prominence, increasing its value tremendously (and be acquired by a large national corporation), or figure in a profitable stock split of some kind.

Mutual Funds

Still others are enchanted with Mutual Funds of the "go-go" variety. These are funds which see-saw unpredictably. Also of interest to these people are Commodities, which is a volatile and extremely speculative investment area. Here you are betting against nature, and the future, specifically in the field of agricultural products, grain, corn, cowhides, and other items.

This book does not purport to be a primer on the stock market, or to concern itself primarily with securities investments; the authors merely outline ground rules and conditions, approaches, and an awareness of the risks involved.

There are two concepts to be considered in evaluating approaches to stock market investing. There is the "fundamental" approach, and there is the "technique" method.

The factor of "TEN" as a base is used in determining price ratio. In other words, $1.00 invested should earn 10¢ in its return to the investor. Stocks selling for $10.00 should earn $1.00. Common stocks, by this standard of measurement, will earn 5% on investments.

The Risks In The Stock Market

Be aware of the risks in stock market investing. It is usually the small investor who gets burned by purchasing nondescript stocks which sound great, i.e., "Got it on a hot tip from my barber!" and "Heard other people were buying that stock!" and "It's bound to go up!" Don't be taken in by emotion.

If this field is interesting to you, study all the books on investing in securities you can put your hands on. Then select a reputable broker, or securities dealer with the proper credentials and affiliations. Study financial records as carefully as you would statistics in your field. Ask a lot of questions. Don't invest on the basis of second-hand information.

Read the established financial publications that cut through the public relations veneer of publicly-owned corporations. Subscribe to these and learn what is happening in the marketplace. And rely on this news rather than what appears in "newsletters" from individuals. Remember, too, that old devil INFLATION has got both his hands in your pockets and will cancel out some of that hoped for profit!

The Difference Between Risk and Venture Capital

While on the subject of risk capital, we should draw a distinction between "risk capital" and "venture capital." These should not be confused.

Risk capital is the money you invest in an enterprise in the hope of realizing a reward or return.

Venture capital, which came into prominence after World War II, is also risk capital, but in a different form. It comes from wealthy individuals, companies, corporations, or groups of investors. It is believed that their investment in *your new product, service, or business* will earn them a profit over a period of time. Usually, venture capital sources will purchase stock, loan money on long-term notes, or make funds available at specific periods of time under various conditions.

Through financial authorities, many small communities in the United States have established venture capital sources to create jobs for people. Numerous individuals with new products but with little or no capital with which to produce their products, have been launched successfully by these communitiy venture capital sources.

Entrepreneurs seeking risk capital fit into three classes:

* Sole proprietorships
* Partnerships
* Corporations

The Internal Revenue Service has explicit regulations on each of these tax categories and types of taxes to be paid on profits made. You can obtain the 192-page "Tax Guide for Small Business" from the IRS, 1111 Constitution Avenue, NW, Washington, DC, 20224, at no cost. It is a valuable guide if you are thinking of starting a business, operating a business, or plan to sell the one you already own. It will tell you specfically how various federal tax laws apply to your venture.

Where To Obtain Risk Capital

Normally, risk capital is obtained in various ways: banks, financial institutions, credit union sources, foundations, wealthy patrons, venture capital sources, friends, relatives, government agencies, or through stock sales of privately-held corporations.

What you must determine is a three part process: 1. What is your financial objective? 2. How do you intend to conduct the operation after the investment transaction? and 3. What is the source of your investment funds (risk capital)?

How The Loan Is Secured

All loans must be secured in some way, not only with banks, but with friends and relatives. Bank loans, personal or commercial, are quite explicit and formal, complying with state and federal regulations. These require sufficient collateral to cover defaults (should this occur) on the original loan. Promissory notes drawn between individuals are customary, and can be prepared simply from stock or prepared documents, or written in great detail.

All of the conditions must be spelled out — the amounts of money involved, interest to be paid, length of time the money is needed, and any other specifiic condition to be agreed upon.

Information You Will Need To Provide

In the case of venture capital sources, as head of a small firm or corporation, you will be asked at one time or another to allocate a specific amount of capital stock with owner-interest percentage indicated to the source, and as assurance of dividend payment if the company becomes successful.

In all cases, you will be asked to detail your own investment contribution in terms of cash to be expended in the venture. You will also be asked to provide a number of related figures (financial records) pertaining to your operating budget, and your projected sales figures. Perhaps at the outset, you may not need to borrow funds to start your business. But somewhere down the line as the venture expands, you will certainly require *operating capital*. This will happen as expenses increase and cash is needed. With months of operation under your belt, you will then have some sort of track record on your operational history to show to potential lenders.

Allocating Your Risk Funds

If you would review your list of "necessities" (your living needs, obligations, recreational interests and desires), you can determine what areas can be placed in a "risk" category to assist you as a guide in your activities. For instance:

1. Housing
2. Food   } Essentials
3. Taxes

4. Utilities
5. Clothing } Necessary
6. Savings

7. Social activities
8. Vacations
9. Insurance
10. Miscellaneous

} One or more of these may be placed at a "risk" level (i.e., the kind of risk related to personality and sophistication of the investor, and reward potential.)

Risk/Reward Relationships

Fortunes are made by exploiting the risk/reward ratio, but usually not the investor.

Example: VERY HIGH RISK/REWARD

Risk: Bet $41.00 you can determine a three-digit number.

Reward: Win $500 for guessing the three-digit number.

Risk/reward ratio: 1/500

Since there are 1,000 numbers available (000 through 999), the odds are 2:1 against someone winning. Hence the tremendous profits in the numbers games and lotteries.

This principle of numbers has been exploited by several state government-approved gambling commissions with high motives and objectives in terms of using the proceeds. For example, Pennsylvania contributes a major portion of funds collected from lottery sales toward Senior Citizens benefits.

Let's examine additional case histories of risk/reward concepts and principles. Earlier, we covered areas of expertise each individual possesses in terms of his/her knowledge, experience, and hobby.

Over the past twenty-five years, a number of women have launched numerous enterprises, some of which have made their founders small fortunes. Their keen knowledge of business and the modern marketplace needs clearly indicate this in all cases, which often spells the difference between failure or a successful venture.

Using Your Knowledge And Experience To Obtain Risk Capital

Once such experience concerns a young New York-based woman who sold electronic copier machines for a major corporation. She did so well in sales that she was promoted to an East Coast sales manager's position. But all of this time, she was planning for the day when she would launch her own operation — new kinds of jigsaw puzzles? The interest had its beginnings in her childhood and had remained strong throughout the years.

Since she had a regular income from sales work, the young woman decided to create a new line of jigsaw puzzles and market them to department and stationery stores. Because she had no plant of her own, and only a modest "nest-egg" (risk capital) of $2,000, she decided to sub-contract the actual manufacturing activity, purchasing packaging and supplies. However, she would do the marketing of the product herself. This was one of her strengths, or the "strong suit" we mentioned earlier.

Over a three-year period, working in her spare time away from the sales position, she sold the puzzles directly to New York retail stores. Later, however, she was able to turn over the sales distribution to established representatives, who, because of their network of customers (hundreds of retail stores located in eastern markets), were able to sell a greater volume.

Now she was at the point of further expansion of her small jigsaw puzzle company. Decisions had to be made. She elected to devote all of her time to the embryonic company. But she would need a commercial loan of a significant sum to staff her small office, increase production, widen sales efforts through travel, and plan new products for the line. Despite all of the competition from large established jigsaw puzzle makers and distributors, her small company was showing impressive sales.

How She Got The Loan

Based on *performance, sales, and her full-time participation and guidance*, she received the loan which enabled the young president to move her company "down the road."

Now, nine years after she first launched her operation, her jigsaw puzzle sales are in the six-figure bracket, and growing at a rate of forty percent each year! She is a hard-working entrepreneur, whose evidence of faith in herself and her product is now graphically reflected in the money she is making. Her risk/reward concept was carefully developed and carried out decisively.

Perhaps the most definitive characteristic of her sales objectives lies in the fact that her company, structured to buffet the currents of inflation, produces products (puzzles) which are *distinctly different* and *more expensive* than the competitor's. She has carved out a unique segment of the jigsaw puzzle market for her own products. Individuals thinking of developing a line of new games and marketing these should study her sales tactic carefully.

Using Current Problems
To Create Risk/Reward
Opportunities: Security Industries

Can an adverse condition create opportunities? You bet! Business crimes, including "white collar" crimes, shoftlifting, business product thefts, industrial espionage, illegal wiretapping, now cost industry and the U.S. taxpayers about $30 billion annually. This figure comes from the Federal Bureau of Investigation and the U.S. Chamber of Commerce, as well as from private security sources. Over the past thirty years, a giant security industry has emerged to provide uniformed guards, K-9 patrol dogs, sophisticated alarm systems, computerized plant access control systems, push-button combination locks, and electronic computerized plastic card "keys" for hotel/motel use, and other safeguards for business and industry. It generates about $2.5 billion in services.

Business owners in this new growing field of plant and office security have developed products which would make a science fiction writer green with envy!

There are dozens of small firms manufacturing sophisticated security devices. And they are financially- and market-oriented to survive the ravages of inflation. An example of the risk/reward principle in this area of industrial security is the story of the development of a remarkable electronic unit. The device, a small "transmitter detector" which looks like a digital wrist watch when worn, is capable of detecting "parasitic" wire taps on any telephone in a business office or home. A thin, pinoted indicator will spin violently on the unit's face if a "bugged" phone is approached by the person wearing the instrument.

The two young electronic technicians who developed this device have sold several hundred units at $290 each. They have also developed tiny radio transmitters for use on the collars of K-9 dogs. These enable security guards to hear the voices of intruders when animals prowl around storage areas at a distance of up to two miles.

A product which brought the pair into national prominence in the security industry was the result of work done in connection with a small radio transmitter development — a sophisticated electronic device. it is called a "Pocket Alarm," and is about the size of a pack of cigarettes. It is used by couriers and messengers who carry large sums of money, stock certificates, diamonds, and other valuables from office buildings to banks in large cities. The couriers in most cases walk from one point to another.

If there is danger of a holdup, the individual carrying this alarm device in a pocket, need only press a button which actuates a radio signal (silent). This is picked up by cruising security patrol cars, monitoring specific city areas. The arrest or apprehension of the person attempting robbery can be accomplished within a few minutes.

These products are being marketed to security industry buyers now by leasing sales specialty firms in the field. The two innovators now have a well-financed and staffed electronics firm with support from shareholders representing affluent business groups. The young executives not only have a number of skilled technicians now on their staff, but as principals, they both draw weekly salaries *comparable to their original product investment*.

Private Detective Agencies

Another young woman recognized an opportune activity and implemented her program. She was a licensed private detective who carried a weapon, wore civilian clothes, and for months guarded show business personalities while on tour. She saw the need for specially-trained uniformed guards who could handle exuberant crowds skillfully, without causing physical harm to anyone.

She made her first move by accumulating her risk capital to start her enterprise by selling two large "luxury" cars she owned. She also used savings from a bank account. In an interview which convinced lenders of her capability of administering and operating the proposed new guard staff, she was able to obtain additional funding from an investor's group

Trained in criminology techniques, the woman also had a good background in office administration. By selecting outstanding security instructors, she molded a group of fifty men and women in a unique protective guard force which commanded top fees from promoters and show business representatives at public events.

Two more divisions were recently added to the corporation: special shoplifting investigative squad operations, and sole distributorships of a special, low-light closed circuit TV surveillance camera and equipment. The risk/reward principle described here in terms of her experience illustrates this individual's high degree of motivation, good knowledge of a specific field of activity, and persistence in carrying out an excellent plan.

Robbery and Burglary Protection

In another case history, two Pennsylvania homemakers who lived in a rather afffluent community were beset by a rash of home break-ins and thefts. They decided to start an unusual enterprise which would be useful to both police and victims in terms of identifying articles taken from a home.

For a fee, the women would come into a residence with their newly-acquired video-tape camera and portable lighting equipment. Touring the house with the owners, they would film paintings, sculpture, expensive bric-a-brac, silverware, clothing, color TV sets, valuble books, and collectors' items. This physical identification, along with a taped vocal description of the article by its owner, was included in each video-taped tour of the house. It was then placed in the owner's safe deposit box for safe keeping, and in case the items were stolen, was turned over to the police department.

Helping The Handicapped

Assisting the handicapped by providing a vital tool to help cope with life's daily demands has been the experience of another innovative person. This is a naturalized American, an electronic engineering school graduate. While working in a small bionics plant, the young engineer assisted in the development of a new electronic "laser cane" for use by blind people who walk on city streets.

The laser cane–a dramatic discovery–employs three small laser beams projecting out from the cane as it is carried. Vibrations alert the blind walker when laser beams probe overhead obstructions, people, or obstacles in the path, or indicate sudden drops at curbside. The new product went through several cycles of development and production, then was virtually abandoned by the firm's original owner who dropped the project because of lack of interest in the market and lack of additional funding.

The young engineer recognized a risk/reward element in the new laser cane, and could see its ultimate acceptance by the blind at some point in the future. He formed his own company by scraping enough funds together from friends. Development costs, however, climbed steadily after only a few months of work, and more cash was seriously needed to purchase supplies.

Because the cane was designed specifically to assist the blind, he found there were avenues open to him through foundations, government agencies, and non-profit associations. These bodies would aid in the final development phase and production of the laser cane. In agreeing to seek funds from a government agency, he did not reckon with the amount of time needed in meetings with agency representatives. These were endless and time-consuming! The laser cane, priced at $2,000 each, had to be demonstrated extensively under all types of conditions.

Obtaining Federal Funding

The initial funding of $500,000 which was finally obtained from the federal agency, required filing of daily forms, numerous periodic tests, weekly review meetings, and "progress" conferences. The problem of sub-contracting the manufacture of plastic parts took almost all of the engineer's time, plus that of two other associates. Then there were constant delays in production. These, however, have been sharply reduced. And the remarkable laser cane, fully approved, has now been delivered to a number of blind people throughout the country for test use. Reports state numerous orders have been received from various agencies. And additional capital has been received to expand facilities and to add personnel.

The engineer still maintains a full sixty-hour work week for himself and his associates. The financial burdens which were nightmarish in the beginning are gone, and his company transactions and business volume are in the black. Other new products are in the testing stage. He reports that time demands for these new items are as great as they were in the early stages of laser cane development!

Risk capital, in this case, was unique in terms of original funding for the product to be manufactured successfully, The time spent in paperwork was a necessary function required in bureaucratic operations. But in solving a risk/reward problem, and achieving the objective, the engineer selected the option best suited to his immediate need, and did so in an expedient fashion.

All effort comes down to an individual's motivation, financial objective, desires, willingness to invest time and effort, and the use of knowledge about the activity in which he/she is so deeply involved.

The Major Weaknesses Of People Seeking Risk Capital

One of major weaknesses facing would-be entrepreneurs, according to bankers and venture capital representatives, is that people asking for venture funds are poorly-prepared to handle proposed products for which they are requesting risk capital.

"I have talked to hundreds of people over a year's time in our bank, who were looking for *risk capital,* or funding, to launch a new business," said a middle-aged banking executive during a recent interview. "And perhaps less than ten percent of those people really had a good handle on the proposition or plan they wanted financed.

"Many people do not have any figures available in an organized fashion; costs, estimated expenses, or estimated profits over a year's time," he said. "And their knowledge or expertise about the field they want to get into amazes me! You listen to school teachers who want to open small pizza restaurants; mechanics who want to establish outdoor nurseries; salespeople who want to manufacture intricate machines; people who want to publish newspapers in areas where there are already about a half-dozen in existence; and people who want to open retail stores without having had any kind of sales experience.

"When I do find someone with a carefully-developed financial program," he continued, "And a detailed outline of objectives, plus experience in that field, I get to work on the loan details almost immediately.

"One important thing for entrepreneurs to remember," he warned, "Be realistic about costs. Most people underestimate the cost of operating a small enterprise. And, unfortunately, get a loan for *less than they actually require!* When they come back in a few months for more money, we can't help them until the first loan has been repaid in full!"

The Pitfalls And How To Avoid Them

If you are at the fateful and final planning step in your venture where you are trying to secure risk capital, it may be vital to the success of your proposed operation to again review your financial needs. Are you *deliberately* underestimating your future operating costs? Have you gone over all your figures carefully? These should include production, supplies, salaries, contingency expenses, taxes, rent, lighting, and all of the other items which will require regular payments.

Remember, some experienced and cynical people will listen to your proposals, study your written plans and program, review your projected financial report, and make a judgement. If you pass this hurdle and get your funding, you are half-way home!

In the case of real estate purchases on your part, the task is not too difficult because buildings and land can be appraised and checked. And if your income is satisfactory in terms of the loan demands, you will probably get the funding, or mortgage money, without too much strain.

Overcoming Resistance From Loan Sources

It is with the innovative idea, program, or product which has not yet "seen the light of day," where you will experience resistance on the part of investors, bankers, or agencies having the funds you need. If you feel you cannot prepare a proposed financial report, then get expert help from an accountant who, for a small expense, can put the figures together in a professional way. Get a business friend to review your program, and ask him/her to make any suggestions. Anticipate the obvious questions and have the answers ready in your mind.

Preparing For Your Loan Request

When you plan for making a risk capital application or loan request, put it aside for a day or two. Look at it again through the eyes of a banker or venture capital specialist. Remember that these people are total strangers who must weigh the decision to make funding available to you. Does your request answer all of the important questions with some oral explanation? Is it professional in appearance? Do you have enough supporting data for reference? Does everything look crisp, efficient, and business-like?

When you are completely satisfied in your own mind, and know you will be at ease, you are now ready to approach the ''money people'' with your risk capital request. Remember, a positive attitude about your program, product, or idea is immediately recognized. Go into your meeting with the knowledge that what you are proposing will not only help you, but will help others. This is the mark of a good entrepreneur!

10 How To Finance A Purchase

You are now at the final point in your transaction: purchasing real estate; investing in a new venture; about to launch a new product; starting a mail order business; or joining several other financial partners in a larger operation. Properly planned, these ventures will bring you an excellent return. This is part of your inflation hedge strategy.

Your next problem: finding the money to take advantage of this risk/reward opportunity. But you will have to ask yourself a few questions before you go in search of funds.

Determining How Much You Will Need

How much cash will you need to finance the operation? Will you need $1,000, $2,500, $5,000 or as much as $25,000? Your estimated financial statement should indicate this. Now that you know how much money you will need, where will you get the money? And for how long a period will you need these funds? If this is "start-up" money, you will need it until you begin to get some kind of monthly financial return from the operation.

The Time Length

The time length is important because it may narrow your financial source choices. Most people have put money aside in their savings or checking accounts which may range from several hundred dollars to several thousands. Obviously, if the sum needed is on the low side, you don't have a problem.

However, if the funds needed are fairly large, you will need to seek a loan from an outside source: a commercial bank, a savings bank, financial institution, venture capital source, private parties, or a foundation. Need for the loan may determine where you will eventually go to get these funds–or its eventual use.

The Rate Of Interest

What rate of interest can you afford to pay for the loan? How much interest on the loan are you *willing* to pay to secure funds? Remember, inflation has boosted loan interest rates at most institutions, to their highest peak in history!

I have borrowed money at a wide range of interest rates from a number of sources over the past fifteen years. These included friends, relatives, commercial and savings banks, insurance companies, and investment syndicates. All of the loans (with the exception of one long-term loan) have been paid, I am happy to state, on profits earned and from sales of real estate.

Sources Of Small Loans

On smaller sums, I would recommend for a variety of reasons, that you get the money from your close immediate sources. If you can get part of the money from your own bank account for your risk/reward opportunity, and then obtain a loan from a relative, or close friend, it may help later with overtures to financial institutions. The interest rate on a promissory note to a relative or friend will not be as high as commercial interest rates. And if you should have to skip a month's repayment because of some emergency, you will not be penalized.

In the case of a friend or relative, unless specified the interest rate in your loan repayment plan should be at least *one percent above* what they would receive from their savings institution. You would offer that person about six and three-quarters percent, which is one percent over their established rates. The gesture is worth the effort, you will discover. And even with the added one percent, you will be *saving* yourself at least *four to five percent* when compared with commercial bank loan rates! Rates will keep climbing.

What you are doing essentially with the friend or relative from whom you borrow money, is keeping the loan arrangement on a business-like basis. Then that person will feel that he/she is not being taken advantage of unfairly. As an entrepreneur, you will find that if *all* business transactions between *lender* and *borrower* (buyer and seller) are business-like, honest, and "above-board" at all times, as all transactions should be, both will benefit from *any* arrangement.

If your relations with a family member are excellent, the problem of deciding the amount to be borrowed, and length of time, should not be a hassle. But always make certain there is a written record of the transaction in the form of a promissory note. The rate of interest to be paid on an annual basis, or monthly basis, if for a short period of time, and the number of months, if the loan is of longer duration, should all be indicated.

When and if an unforeseen event occurs–death, illness, or a sudden departure from the area–there will always be a record of the debt to be paid, or *proof* that a loan has been fully repaid! Too many times, original family witnesses to a loan transaction move away, or suddenly forget the incident, and then the borrrower has a problem.

The Mechanics Of Obtaining A Commercial Loan

What are the mechanics of obtaining a commercial loan? Let us assume that you have a successful, part-time mail order business, selling small imported bird cages, supplies, and feed. You have repaid an initial loan of $2,500 from an uncle to start the venture almost two years ago. Now you discover you can purchase 1,000 small cages at half price, from an importer, if you do so within sixty days! That means you will triple your sales volume to your supplier/customers. But you need $3,000 to buy these at wholesale from the manufacturer. You also discover you must now rent additional storage space in a small warehouse, about 3,000 square feet, to take care of this material, plus cartons, wrappers, holders, and related items.

With the expanded business, you will need a new mail scale, automatic tape dispenser, two additional tables, office files, and the service of a part-time stock room clerk to fill these orders. You cannot handle all of the work yourself, since you also hold down a full-time office job. With a careful review of estimated cost, including the cages, you find that now you will need about $5,000 in cash to cover warehouse rental, employee wages, and all of the items in order to keep your operation moving ahead successfully.

Financially, you are in "the black," according to your brother, who is an accountant, handling your bookkeeping records. On this basis, you decide to approach a commercial bank because you have a good, beginning track record. You will bring along a financial statement covering two years of operations, a record of your mail order customers, and your proposed sales program. You also feel you can repay the loan within a year.

The Initial Meeting With Your Banker

Your meeting with the bank officer is a friendly and illuminating one. He is impressed by your business volume in such short a period of time. He likes your financial statement, and tells you that your approach is a professional one. On the proposed loan request, he reports the following: since you do not own the building from which you are operating your mail order business, you must pledge some kind of collateral covering the $5,000 you want to borrow. This is known as a *collateral loan*.

He also notes you have a full-time job with a regular weekly salary. You also have a stock portfolio worth about $3,500. Then he asks about your home, which has no mortgage. The bank could place a lien against it for the amount of $5,000 until that has been paid. You have several options open to you in terms of the proposed loan.

Then you learn the loan will cost you about 13% over a twelve-month period. And you also learn there are about ten different kinds of commercial loans you can initiate, ranging from "on demand" loans to "limited commercial" loans. These extend from month-to-month, if needed.

"What about considering a 'personal loan' over three years?" he asks you. This could vary from 11½% to 13½% annually, or slightly higher. You would need to guarantee this by pledging collateral in the form of stocks, bonds, your savings account, or real estate, to cover the principal.

You tell your banking representative that you want to think about the various loan options, and will come back with a decision within a week. He gives you all of the loan application forms, some explanatory data and folders, and his card.

You arrange a meeting with your brother, and discuss the proposed loan options. You also review the various rates of interest. He advises you that loan interest rates are about the same at most commercial banks. But he recommends that you "shop around" for a few more days for other loan sources, and then make a decision as to where you will secure your loan.

"Shopping Around" For Loans

Are there other sources of loan funds? Yes! There are at least twenty-five to thirty-five sources of capital in the United States. Depending upon the size of the loan, you can try numerous institutions and agencies. What about a credit union, of which there are many throughout the country? They loan members money, but they also make short-term and long-term loans to responsible people. Generally, their interest rates on loans are around 9¼%.

Other Sources Of Loans

In addition to the banking and financial institutions, there are state and federal agencies for minority entrepreneurs; mutual funds; investment bankers and advisors; pension fund groups; factoring companies; and venture capital sources, to name a few. And there are union treasuries in many states which are authorized to loan money at "competitive rates." There is also the Small Business Administration agency, but it may be difficult to get a loan here on a new venture.

After much thought, you make your decision to go with the credit union people who approve your loan application for $5,000, on the basis of your stock portfolio and your savings account, plus a review of your financial statement. It is a two-year loan at 9¼% with renewal provisions, if required.

And now you are able to purchase all of the 1,000 small cages, get additional warehouse space, and your supplies. Your first sales are excellent, and you know you will be able to pay off your credit union loan without difficulty.

Venture Capital Considerations

On a new venture, you must get "start up" money. This money is available from venture capital sources, investment syndicates, government agencies, commercial banks, educational institutions, and some corporations.

Commercial banks, as outlined earlier, will demand the most from you in terms of collateral–stocks, bonds, property, savings accounts, passenger cars, machinery pledged. They take the depositor's money, invest it, return a portion of it to depositors, and then pass on the balance earned to the directors and stockholders which is profitable for the institution.

Financial institutions will do a complete "rundown" on your personal finances, as carefully as the FBI does on an individual's criminal background. Your credit rating will be probed; your mortgage checked; and your monthly obligation payoff record to your regular creditors examined. They will check your place of employment to confirm your salary figures and length of time with the firm.

However, once you have "cleared" or paid off the commercial bank loan, or loans from any financial or investment institution, you will have established a good credit base for future entrepreneurial operations. And when you are successful, these institutions will attempt to sell you every type of financial service they offer.

Borrowing Against Your Insurance Policy

If you want to take another route for the purpose of obtaining a business loan, you need not (as pointed out) approach a commercial or savings bank. Perhaps you have a large insurance policy (not "term") that represents a significant amount of equity in terms of cash surrender value. You can borrow against this insurance policy at a low rate of interest, but at the same time still have the financial protection for your family. A talk with your insurance representative on "cash surrender" provisions may be in order to give you the loan your need for your venture.

Your Home As Collateral

Your home, or other real estate property, is another excellent source of collateral in borrowing funds for a risk/reward opportunity. We discussed the use of real estate as property in terms of bank loans.

If a fairly large amount of money is required for your venture, you may want to go directly to a venture capital source, or incorporate. A list of these sources can be found in the book by Ted Nicholas, "WHERE THE MONEY IS & HOW TO GET IT."* There are additional directories at large city libraries and eductional institutions which also list foundations.

If you get a bank-granted mortgage (a regular mortgage), it usually has no strings attached to it, and the money can be used for virtually any purpose, providing of course monthly payments are met on time.

If your investment opportunity lies in the purchase of real estate of some type, local commercial banks and savings institutions should be at the top of your shopping list. It may depend to a great degree on what part of the country you live in that determines the type and scope of real estate mortgage you may get on your entrepreneurial investment property.

The New Types Of Mortgages

Recently, there have been numerous and revolutionary changes in the types of mortgages available for new homes, used homes, and commercial property. As is customary, new types of mortgages came about in the West, notably the "flexible rate" mortgages. These have been approved by federal lending agencies and banking departments for issuance by savings and loan associations. These are primarily for "Young Marrieds" who want new housing, but are not yet in the peak earning periods. As a result, their mortgage

*Available through Enterprise Publishing Inc., 725 Market Street, Wilmington, DE 19801.

payments on expensive homes are tailored to meet their incomes, but will increase in proportion to rising incomes on a flexible basis.

You will find, as you begin to purchase more investments, or add to your business investment operations, that financial institutions may be your best source of financing. *First:* you will have a track record of collateral equity owned; *Second:* you will, by now, have established an excellent credit rating by having repaid all of the loans satisfactorily obtained from that source. As a result, your credit line (limit) will be increased, particularly on short-term loans.

Also, build a reserve of cash savings against which you can borrow when necessary. This will add to your strength of financial leverage. And in these inflationary and recession-tinged days, the cash will give you a high degree of flexibility in order to take advantage of expedient opportunities.

Maintaining The Proper Perspective

It is important that you keep all of your investments in their proper perspective, especially now and in the short-term future, in view of inflation's effects on our economy. Constantly review and examine your holdings (stock portfolio, coins, art, real estate, certificates, and antiques) in terms of what is happening *now* and what will be happening *tomorrow*. With inflation hitting the 14% mark and still moving upward, your loan interest rates will change in relation to this. Obviously, obtaining financing then becomes more difficult.

When To Sell

If your investment is not making any money, excluding raw land being held for future development or re-sale, sell it. Being overly sentimental is not a characteristic of a successful entrepreneur. Re-invest in another opportunity quickly.

How To Generate Income While Property Appreciates

A New Jersey entrepreneur had been holding a 200-acre tract of land, a former fruit orchard, for about five years, with the idea of developing the entire acreage into an industrial park. He had purchased the orchard at auction for $75,000, or about $375 per acre. The area was near a railroad, and close to a liquified petroleum gas plant, with two state highways bordering the tract.

The owner had sub-divided plans completed and approved by the local township zoning board. He needed around $50,000 in cash for sewer and water line installations, plus a partial road-building operation. Since he had limited cash reserves, and already had a mortgage on his property, he looked for an alternative program to generate capital. Then he found that soybeans were bringing farmers in the area an average of $200 per acre!

Since he had the land on which to plant, he estimated that he could grow a profitable crop of soybeans on his acreage during the coming season. With the help of a farmer friend, he purchased soybean seed, and planted the entire tract. At harvest, the soybean crop (which measured up to his expectations) was purchased by a grain buyer which brought the entrepreneur a total of $35,000. With that amount of money, he was able to borrow an additional $15,000 from another source, which enabled the industrial park development work to move forward during the fall and winter months.

With his first industrial lease, he paid off his loan, and also leased five additional industrial plots for a total of $90,000! Today, there are ten business offices, plants, and warehouses located in the industrial park with room for about fifteen more buildings. Because he decided to leave the area, the entrepreneur recently sold his industrial park to a real estate syndicate for $750,000! He had increased his original investment *TEN times*. This is a classic example of capitalizing for increasing funds.

Generating Capital From Sideline Activities

Another opportunist, a lone truck owner who specialized in the hauling and delivery of concrete and cinder blocks to construction sites, was interested in purchasing a small, profitable "golf practice" enterprise. The property was located at the city outskirts on a three-acre tract of ground.

He had problems in obtaining $10,000 in cash as a down payment on the purchase of the $35,000 recrea-

tion operation. He could not negotiate a bank loan for this amount because of an unpaid mortgage at that institution, although his credit remained good.

A friend told him about a landscaping contractor he knew, who was deeply involved with the planting of trees, shrubs, and lawns of a large, luxury housing development several miles away. The landscaper feared he would not complete his contract for the project by the contracted date, because top soil deliveries were arriving at too slow a rate at the site. Regular truckers were asking prohibitive sums to deliver ground to the site, and would do it only on a five-day-a-week basis.

In order to take advantage of weather conditions, the contractor doing the landscaping work was forced to work around the clock on a seven-day-a-week basis. If the planting work was not completed by the agreed-upon date, the landscaper would be forced to forfeit a good part of his profits.

Interested in the story, the block hauler met with the landscaper contractor at the job site. He proposed to the landscaper that he could haul topsoil in the evenings, after his regular deliveries, and also on weekends at a "truck-delivered" price. He also offered the daily rental of his second truck when it was not being used, and for weekend use. The two quickly struck a deal.

The top soil was delivered by the truckloads over a periods of two months. Rental for the second truck, plus payments for the soil delivered, brought in about $5,000 that summer for the entrepreneur. Then the landscape contractor offered the block-hauler an opportunity to haul grass sod to two other housing sites, in his spare time.

By late fall of that year, the block hauler was able to make his $10,000 down payment on the "golf practice" enterprise, and worked out a financing program for the balance of the cost. He also established a friendship with the landscape contractor, who continued to rent his second truck. At the same time, he created a ready source of income for needed funds.

Here is another example of benefiting from an operation on the part of two people. When needs are met, *everyone* profits from the relationship.

Sources Of Emergency Cash

Reviewing my own past history of trying to accumulate additional funding, I can recall owning a twenty-five acre tract of tree-covered land, a heavily wooded section. There were hundreds of pin oak, beech, chestnut, and tulip poplar trees growing on the site, with some of them reaching eighty feet in height. Since the trees needed to be thinned to make room for the new road I wanted to construct for access to an adjoining section of land, I had a farmer cut down about fifty trees.

These were cut into logs, and later into cordwood and stacked into large piles. I was then faced with a sudden emergency which required me to make a $6,000 payment within a week!

Since I was committed to several loans, I had to find another source of funding. I remembered that firewood was selling at $60 a cord in the area. I contacted a dealer who had been looking for a new source of firewood for his customers. He quickly offered to buy the entire supply of wood–amounting to six huge truckloads in volume–for $6,500! He also agreed to truck the firewood out of the site. My financial needs were met on time, as a result of this transaction.

As a result of this profitable wood sale, I decided to carefully harvest the remaining wooded acreage. Since I had hoped to sub-divide the acreage into large building lots within two to three years, many of the centrally-located trees would have to be cut down to make room for construction. However, I was determined to preserve the larger, more attractive chestnut and pin oak trees.

The following year, I harvested several thousands of dollars of firewood from the tract. Since that time, I have recommended wood harvesting to a number of friends who have wondered how to capitalize on raw, tree-covered land they have purchased over the years. As a matter of fact, many farmers throughout the country now have profitable side incomes from cutting and selling firewood from their tree-covered acreage, along with the sale of evergreen trees for Christmas use. This is in addition to *trout farming* businesses, which many pursue!

How To Raise Cash When You Do Not Own Land

What if you *do not* own farmland, wooded sites, or land on which to grow cash crop? There are other resources which you can use to develop an income source. What can you convert to raise investment funding? Certainly it is easier if you own property, stocks, bonds, a business venture, vehicles, a coin collection, or valuable antiques. Inventory your resources, not necessarily material things, but your expertise in a specific field, knowledge of business or industry, or experience with a specific hobby.

Become A Consultant

Can you put any of these to work for you successfully on a consulting basis, which could earn you a profitable hourly or daily rate from someone who could use your services? There are teachers who use their educational talents in numerous ways during vacation periods. They assist young people who must make up work for junior and senior high school terms through tutoring. Other teachers have established neighborhood "tutoring workshops" in former retail store buildings, which are successful and profitable. Others contact corporations to do translation work, or work with publishers in editing scholarly works.

All of these efforts enable these teachers to earn additional income, needed during inflationary periods. Some take this income and use it for investment purposes.

One eastern junior high school principal earned enough money during his summer months to start a profitable antique business. This was his hobby. With retirement only a few years away, he will make a profitable transition into his expanded antique sales enterprise which now employs four people.

Summer Jobs In Your Field Of Interest

The original start-up capital for this project came from his summer months, where he worked cataloging antique furniture for a regional publisher. He not only earned a good income for doing this, but he acquired valuable knowledge for his avocation. His retirement years will now be considerably eased in terms of coping with inflation's costs. His planning and implementation of his program were all developed with a specific goal in mind.

Use A Variety Of Income-generating Activities To Reach Your Goal

There is no *one* method or standard way of financing a venture. With the pressures of inflation, we need to recognize that greater effort and motivation will aid us in seeking out capital sources or funds.

Certainly all of us are different in terms of needs, lifestyles, objectives, and age. However, our objectives are the same: to survive financially in the calamitous inflation period bearing down upon us.

11 Can Financial Partners Assist You?

A recent study of the 519,834 millionaires in the United States, conducted by a Princeton, N.J. group, indicated that about 1,000 persons are being added to this select group annually. It was revealed that more than 40% became wealthy through financial partnerships![1]

How many more entrepreneurs will become millionaires in the next decade through their new businesses in fields such as energy or medical technology? This is, of course, an unknown factor, but it is safe to assume that a number will attain this rank because of help from partners who fund new ventures.

If you need a partner to help you financially with any type of loan (from as little as $1,000 to as much as $500,000), you should first consider all of the "pros and cons" of such an arrangement.

The Advantages Of Having Partners

What are the advantages of having a financial partner?
1. The partner *shares your risk*.
2. A partner will *provide the necessary funds*.
3. In many cases, a partner will *provide business knowledge*.
4. By furnishing a substantial financial contribution, a partner *enables you to participate in a larger operation where hoped-for rewards will be greater*.

[1]Source: Heritage Research Group, Princeton, New Jersey.

The Disadvantages Of Having Partners

Now here are some disadvantages of having a financial partner in your operation:
1. Your partner's personality and temperment may clash with yours. Decision-making can be rough.
2. Your partner's financial objectives may be quite different from your own plans.
    (a) He/she may want a faster cash return on the funding.
    (b) The partner may opt for a slow cash return.
    (c) He/she may seek short capital gains versus your long-term capital gain objectives.
    (d) He/she may opt for a brisk current development of the business operation, as opposed to your delayed development program.
3. The biggest disadvantage is that your partner can bind you personally to obligations without your knowledge. Incorporating a partnership, however, makes this virtually impossible.

There are many partnership experiences one hears about, which can fit any category from "heavenly and profitable" to "horrendous and disastrous." Let me give you an example of how one partnership worked out in terms of a significant investment venture. This was a nursing home, involving several financial partners working with me.

Fulfilling Each Other's Needs

On this particular venture, I had the ground site for a proposed nursing home. My contribution, in addition to my own investment funds, was my medical expertise. My financial partners had current cash fundings available. In addition to their money, they had excellent access to mortgage funding. Also, these individuals had wide experience in financial matters, which is extremely important in any expensive real estate development.

Having Similar Financial Goals

Our financial goals on this proposed project were uniformly similar. We were looking for long-term capital gains. The nursing home was designed under my direction, since I was acting as general contractor. This enabled us to control building costs. Eighteen months later our structure was completed and occupied.

The normal cost of nursing home building is "cost per bed"-valued. At the time, the rate of construction was $10,000 per bed. Our construction cost was $4,000 per bed! The reason for this low cost was sub-leasing of contracts and control of building operations.

Six months after beginning operations, we reached our "break-even" point in terms of financial return. Then, thirty months after its formal opening, the nursing home was sold to an organization which needed a successful, extended-care facility. The sales price to the buyer was on a $9,000 per-bed factor, returning an excellent profit to our group–the original partners.

The Right Chemistry

To this day, those former business investment partners are my friends. At the time plans were being drawn up for the new nursing home project, we were unknown to each other, except by recommendation. In this case, the chemistry between us was right!

Perhaps there is a lesson to be learned here. First, you do not have to depend upon friends for financial contributions in terms of partnerships. In some cases, this might be a disadvantage. Where difficult sometimes frustrating decisions have to be made, and where bluntness and seemingly curt conversations are conducted, a friend might be offended or hurt. The result could be that the entire operation could be wrecked through misguided emotion!

When Not To Take On A Partner

Here is another case history of a partnership arrangement on a real estate investment venture. A forty-acre tract of ground was being auctioned at a reasonable price. Two friends had told me they wanted to invest in real estate. But they lacked real estate investment experience, and were reluctant to share the substantial financial risk. They indicated they could not spare the amount of time required in meetings, in tracking down documents, or in researching information on deeds.

On this basis, I looked elsewhere for a financial partner for the 50% help I needed to acquire the forty-acre tract. I had made a downpayment on the sale price at the auction, and I needed the balance of the funds.

Similar Knowledge And Expertise

The Realtor involved in the tract auction was quite interested in my purchase, and foresaw a rising land value. On the basis of his interest, I felt he would take an active role in raising the value of the ground should he become a financial partner with me. I made a proposition to him, offering him a partnership, which he accepted.

About eighteen months later, we sold the tract to another buyer for about *three times* the amount we had paid! We then took these funds from the sale and purchased a large, 100-acre farm. The entire acreage and farm buildings have been rented out to cover taxes and attendant expenses, and has been allowed to appreciate in value.

This 100-acre tract of farmland is now worth 300% more than its original price when we purchased it *seven years ago!* And if indications are correct, it will continue to appreciate in value significantly. A FORBES Magazine report stated that farmland from the period of *1968 to 1978* has appreciated more than any other group investment!

Sharing The Responsibility

Partners should have the ability to assist you in several different ways, so that the total investment can become profitable and viable. You need to have a clear understanding of responsibilities with your partner. Equal shares require equal work on the partner's part, to insure the operation is going in the right direction. There are some exceptions, however. If you have a relative who agrees to loan money or make an investment, without taking an active part in management, this relationship should be clear at the outset.

The more expertise a partner has, the better the chances are for making the venture a success. If a partner is an accountant, a lawyer, a real estate broker, or a sales representative, that is a plus for you.

Setting Realistic Goals

There are times when partners establish unrealistic goals for both you and themselves. This happened to me and a group of partners a number of years ago when we undertook the establishment of an industrial feeding venture. We were tying this into a feeding program for nursing homes. A partner, who did have experience in this field, had unfortunately underestimated food costs (our raw materials) in terms of inflation. While costs did not move upwards as rapidly as today, they increased over a period of six months during each of the two years.

When To Recover Your Investment

When an established budget for an operation does not match current expenses of the operation, you have only two options. Either halt everything and do a critical analysis of what you are doing and what it is costing, or move to your second option—sell or liquidate your investment before losses reach a danger point. We elected to sell. There were buyers waiting for our operation to go on sale. In a calm, unemotional meeting with representatives, we recovered our original investment without any profit.

You can learn much from the business experience of others. Many have learned that you cannot become wealthy in a mail order operation, even with partners, unless you become a publicly-owned corporation with a cash flow in the high six figures or even on the million-dollar level.

According to mail order trade publications, about half of all mail order operations gross only around $100,000 annually. With a net profit of 10% after all costs have been met, a split with one or two partners doesn't leave you with much of a profit for all of the work involved. Hundreds of smaller mail order firms show a gross volume of about $25,000! You can make more money cutting and selling firewood.

Here is an interesting and informative case history about three partners who built a medium-sized shopping center in a small eastern suburb. Two of the partners were experienced real estate brokers who had made a considerable amount of money in real estate development operations. These included residential housing, small industrial parks, and retail stores. The third partner was an experienced building contractor who had specialized in commercial construction, including small apartments, commercial garages, business office structures, and other projects.

The Type Of Partnership To Avoid

One of the real estate brokers had been having spectacular financial success in developing and leasing small retail shopping centers in small towns and communities within a twenty-mile radius of his main operation. In an effort to finance one or two new developments, he would "lever" his equity in the three small shopping centers for mortgage money. Acting as a general contractor, he was able to sub-contract construction phases, spreading over his payments. Some of these contractors would not receive any money for as long as ninety days!

While he was completing final plans on a large shopping center, he joined with two friends (the real estate broker and the builder) in purchasing a five-acre tract in a well-to-do suburban community which offered no large shopping facilities. Within months, the three partners had constructed a supermarket with ten adjoining stores. The cost was $350,000, and all of this took place in 1958.

Warning Signs

However, the first real estate broker still continued his wide range of independent development projects, using the speculator's method of financing, or what is commonly called "shoestring" or "jack rabbit" financing. This is where funds are taken from one leased venture from store owners. Part of it is applied to bank payments and the other part is used in the financing of new real estate operations. It is "leverage" in its more exaggerated form. And it is risky!

His two partners, who were getting an excellent return on their joint venture (the shopping center in the affluent community), were more conservative in terms of investments. They voiced disapproval of his other ventures when they held their monthly meetings. But the entrepreneur brushed off their concerns by telling them they were "old ladies" and were missing many opportunities.

The real estate broker, who now owned five shopping centers, a large industrial park, and the joint venture with the two partners, felt his first terrible financial crunch in 1968. Several sub-contractors refused to finish work on two new industrial plants unless "thirty-day money" was forthcoming. Shortly afterwards, two large commercial banks would not renew notes, but demanded large cash repayments. Building suppliers demanded one-third cash with his large orders.

The 1969/1970 recession hit the construction field like a bolt of lightning! And now the "jack rabbit" financing plan worked in *reverse* for the real estate man! Work halted in numerous areas when no credit was granted. Banks demanded quick payment of twelve-month construction loans, and the two industrial parks (one that was in existence for five years, and a newly-started venture) were liquidated to satisfy banking demands. Creditors short of cash now hammered on his office doors! The "Domino Theory," well-known to speculators, flattened the real estate man financially, except for the small shopping center which was jointly-owned. He had to liquidate $6.5 million in real estate property and shopping centers to meet creditors' demand for $2.7 million in cash!

The last transaction was the sale of the jointly-owned shopping center. The price was $1.2 million after eleven years of ownership. The two partners, who were quite solvent because of their conservative investment philosophies, were reluctant to sell. But out of sympathy for the free-wheeling broker (whose only remaining cash holdings were in his share of the center), went along with his plea for aid.

Today, this real estate broker owns a small office building with three offices, one of which is his own. His former partners are now retired in Florida, living comfortably on condominium incomes.

The Moral Of The Story

The moral of this story is obvious. You must take risks to attain your financial objectives, but taking unwarranted, overly-risky chances on a thin line of financing is courting disaster. Contingency planning is imperative!

Success After Failure

Ten years ago, one man sold his stock in a publicly-owned commemorative coin minting operation for $10 million. This was a venture he had personally founded out of a coin collecting hobby. Five of his previous business ventures were failures. When he approached business associates and friends (who had financed ventures with him in the past, only to lose their investments), they turned him down on the coin-minting venture. But the coin collector hobbyists were more receptive to the plan. They saw rewards in the proposed commemorative minting operation. Partnerships were formed to create the "front money" required to start a small plant. The $2 million "nest egg" contributed by a dozen financial partners was soon spent on expensive, imported coin-stamping machines, various types of metals in large quantities, and salaries for metallurgists, numismatic experts, and other mint personnel.

Several millions of dollars in commemorative coin orders enabled the partners to secure substantial loans. All of the original partners had accepted stock, rather than repayments in cash. When the firm went "public" with a stock issue, and shares were over-subscribed, partners became wealthy! The original entrepreneur now shuttles between Florida and the French coast on a leased private jet, enjoying the fruits of his labors.

Your Spouse May Be Your Best Partner

Across the nation, thousands of women are "partners" in business ventures as well as in marriage. True, some of the ventures are modest in terms of gross business volume, but have good potential for expansion, particularly in service-oriented businesses which are bound to survive inflation's "belt-tightening."

As one owner of an automotve engine repair operation pointed out, "My wife is a financial partner–

and my only partner. She is the chief bookkeeper, supervising two other women we employ. When I am called away on special projects, she is able to determine work output in our shop, and knows what is going on administratively at all times. After five years as a business associate, she could carry on this business successfully if I should become incapacitated or die.''

Interestingly enough, some spouses with inherited incomes of their own from families, have financed their mates in various ventures. These range from beauty product manufacturing to small charter airline service companies. A number of these businesses have become successful financially. Who knows? Your best financial partner may be your own spouse!

Incorporating Your Partnership

Many partnerships develop into corporations for a number of valid reasons, including the burden of "distributive shares" as defined by the IRS. Bank financing of an enterprise is easier in many cases, when the company is a corporation. An excellent financial record of a partnership will always be instrumental in getting a bank loan.

Partnerships have a great degree of flexibility which you can enjoy without the restriction of corporate functions. You can form a partnership in an hour, sign your respective agreements, "bank the checks," and you are in operation. Forming a corporation, though no less difficult, takes a bit more than an hour to come into existence.2

Once you and your partners have achieved your financial goal in terms of a specific investment, you can dissolve the partnership when a sale is made. You do, however, report profits to the IRS and pay the appropriate tax.

You can form a number of partnerships in a year's time if this is a financial advantage, particularly if the investments are in a variety of business fields. Again, it would depend upon the amount of the investment funds available to you. Each case is totally different, as are investments.

Partnerships have been formed by individuals living in various parts of the country, and the people concerned confer by telephone, or Telex, or by computerized forms of communication. On vital issues, no

2See HOW TO FORM YOUR OWN CORPORATION WITHOUT A LAWYER FOR UNDER $50 by Ted Nicholas. Available from Enterprise Publishing, Inc., Wilmington, DE.

information is transmitted over telephone lines or other means of communication. The partners meet to make financial decisions on promising real estate development propositions, or to purchase a New York office structure!

Another interesting group of partners who have their own corporate niches, meet and purchase two to three small corporations every year. These corporations' annual sales reach as high as $30 million as each one's share of the partnership investment. The rewards, based on these risks, are (as you may have guessed) quite large and profitable.

We are not guaranteeing that you, too, will become a millionaire or even make a profit by reading this book. That is not the purpose of relating case histories of successful entrepreneurs in various chapters. What we are saying is that if you really learn everything you can about a specific field and know how to finance the venture, work hard, maneuver through the dark days ahead that will come because of inflation, you will *survive* and perhaps make money!

Partnerships offer that opportunity if you elect to go that route. We discussed personalities earlier in relation to your own, and it is obvious that unless you work well with people–strangers in many cases–partnership arrangements may not be for you. That decision must be yours to make.

Combining Talents In Partnerships

Partnerships are extremely helpful in some fields of endeavor. For example, let's look at a small advertising agency. There are three individuals who are extremely creative in a field where creative work is a necessity to survive. One of the partners is a young woman who is an outstanding artist, and knowledgeable in many forms of art. She has a commercial sense of blending artwork with typography to produce an arresting advertisement. The second partner is a top copywriter. He can write advertisements which will make a reader review all the compelling prose, and then fire off a check to purchase the product! The third partner is a skilled salesperson with a good knowledge of advertising. Neat, personable, and convincing, he is able to communicate with executives intelligently. He advises them that unless they advertise their product with *his* agency, sales will remain on a plateau!

These partners compliment each other with their respective talents and expertise, and their progressive business growth reflects this compatability. Ideally, all partnerships should work that way.

The Need For A Written Agreement

What if a partner becomes incapacitated or dies? This happens hundreds of times every year in every part of the country. Obviously, a written agreement covers survivor benefits to safeguard an investment. Where a partner is full-time and active, the loss is more severe. What eventually happens is that the late partner's share is sold, unless there is a binding agreement otherwise. The funds, plus a percentage of the profits, are then paid to the survivor, because a management replacement must be found to keep the business in existence.

Investment partnerships between entrepreneurs usually do not require full-time participation, so that, should a partner die, his/her share of the investment is still held by the surviving spouse.

Partnerships can be important and helpful in various fields of endeavor. Two partners can handle business demands if a third partner elects to go off on a trip on his day of grace! And partners can bring fresh, new ideas into a business proposition, the process of which may be fatiguing to a tired investor.

There is a classic story of a strange partnership formed by two friends, veterans of the Korean "Police Action." One was Black and the other white. Both had been in the Army Reserves and were sergeants who later served in the same ground units. Both saw a considerable amount of fighting, almost side by side. In one action, the black sergeant saved his buddy from a North Korean machine gun attack.

When both returned home to the same state, the white sergeant took over a small machine shop his father had left him. The Black sergeant, interested in food marketing, went on to college to earn a degree. Now a small manufacturing operation owner, the white sergeant expanded his machine shop into a metal fabrication operation, and was showing profit within two years' time.

The Black college graduate developed a new method of freezing desserts, and needed funds to establish his own business. He obtained a limited amount of initial investment funds, but not enough to attract a volume order. He visited his former Army associate, and laid out the details of his food processing plan.

Needing at least $10,000 in additional funds, he made the request.

After a lengthy discussion, the metals fabrication owner agreed to make the loan–but only if it were applied as an investment in the fledgling firm. He would not have any time to advise or assist in any way, since his own company demanded all of his time and effort. An agreement was outlined and signed.

Nothing was heard from the Black food processing entrepreneur for more than a year. Then into the second year, the metals fabrication owner received a letter containing a check for $10,000. The letter stated that the check was the first of two payments–*earnings* on the original investment. The food processor was processing desserts for eight companies, had developed a line of specially smoked turkeys, hams, and bacon, and had thirty-five employees in an expanded plant. The plant had been built for him by a southern city which needed jobs for its residents.

The partnership has continued over the years with both men visiting each other's operations. Both have prospered in their respective fields. They do not always agree on ideas, but the trust and respect born back in Korea still remains with them.

Then there is the story of three well-known motion picture stars who talked about building a "Tree Top Hotel" in an African community for wealthy people. In 1963, they formed a partnership and pooled about $2 million for the purchase of land, construction of the elevated structure, and a small airstrip for a shuttle aircraft.

The project was a success from the start. Its gala opening was featured on the society pages of European and American daily newspapers. It was perhaps the most expensive *tourist stop* on the continent! And the share of the profits was welcome income to one of the partners whose fame had dimmed in Hollywood. He also shared in the rotation of management, spending weeks at the site, as did each of the others. Finally, all the partners could not refuse a generous financial offer proposed by a wealthy Swiss banking official to buy out the business. Their investment risk resulted in an excellent return for all partners. Two have since passed away, but the third partner still recalls the novel venture.

Your own investment objective need not be a remote vacation site. But whatever it is, if you need a financial partner, get the best qualified person you can find!

12 Measuring Investment Returns

Perhaps this is one of the most difficult periods in the history of the U.S. economy since the end of World War II in analyzing an investment in terms of capital return. The reason it is so difficult is that values of everything, from gold to land, have been altered significantly because of the annual compounded rate of inflation. The rate of inflation is now at a mark *far above* many conservative investment returns!

The New Investments

With the prime rate of commercial banks having been raised to the highest point in history, as a result of the Federal Reserve's credit tightening policy, investors will take funds out of banks and thrift institutions. They will invest in money market funds where high yields of from 9% to 11% are being paid annually. Others will attempt to lever investments for a 15% to 25% return by investing in everything from silver to Chinese ceramics. With collectibles, coins, stamps, and old-master paintings, you might have to wait for at least three years just to come out evenly, but perhaps after that, your return would be profitable.

Some economists are even indicating that common stocks will be one of the best hedges against inflation in future years.

Gold As An Investment

If you want to consider percentage returns on gold, for example, you would have to go back ten or twelve years, before inflation became a real threat.

Unless you were an international speculator or coin collector, gold was merely a commodity like lead, sow bellies, sugar, cow hides, and silver. As a matter of fact, gold is used primarily in commercial manufacturing of jewelry, dental work, artifacts, electronics, and other uses. About 70% of refined gold goes into commercial products. The remaining 30% is left in the form of bullion for investment purposes.

Would you have had the patience and the financial sustenance to have invested $5,000 in gold bullion back in 1968? While gold was fixed at $35 per ounce in the U.S., and then later moved to $38 per ounce, the foreign exchanges were quoting "free" prices of $70 per ounce! And you would not have been drawing one cent of interest on this investment–nor receiving any dividends–as you would, had your money been placed in savings, common stocks, or bonds.

When gold "went through the roof," breaking the $400 per ounce barrier, speculators, investors, and Middle Eastern governments got caught up in the "buy-sell" syndrome. Many rushed in to buy gold bullion or coins and suddenly got caught in the whiplash of bouncing prices. Many sold when gold slipped downward on foreign exchanges and got "burned"– not a good percentage return!

If you began collecting U.S. gold in the 1960's in the form of $1, $2½, and perhaps $5 coins, dating back to the early 1900's, and then sold these in 1979, some of them would have given you a return of more than 900%! True numismatic worth of these gold coins, and speculative prices, have little relationship.

WHAT HAPPENED TO AN ORIGINAL
INVESTMENT OF $100

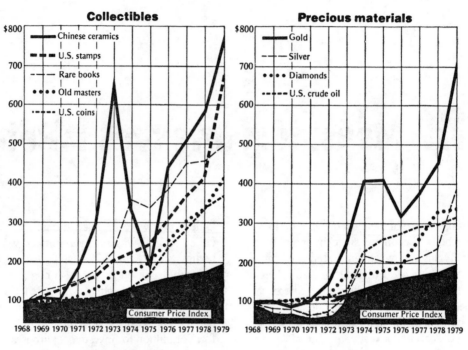

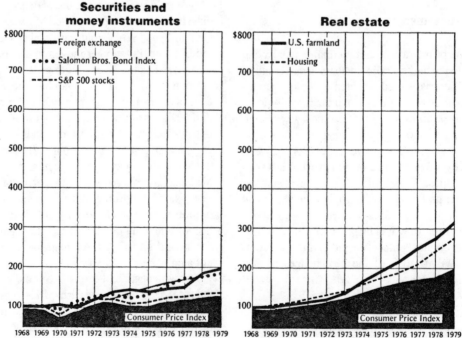

Those Who Advocate The Purchase Of Gold

There are some financial advisors who are advocating the purchase of gold coins for use as a hedge in future years should inflation get completely out of control and the currency is devalued. There are several classes of economics advisors: the Keynesians, the Monetarists, the new reform "FinTechs," and the broad conservative "Establishment Economists" who believe that only the Federal Open Market Committee (a branch of the Federal Reserve System) can correct the nation's economy. And there is another new and growing group of advisors known as the "Scareconomists" who predict that dire, catastrophic events will hit this nation within the next decade, shattering the economic system, pitting group against group. They advocate the storing of reserves of food, ammunition, medicine, gold and silver coins, and the burrowing into a cave to await the "dawning of the new U.S. day!"

Our Future "Currency"

The "Doomsday" spokesperson can be commended for frightening members of the banking community and some government agencies, but they completely overlook our systems of checks and balances, and a totally new concept of future currency: *credit cards*. Because of our computerized "instant" cash balance technology, paper currency may pass into limbo, replaced by $1 and $5 coins. The personalized, electronically-striped plastic card will contain your Social Security number and some specific demographic data. This will enable every merchant to grant instant credit or exchange, since money in the form of "credit banks" will be "moved" electronically. Coins will be used for special out-of-town areas not covered by computerized systems.

Since currency will move out of existence, the enormous time lag in attempting to take corrective measures to crush inflation's effects, will be dramatically shortened because of the computerized monetary policy. The fiscal policy of the U.S. economy will be mated to this new system and both will be successful. But we must always be aware of the fact that politicians are virtually unpredictable.

Predictions Based On Past Events

Almost all of the contemporary economists are at a loss when predicting the future U.S. economy. The reason is that all of their prognostications are based on *past events* in the U.S.! And since we have gone through tremendous industrial and technological changes in this country since World War II, nothing has remained the same economically. Who would have thought that a *recession within an inflationary period* could come to pass?

It is one thing to agonize over the nation's $800 billion national debt, but quite another to put serious economic problems in a totally new perspective and solve them!

Many people, aware of all the complex financial problems and conditions caused by inflation and the recessions, point out the following: Americans in the United States are *unique*. We will weather this terrible economic storm! And we will do it through our unique financial creativity, and by harnessing our vast, tremendous productive ability and power.

All of this is being presented to give you a rational balance of measuring percentage returns as a business person.

Let us review and study investments in land, buildings, and ground rental in terms of measuring percentage returns—past and potential.

Returns On Land Investments

If you have any doubts about land values, take a leaf from foreign investors' notebooks which report they have invested about $200 billion in farmland and real estate in the U.S. over the past twenty-five years. Okay, dollars have been cheaper, but wealthy individuals from Italy, Germany, Japan, and the Middle East, plus numerous foreign corporations, have snapped up expensive farmland from Pennsylvania to California. They recognize that it will appreciate over the next decade because of increased demands for food.

Steps In Acquiring Farmland

Consider acquisition of farmland in terms of this dictum:

1. Farms are usually sold on a cost/acre basis.
2. Large tracts of land usually can be visualized in terms of utility by the investors who recognized multiple uses.
3. Each of the uses of the ground will have a different value.

4. The sum of the values of the individual uses usually exceed by far the blanket price paid by the buyer.

5. The "end user" is willing to pay full market price if the ground can be utilized immediately.

6. The large tract of ground or farm should be visualized as being bought "below wholesale" cost.

7. The preceding trading guide conforms to the old axiom: "Buy *low*–sell *high*, or buy *wholesale* and sell *retail*."

8. The entrepreneur purchasing land will have to *invest*...
   (a) thinking in terms of return
   (b) planning uses
   (c) getting municipal approvals on uses

9. Make use of the information and expertise readily available to you from real estate brokers, municipal representatives and authorities, builders, developers, and regional planners. These individuals will help you for their own reasons, but it is to your advantage as well.

Let's take a step-by-step chronological history of an actual transaction to determine the rate of return:

A small thirty-acre farm had been posted for sale for at least four years with no buyers. The house had been completely vandalized, and the farm ground was overgrown and visually unattractive. The total picture was negative with a "Tobacco Road" touch.

However, from an entrepreneurial point of view a thorough inspection and study indicated:

1. The farm was located in a developing residential area.

2. The farm was surrounded on almost all sides by paved roads, unlike other nearby farm properties.

3. A study of the highways revealed that one of these roads ran over a sewer line which had been constructed two years ago.

4. The farm was owned by an out-of-state executor of an estate, who would not subdivide the property.

5. The executor would not agree to, or accept, a conditional sale.

6. The farm was finally purchased at "fair market value" of acreage: $100,000 for thirty acres.

7. Following settlement, the Township Manager was consulted relative to zoning recommendations in terms of "What would the community like to see developed out of this 'eyesore'?"

8. An engineer was hired.

9. An expert in planning, the engineer reported that he felt three phases of development would be most easily accepted by authorities. This would also help spread expenses.

10. Phase I was completed within a six-month period.

11. Homesites of 20,000 square feet each were made available, with sewage facilities on one of the road frontage.

12. A builder was located who wanted homesites with building permits.

13. All sites were sold on an "investor-basis" rather than individually. This made the developer capital gains incomes versus ordinary income.

14. Lots were sold after long-term gains had been established.

15. Transaction: ten lots comprising 15% of the farm acreage were sold for 100% of the investment of $120,000.

16. One lot was held to provide access to the farm buildings.

Phase II Plan Record

1. Phase II was started when Phase I was being completed.

2. Development of three one-acre building lots was completed.

3. Development of an eleven-acre farm tract was accomplished.

4. Development of a ten-acre tract on the third road with 1,100-foot frontage, was accomplished.

5. The Phase II "package development" was sold to a builder as soon as it was approved by the Township authorities. The sale produced $45,000 for the lots and tract–three in all.

Phase III of the total development is now underway. This is specifically designed to create lots, but will be delayed until such time as the funds can be put to use. This phase might also be affected by a plan change which involves the possible swap of nine lots.

Summary Of Financial Transactions On The Thirty-Acre Farm Purchase:

1. Cost of land $100,000
2. Settlement costs   1,500

3. Engineering cost 7,000
4. Municipal costs
    a. Sewage hook-up 3,500
    b. Park assessments 2,500
    c. Road-grading assessment ...... <u>2,500</u>
                Total costs $117,000

<u>INCOME</u>
    1. Ten lots @ $11,500 .... $115,000
    2. Three lots @ $15,000 .... <u>45,000</u>
                Total Income .. $160,000
                <u>Profit</u> 43,000

Residual Assets
1. Lot & Sewer .... $ 17,500
2. Ten-acre lot (undeveloped) 50,000
3. Twelve-acre farm (undeveloped) ... <u>60,000</u>
           Residual Net Value . $127,000

The farm was financed with a $25,000 cash downpayment and a $75,000 note. $25,000 plus one year's interest yielded $43,000 or a *profit of 172%*.

Excellent capital returns from realty values and utilization of land will depend, of course, on the location, the nature of the land, and its ultimate uses. Improved property (complete with road, sewage facilities, water, and electric power access) gives land a desired value in terms of sale offerings.

Steps In Converting Acreage

Let's look at another actual case history of ours in converting land acreage:

1. Seven hundred acres of wood and hunting land in central Pennsylvania was purchased. This included a small mobile home with a well, septic tank facilities, and a small family home.
2. The tract was purchased in the mid-1970's
3. About four years later, 550 acres of the mountainside acreage were sold (in 1977) for *180% of the initial* purchase price of the site.
4. The mobile home site was *sold for 40%* of the purchase price of the entire tract.
5. Remaining 150 acres were *sold for 40%* of the purchase price.
6. Return on original investment in four years: *260%!*
7. Sales transaction financed in the following manner:
    a. Bank loan

    b. Purchase of money mortgage
    c. Ten percent cash downpayment

And while we are looking at percentage returns on investments, you need to look at the "broad picture" of potential investment opportunities. You also need to be aware of some basic premises:

The Basics Of Investing In New Ideas

1. It is always good to "get in on the *ground floor*, but it is not always good to be the *foundation*."
2. The earliest entrepreneur of a new concept, product, or service provides others with an idea which they may embellish, and, after the market has been defined, may *capture* the most significant portion!
3. Don't forget that *all* new ideas follow the bell-shaped curve, illustrated below:
    a. First, *the idea*. The market is being defined, the population is becoming aware of the idea, and the value is starting to be recognized.
    b. *Rapid growth* of the program. Early excitement is being developed, but full awareness is not yet recognized.
    c. *Maximum growth*. There is full awareness of value, a massive effort to "get on the bandwagon," and people are "chasing" the idea, and starting to develop programs to lure unknowledgable investors to "climb aboard" passively.
    d. *Idea has "peaked."* Too many people are getting involved.
    e. What was once a "good idea" is not turning into a "get rich quick" scheme. This phase is the *"over-the-hill"* concept.
    (Some entrepreneurs who are discerning will realize that bargains may be secured in this stage in the secondary market).
4. What about new ideas which will earn you a high percentage return?
    a. Are people turning to different forms of dietetics, or new international food fads? (Will Pita replace Pizza?)
    b. What does the new market need for support? For example, can you take advantage of the change in housing concepts? Do you, in fact, even recognize current changes?

c. Can bargains be secured in old urban housing for refurbishing programs? Examples: "Society Hill," Philadelphia. Areas in Boston, Baltimore, Bronx, Miami Beach, and Chicago are all examples of new, urban housing programs entrepreneurs have started.

5. Ideas to _extend_ the purchasing power of the dollar:

a. _Wholesale food_ purchasing programs to enable families to obtain more vegetables, fruits, and meat for their expenditures. New purchasing concepts to be established.

b. _Home entertainment_ (visual aids, games, and television) to keep families occupied at home, avoiding unnecessary purchase outside.

c. _New health ideas_ to treat or prevent simple maladies to reduce the cost of medical bills. (Note: the sale of common aspirin is an acknowledge barometer of the economy. When sales are _increasing_, we are in an economic _downturn_. This is an indication that the population is reducing spending on possible unnecessary medical expenses by trying to cure their own minor medical problems!)

6. Entrepreneurs, now successful in their respective fields. point out that unusual, exotic, or extravagant (sometimes outrageous) ideas will be successful by virtue of their inherent novelty.

a. Skateboard arenas, paper underwear, portable "johns," organic flower pots, CB radios. "Drive-a-Wreck," salad restaurants. and other unusual ideas and products have caught on in the last decade.

How will owners of the above enterprises and product innovators assess their percentage returns? After a period of several months, the "flow" of funds–in and out–will quickly indicate the amount of profit accumulated.

Measuring Returns On Coins And Commemoratives

What about returns on investments in coins and commemoratives? If you began collecting mint proof coin sets back in the 1960's, along with _gem quality_ Peace Dollars, and selected commemorative _gold coins_, and perhaps 1893 Morgan Dollars, your investment return–providing it amounted to $1,500 then–would now be over 1000%

However, today if you wanted to buy a bag of $1,000 face value Morgan Dollar coins (brilliant, uncirculated) for investment from a coin dealer, it would cost you _$23,000!_ A 1973-S Eisenhower Dollar in clad metal, gem quality proof will cost you _$86!_ A bag of Franklin half-dollars coins with a face value of $1,000 will cost our about _$9,500_. A Liberty head type U.S. gold dollar, billiant, uncirculated, will cost you _$950_. And if you can find a bag of Mercury Dime coins (worn, used), the prevailing price will be around _$3,500_.

The average person will have a difficult time making a quick profit on coin investments in these inflationary days. First, his/her investment must be substantial to seek out scarce historical coins at an auction. Well-financed dealers and wealthy numismatic collectors will outbid the small collector at every turn.

Coin Investment Clubs

There are coin investment clubs now in existence, built around the mutual fund concept, which begin at around $50 per month. And there are independent collector groups who purchase expensive collections. Investments here are similar to those made in the stock market. There are no guarantees that coin values will continue to rise. If you are seriously interested in the area of rare coins as an investment, get all of the coin publications and books available on the subject. Talk to dealers, talk to collectors, then make your decision. It could take several years before you receive an appreciable return on your original investment!

Books, Antiques, And Artwork As Investments

What about returns on other collectibles? If you collected $100 worth of rare U.S. stamps over an eleven-year period, from 1968 to 1979, your collection would have had an annual compound rate of return of 18.9% each year! In a report compiled by MEDICAL ECONOMICS magazine, gold appreciated at the rate of return of 19.4% annually since 1968. Chinese ceramics also performed at an excellent rate of 19.1% annually in terms of return since 1968.

If your operation is being built around collecting rare books, antiques, prints, or artwork, dealers who are reputable, warn about numerous "fakes" peddlers are anxious to unload on unwary buyers. Even in the numismatic field, there are numerous reports about gold coins actually being counterfeited in the Middle East and in some areas of the United States, worth one-third (or less) in value. These are then sold as "authentic gold coins" to inexperienced collectors!

Anyone who has established his/her own business knows that *investigation before investing* is mandatory.

There is an excellent market for old prints, old toys, old clocks, antiques of every type and variety, rare books, and stamps. A lucky find can bring a high return to the collector.

Sources Of Information

Galleries, auction houses, and antique dealer groups are an excellent source of information. In addition to furnishing a market for collectibles, they are able to outline prices and establish values for you.

There are many books and trade magazines on these subjects, specializing in vertical areas of collectibles.

Antique Cars

If you began collecting the original Ford Company T-Bird back in the 1950's, your percentage return would now be around 600%. Many people are in the antique passenger car collecting field. Initial investments are moderate to expensive, depending upon the specific model of car you seek.

Replica Cars

There is even a new market for "replica" cars—copies of English roadsters, Stutz Bearcats, and other exotic vehicles. People who purchase Fiberglas® bodies and attach these to Volkswagon chassis, find a ready market, netting a high percentage return.

Three Steps To Insure Protection

Before investing in any area, however, it is important to perform a thorough investigation, seek advice, and know the basics of measuring your potential return. These three steps are your best insurance for safeguarding your investment.

13 What About Taxes?

A distinguished European business executive who had just acquired a $600 million food processing corporation, was waiting for his return flight in New York, while being interviewed by a financial writer.

"I never cease to be amazed at American business people," he told the writer. "They are innovative, excellent at building fortunes from small beginnings–true entrepreneurs–skilled at bargaining. But many of them, including professional persons, have a peculiar...attitude toward income taxes. This is hard to understand!" We suppose what is difficult for the European to understand, is American business people's resistance to the idea of taxation. Europeans can pay as much as 90% of their income in taxes, so it surprises them to meet with resistance to taxation from Americans.

The American Spirit

The spirit of American business people is reflected in their anti-tax position. This attitude is perhaps a carry-over from the founding fathers of the United States who founded this nation, in large measure, because of King George of England's oppressive tax policies. So we, as "rebellious" Americans, are almost innately resistant to the mere idea of taxes.

The attitude has been so strong among some Americans, that they have gone to jail, rather than pay what they feel are confiscatory taxes.

Of course we are not advocating this approach. Nor are we advocating tax evasion, which is illegal and can get you into all kinds of trouble. Our aim is to provide some basic guidelines which will help you determine your minimum amount of tax. This is a prudent and intelligent move for any business person.

Common Problems With The IRS

The problems business people most often face in dealings with the Internal Revenue Service, are those where there are disallowances of deductions. Most business owners use the policy of: "when in doubt, deduct." This is usually a good idea. Despite your personal feelings about *how* the federal government funds are sometimes expended or the political party in "power" at the moment, income taxes should be paid in accordance with existing laws. Of course, all legal "loopholes" should be considered. Whatever innate resistance you have toward taxation, might be better channeled toward working with your congressional representatives (and in electing new ones) to legislate more equitable tax laws and distribution of tax funds.

Regardless of whether you are in the 40%, 50%, or even the 70% tax bracket, you will still be paying income taxes out of the profits of your business. This is a key point to remember. Of course, profit potential after taxes must be great enough, so you will want to take the risks necessary in any business venture. Otherwise, you would be better off investing your money in a good dividend-paying stock or bond.

The Quest For Tax Shelters

Thousands of business people seeking to escape a significant income tax, but wanting to do this legally, look for tax shelters. They look for an investment strategy which will help them defer payment of taxes until some time in the future. This motivation is sometimes linked to the desire to convert profits to long-term capital gains. Some of the popular tax shelters, however, which have been proposed by tax advisors (cattle raising, movie deals, professional hockey team ownerships, etc.) have fizzled out completely. In other cases, these tax shelters have performed so badly that funds would have appreciated more in a standard savings account.

For the successful person, the major tax problem in terms of income lies in the area of *short-term* versus *long-term* capital gains. There have been significant changes in federal income tax laws in the last decade which could affect business people markedly, if adherence to specific IRS definitions of capital assets (either in the gain or loss areas) is not achieved. Tax accountants are aware of these important changes, but you may not be aware of the IRS's discarding of the so-called "six-months" provision on disposition of capital assets. Here is the present definition as enacted by the federal government:

"If you hold a capital asset *one year or less* for tax years beginning after 1977, the gain or loss from its sale or exchange is *short-term* (except for an invention, or property which has been in family ownership). If you hold it *longer than one year* for the tax years beginning after 1977, the gain or loss from its sale or exchange is *long-term*."

This, of course, means *366 days* of continuous ownership qualifies the asset for *long-term* gains provision.

Qualifying For Capital Gains Treatment

In terms of sales of land, you must exercise caution so that, by selling lots on a regular basis, you do not become a "dealer" similar to a real estate broker. Proceeds from these sales are treated as "ordinary income" by the IRS. If it is held for an investment account or for your use in business, it qualifies for capital gains treatment.

Numerous changes in federal income tax laws have come about because of certain tax deductions over the years.

Recent Tax Law Changes

One area that has been changed drastically as a result of overuse, is the *"at risk" deductions*. In former years, these permitted an individual to risk $5,000 in some new venture to obtain a $25,000 deduction. Under new IRS regulations, in order to deduct the $25,000 on your personal income tax, the $25,000 must be a bona fide *loss*. This can sometimes discourage investments for the express purpose of trying make a profit, if the investor is in a high income tax bracket.

Successful entrepreneurs should be wary of "new" and unusual tax shelters, such as buying teak wood in South America and storing it in warehouses for five years; sheep ranches in Australia; cultivating bullfrogs in Louisiana; and theatrical "talent" foundations. These examples may amuse you, but they are actual cases. You are better off purchasing Municipal Bonds, or long-term savings certificates! At least you will not lose all of your tax shelter funds as you would in dubious tax shelter proposals.

The Keogh And IRA

If you are self-employed and successful, you should take advantage of establishing a Keogh (H.R. 10) self-employed retirement plan which permits you to set aside 15% of your annual income, up to $7,500 annually. Or you may elect to set up an Individual Retirement Account (IRA), setting aside up to 15% of your annual earnings. You can get complete details on these from the Treasury Department's Tax Publication division. Write for Publication 590, "TAX INFORMATION ON INDIVIDUAL RETIREMENT ARRANGEMENTS." These tax shelter programs should be of concern to the lone entrepreneur. A competent tax accountant should give you all the details and advantages of these tax shelter retirement plans.

Here is a typical example of determining gross profit for a person who owns a hobby shop:

Profit and Loss Statement
Year ended December 31, 19--
(1) Sales
    (less returns and allowances)   ... $77,060

(2) Less–Cost of Goods Sold:
>   a. Inventory 1/1/-- $7,845
>   b. Purchase (less personal items) . 60,250
>   c. Goods available for sale 68,095
>   d. Less inventory 12/31/-- 7,955
(3) Cost of Goods Sold $60,140
(4) Gross Profit $16,920

Reviewing the above example, to arrive at gross profit, subtract #3 (Cost of Goods Sold–$60,140) from #1 (Sales–$77,060). The difference will be #4 (Gross Profit–$16,920).

Again, you are in a retail business and it is imperative that you maintain efficient and detailed records of all transactions, sales tapes, invoicing system records, sales taxes collected, purchase data, payroll records, Social Security withholding tax records, and all city and state tax records.

Qualifying For "Net Operating Loss"

What about Net Operating Loss in an operation?

While business losses are the dominant factor in operating losses, other types of income and deductions must be considered in determining the net operating loss deduction factor. In IRS definition, a net operation loss is: *"Excess of allowable deductions over gross income after certain adjustments are applied to that excess."*

You may carry the loss as a deduction to certain other tax years to reduce your tax liability, or to obtain a refund of all or part of any income tax paid.

Some of the deductions could include: casualty and theft losses, moving expenses, state income taxes on profits, employee business expenses, loss on rental or business property, to name a few items.

Sadly enough, our present inflation has boosted us into higher tax brackets without boosting our increased buying power. There is a term now being used by business analysts, politicians, and entrepreneurs called "taxflation." An individual moves up into higher income brackets, he/she is required to pay considerably more taxes to the benefit of the federal government. As a direct result of our raging inflation, it has been estimated that about $37 billion in additional tax revenues went into the U.S. Treasury at the beginning of this decade!

Some legislators are fighting for cuts in Social Security taxes for entrepreneurs and business corporations, plus a provision to reduce corporate taxes for the purpose of new plant investments. Politically, it gives the federal government more funds with which to play in departments aiding the party in power, and which critics contend actually _adds_ to inflation. It creates more money in circulation!

What It Means In Dollars and Cents

At the present time, 18.5% of an average earner's pay of about $28,000 annually will go to the government in taxes. The final "take-home" pay meanwhile has dropped in "spendable income" to about $14,000!

If you and one or two others decided to launch your own operation, here's the definition of a partnership from the IRS for tax purposes:

"Partnership" For Tax Purposes

> "A partnership is not a taxable entity. However, it must determine its income and file its return the same as an individual, except for certain items that must be separately stated. Form 1065 is used for filing its return."

Further, the IRS explains, that for income tax purposes "partnership," as a term, includes "syndicate," "group," "pool," a "joint venture," or any other type of unincorporated organization which is carrying on a business function. It is also the combined efforts of two or more persons who join together to carry on a trade or business, with each person contributing money, property, labor, or some skill. Each expects to share in the profits or losses, regardless of whether a formal agreement has been executed.

A "principal partner" is one who has five percent or more interest in the profits or capital of the partnership. As partners, you should also know that you must include in your income, _distributive shares_ of partnership items, plus any guaranteed payments. This would include salary or interest received or accrued from the partnership, ending with your tax year.

With your partners, you should also check with your tax accountant as to the accounting method you are going to use in your operation. You may elect to follow the fifty-two/fifty-three week tax year. The date your partnership is formed and your business is in operation. is the date from which your tax year will begin. unless the IRS gives you permission to follow the calendar year. Your accountant should establish this for you.

The Privately-held Corporation

The third type of business structure many entrepreneurs who launch new business form, is the privately-held corporation. A corporation is an entity, chartered by state agencies, as a legally constituted business operation with duly elected officers. Their investment in terms of cash is represented in the number of shares of capital stock issued.

For tax purposes, individuals who are officers in the corporation may assist in the compilation of income tax returns. on profits and losses, under the aegis of the treasurer. However, you also file your own personal income tax return on the salary you receive from your corporation, your bonuses, interest, and other items if you are president or an officer.

The Benefits Of
Incorporating Your Business

One of the advantages of being president of a small corporation is that you will have no personal liability (unless of course fraud or some other crime is involved), should the business fail. Your home or bank account will not be affected, and creditors can only seize assets of the corporation.

The degree of personal liability has been reduced if you head the corporation as its chief executive. There are broader benefits in terms of deductions allowed, which are not possible in a proprietorship or partnership. Additionally, a privately-held corporation can sell shares of stock to raise capital and expand operations.

Corporations are formed because of the numerous management responsibilities that come with expansion of operations: production, development and research, marketing, finance, and personnel. Corporate responsibilities can be delegated more easily and more efficiently because there are enough funds to carry out these activities. And from a *tax* point of view, there are distinct advantages in terms of retaining earnings, capitalizing expenditures, and through various accounting procedures.

Raising Cash By
"Going Public"

A privately-held corporation can also go "public," if this decision is unanimously approved by officers and stockholders. A public offering of stock is made by an underwriter with a per-share stock price stated, when all state and federal Security and Exchange provisions have been met. The monies received through these stock offerings, handled by securities dealers, are used for working capital, and at the same time, provide some "ownership" to individuals in terms of risk/reward opportunities: dividends. Obviously, this transaction sets up another series of tax structures which require knowledgeable accountants to work out tax reports and payments.

There is another type of corporation which, from a tax point of view, you need to be aware of in corporate planning. This is the *Subchapter S Corporation.*

The Subchapter S Corporation

According to the IRS, some corporations (commonly known as Subchapter S Corporations) *may elect not to be subject to the income tax.* If a corporation qualifies under IRS tax guidelines, its income will generally be taxed to the shareholders. However, if such a corporation has capital gains in excess of $25,000. it may be subject to a capital gains tax and the minimum tax.

How can your corporation qualify for these exceptions as a Subchapter S entity?

1. It must be a domestic corporation (a U.S. company).

2. It must not be a member of an affiliated group (a company subsidiary).

3. It must have only one class of stock.[1]

4. It must not have more than fifteen shareholders.

5. It must have only individuals or estates as shareholders.

6. No non-resident alien can be a shareholder.

---

[1]One class of stock means stock in which the voting rights, dividend rights and liquidation preference applicable to each share, are equal.

You must determine for yourself which type of business entity is best suited for your operation. A knowledgeable tax accountant or attorney, versed in tax structure and business operations, can assist in making this determination for you.

Travel Expenses

Many business people find they must do a great amount of travel in an effort to market products, services, or programs. Some of the best customers are sometimes located in areas miles from the operation's base. In filing of income taxes, deductible travel expenses are important.

The IRS states that deductible travel expenses are the ordinary and necessary expenses of foreign and domestic travel away from home, in pursuit of your profession, trade, or business. Expenses must be substantiated in the form of paid receipts in chronological record form. However, *travel* expenses should not be confused with *transportation* expenses, which is another subject entirely.

Costs You Can Deduct

Deductible travel expenses, says the IRS, would include:

* Meals and lodging (en route and at your destination).

* Baggage charges.

* Cost of transporting sample cases, display materials, or related items.

* Cost of maintaining and operating your passenger car.

* Cost of maintaining and operating your house trailer.

* Telephone and telegraph expenses.

* Reasonable laundry and cleaning expenses.

* Cost of a public stenographer.

* Cost of transportation from airport, railroad or bus station to your hotel; from your hotel to the airport or station; transporting a customer from office to warehouse.

* Reasonable cost of travel between your hotel, motel, or restaurant to your customer's base of operation.

* Reasonable record of tips.

* Travel expenses at a convention for yourself, but *not* for any other family members if they attend with you.

* Travel expenses *do not include* entertainment expenses that are incurred while you are away from home.

* Travel expenses on a business trip outside of the United States must be substantiated by purpose, nature of trip, and supporting receipts.

You need to devote enough time and study to your business records to know and determine which business expenses can be deducted from your income tax report. The accumulated figures, presented in an organized fashion, will reveal whether you will report a net income or loss from the business operation for the past year.

Deductible Business Expenses

As a business person, you need distinguish between capital expenditures and business expenses. Under IRS regulations, you may not deduct capital expenditures. To be deductible, a business expense must be *ordinary* in the business, trade, or profession in which you are involved, and *necessary* for its operation. Defined in IRS terms, "ordinary" refers to an expense that is a common and accepted practice in your specific field of endeavor. A "necessary" expense is one that is *appropriate* and *helpful* in maintaining in trade or business.

Employer Taxes

Social Security taxes are a major concern for all businesses, large or small. Under the Federal Insurance Contributions Act, Social Security provides for old age, survivors, disability, and hospital insurance. These payments are financed through FICA taxes (Social Security). Except for income from cash or charge tips, they are levied on *both* you and your employees. As an employer, you are liable for collection and payment of the employee tax. Under the law, you must withhold it from wages. You are also liable for *your own* share of FICA.

The Social Security withholding tax rate moves upward each year. In two previous years, it moved from 6.05% to 6.13%. Wages subject to these taxes were limited to the first $22,900 in 1979.

Filing Tax Returns

As an employer, you must file a quarterly return on taxes withheld for the federal government, and make deposits into an account at a federal reserve bank, together with the necessary tax forms. The IRS can answer any questions relative to procedures, types of forms, and necessary schedules.

If you are a lone entrepreneur in a small business, you will be subject to the Self-Employment Tax. This tax is part of the system for providing Social Security coverage for people who work for themselves. Under the law, all self-employed individuals must pay self-employment tax each year on part or all of their income. This helps finance Social Security benefits which are payable to self-employed individuals as well as to wage earners who work for companies. Schedule SE Form 1040 is used to compile this tax on a return.

Many small businesses all over the country are affected every year by losses over which the owners have no control. Quite obviously, if these losses are not covered by adequate insurance, or some state or federal help, the business could become a total loss. This is known as a "casualty loss," under tax definition.

Casualty Loss Deductions

A casualty loss is the complete or partial destruction, or accidental and irretrievable loss, of property resulting from some sudden, unexpected, and unnatural event — hurricane, flood, storm, fire, explosion, etc. With property insurance, virtually all of the damage loss would be covered by private insurance companies, depending upon the deductible arrangements in the policy. In many cases, however, only a portion of the damage may be covered. These losses are deductible on your income tax return.

The following are casualty loss tax deductible items:

* Auto accidents, damage to business passenger cars or trucks.

* Sonic boom damage from aircraft.

* Loss due to vandalism.

* Mine cave-in damage.

* Smog damage from chemical fumes.

* General decline in market value of the property.

* Loss of potential profits (i.e., ice storm damage to fruit trees, timber, evergreen trees for commercial sales, etc.)

There are other loss items which your tax accountant, attorney, or the IRS can clarify for you, which would affect your income tax.

Bad Debt Deductions

If you remain in business for a period of several years, you will, at one point or another, encounter the "bad debt" problem. Some individual, some company, or some corporation will vanish from the scene, owing you money for a product or service which was purchased or performed, leaving you with an unpaid bill. This is called a "bad debt." Depending upon the amount involved, it could affect your operation or it could be a nominal sum easily absorbed. At any rate, bad debts are deductible on your income tax if they are bona fide and can be supported by evidence. For example, a company goes into bankruptcy and cannot meet any of its obligations. You would need evidence verifying the fact that the company went bankrupt.

There are numerous and special provisions for each type of business entity and operation with which you should familiarize yourself under federal tax laws.

Changes In Your Operation

Let us assume you change your business structure or the way you do business. You become a wholesaler or distributor instead of running a retail business. You add partners, increasing your volume considerably. Obviously, your tax structure and method of accounting for tax purposes will also change.

Liquidation

What if you decide to liquidate your business operation by reason of retirement or disability? You must still file all necessary tax returns through the last year of operation, and make all payments due.

Then there are sales and "lease-back" provisions in some types of businesses, which require special handling of tax information. There are trades of old machines for new machines which may give you certain tax credits, plus depreciation provisions. These are important.

Depreciation

If you own the building in which you produce a product for a specific market, there are depreciation provisions you should be aware of, in determining your income tax. If you materially improve your property, this will affect its market value. If it is in a declining neighborhood, this will also affect its basis for deductibility on your income tax. The machines you use in your operations can be depreciated using specific tax provisions.

Real estate depreciation can be figured on a "straight line" rate. This includes real estate in the category of commercial buildings and industrial structures, acquired after July, 1969. A declining-balance method-of-depreciation rule has been established by the IRS. Your tax accountant can investigate this for you.

Maintaining Records

Business advisors, including bankers and specialists of the Small Business Administration, point out that many people fail in their business operations because they do not maintain proper, efficient records. *This includes tax records.* Unless you understand basic tax law fundamentals and requirements, get the expert help of a good tax accountant before you begin your operation.

Non-payment of business or income taxes is a serious matter, and can cause horrendous problems. Nobody enjoys paying taxes, especially when you feel as if your money is being used improperly by the government. But it is an intelligent move to become as knowledgeable as possible (and practical) in tax matters affecting your business. Know how to avoid paying unnecessary taxes, and plan accordingly.

We would recommend a conference with a tax consultant, and the purchase of a good, basic book on accounting before you begin.

This information will actually help you avoid taking certain actions in your business operation which may be detrimental. And, perhaps it will help you earn better profits by following specific tax procedures.

Part Four:

What To Do Now

14 Recognizing Other Areas Of Investment

In earlier chapters of this book, we discussed a variety of investment areas and businesses which will prove to be inflation proof, or will act as inflation hedges in the months and years ahead. More specific business areas to assist you in surviving financially (in view of opportunities available) should be examined and considered.

The Best Inflation Hedge: The Small Business

The premise that privately-owned businesses, headed by their entrepreneur/owners, with their low overhead, part-time employees or "independent contractors" (employees who work for a fee, not a salary), will not only cope with inflation, but may even become profitable. This is a prediction supported by many economists, bankers, and members of the business community. Price flexibility, shifting of market approaches, and the ability to "maneuver" in any type of business condition gives the small operator a decided advantage during inflationary times!

The Best Fields To Be In

Perhaps the greatest opportunity for many people about to start a venture or business, will be in the fields of energy, energy conservation, and in unrelated fields of pollution and chemical waste disposal. The production of synthetic fuels is included. Vast industries will emerge from this new sphere of activity, creating millions of new jobs and thousands of new business enterprises in the decade ahead.

Grants From Uncle Sam

The U.S. Department of Energy recently awarded eighty-three inventors grants totalling about $607,000. These grants were to be used to finance their ideas on energy-related projects and activities. Some grants went as high as $49,800, with both men and women sharing in the awards.

These entrepreneurs submitted ideas and proposals for cash grants, which included such feasible and workable ideas as roof shading and surface glazing for reduced peak building heating and cooling loads; new types of windmill generators; self-insulating passive solar heating systems; improved capillary refrigeration systems and techniques; solar greenhouses; and other energy-related ideas.

Established corporations such as Du Pont, General Electric, and Westinghouse, who normally discourage the submission of ideas from inventors, are now seeking suggestions from this group in areas of solar-heating; methane gas development; cold light electric light bulbs; new types of electric storage batteries; and laser beam power transmission, to name a few needed items.[1]

The Good News For Inventors

Entrepreneurs with just a patented, scientific idea that is proved to be feasible and practical in terms of generating or conserving energy, will be able to establish their own businesses from "scratch" with little or no capital.

[1]*Inventor's Journal*, March, 1979.

Perhaps this is the first time since World War II (when inventors were sought after and paid handsomely for new and novel inventions which could be used by the Armed Forces successfully), that entrepreneurs with scientific, engineering, or mechanical expertise can find a market for their ideas.

Recycling

Recycling of materials has become a multi-million dollar industrial activity over the past eight years in the United States, with both small and large companies involved in recovering metals (aluminum, steel, and tin); corrugated paper; plywood lumber; glass; and now even plastic containers converted to shredded packing materials. Many opportunities exist for you in this growing field.

Such cities as Milwaukee, Wisconsin have established massive sewage recycling operations in which processed sewage is converted to organic fertilizer high in nitrogen. The conversion is performed safely and hygienically. The final product is bagged and sold through farm supply and garden shops throughout the country, and returns high revenues to that city's government.

Small operators have established profitable ventures, securing and marketing organic materials obtained at low cost from sewage authorities in many states. These are sold by the bushel or truckload to nurseries and landscape gardeners.

Franchises

Returning to another investment area: *business franchises*, this is an area in which many have made a great deal of money, while others have lost substantial investments. As one eastern business editor reported, "We don't plan to *fail*, we simply fail to *plan*!" There are many bona fide franchise programs available for those people who feel they cannot develop a new venture from "ground zero" because of their lack of temperment, lack of time, or a desire to link up with an established trade name.

Reputable business franchises can cost you as little as $300 or as much as $150,000. And the obvious question emerges: why pay $150,000 for a franchise when you can buy an established business for that amount? The answers include: new challenge, unlimited profit potential, and being a part of the "action" in an established but growing activity or enterprise. What kind of franchise can you get for $150,000? Well, for example, in the "fast food" field, it will get you into an operation like "Wendy's Hamburgers," "Burger Boy," "Denny's," "Pizza Boy," "Burger Chef," and other related food enterprises. A small motel, a retail operation, or a building supply firm would also be available at that price.

Building services, which would include a franchised janitorial service, could cost you about $8,000 for an exclusive area, the right to advertise a national name of your truck, letterheads, invoices, business cards and advertising.

Almost every field of endeavor, ranging from automotive products to water conditioning, now has franchised "deals," or business opportunities for people with the necessary funds. If you do not have the business experience in a particular field, you will get the training through seminars, study classes, training manuals, and tape recordings. You will receive books, authorized manuals, charts, graphs, completely indexed advertising and promotion programs, decals, signs, and posters.

And if you elect to invest in any of the hundreds of retail, repair, service, or industrial franchises, you will be making a significant financial commitment, in addition to your original cash investment. Obviously, any of the franchises require full-time services of the franchise owner, and quite possibly, it may require the services of others (employees) to make the venture succeed financially.

Ultimately, it is *YOU* who will make the venture a success — regardless of how much promotion, or name trade-on value you may have bought.

Then there are those people who are more daring and, more realistically, they lack the necessary funds to purchase a franchise. But they like the market and the specific type of business opportunity offered. So they launch their own enterprises in that field — patterned after an established franchise business, but using another name, or their own legal name. There is nothing illegal about this, providing that no registered name, copyrighted slogan, or patented processes are used. Factor in effects of inflation on prices and costs.

What about investing in a one-person enterprise or business activity? Are these ventures successful financially? Inflation-proof? Yes, indeed!

One-Person Businesses

Child care day centers, or nurseries, have been expanding nationally both in the public and private sectors. This is primarily because of working parents. If your home or yard is large enough and you are physically able to care for up to twelve toddlers or young children, here is an enterprise you can operate from your own home! First check with your zoning department and also with your local health department. You may need a license to operate, depending upon the day care center laws in your state. Calls to local church groups, and Health and Welfare Departments, can indicate to you whether a venture of this type will be successful in your area. If so, establish daily fees which would include the feeding of youngsters. Also check with your insurance agent on coverage to find out the degree of liability involved on your part.

Day Care Centers

In the years ahead, day care centers will mushroom because both parents must now work to combat the high living costs of families. Two, and sometimes three incomes, are necessary to keep a growing family solvent, and to put food on the table.

Newsletters

A relatively new field — newsletters — has developed as a profitable field of endeavor over the past ten years. This is a one-person operation and now accounts for about 8,000 separate and distinct newsletters in print today? The good news about this venture is that some established newsletters in the financial, industrial, aviation, and hobby fields gross about $100,000 for their publisher. One, who puts out sixteen different newsletters, reports that he will gross about $2 million this year.

Now for the negative aspect of the newsletter business. First, unless you have extensive journalism background, or experience as an advertising copywriter, public relations writer, trade paper editor, or freelance writer, do not attempt to launch a newsletter. Your investment in such a venture will cost you (on the average) from $20,000 to about $30,000 to start, and possibly as much as $100,000, depending upon what you invest in printing, mailing, and advertising. Also,

you must be able to support yourself for up to two years until the revenue from first-year subscription renewals comes flowing into your account. No newsletter is successful unless a large percentage of satisfied subscribers renews.

Newsletters are published daily, weekly, biweekly, and monthly, with subscriptions costing as much as $295 annually, as do several newsletters for "gold bugs" — people who buy and sell gold futures, bullion, and coins. There are more expensive newsletters.

About 75% of the cost is directed toward promotion of an individual newsletter to obtain subscribers. Subscriptions are the only revenue to be realized. The amount of editorial work, research, detail work, promotional activity, printing, and production time required can demand up to a seven-day work schedule.

You can get additional information on newsletter operations by writing to "The Newsletter on Newsletters," Rhinebeck, New York.

Copier Services

Other profitable one-person operations include copier services from your home or office. Establishing an employment agency from your home or office requires only a small investment, primarily for advertising and promotion, unless you purchase an established employment franchise which could cost $5,000 and up.

Exterminating Services

One-person exterminating services have proved profitable to many entrepreneurs, both as a part-time and a full-time operation. Costs include purchase of chemicals, transportation, advertising, and insurance. Investment here can start as low as $150 for the operator.

Repair Services

Office equipment and copier repair services are a growing field for thousands of skilled machine mechanics who receive as much as $20 per hour for their services! It is also an excellent field for retired people, since they can work out of basement or garage workshops and have machines delivered to them, and picked up by office equipment dealers.

Training in office equipment and copier repair can be acquired at schools established in numerous parts of the country by national office machine manufacturers. Tuition ranges from $150 to $350 for two- to three-week courses, plus food and lodging costs. Also, vocational and trade schools in most larger cities offer office machine repair courses open to anyone for a minimum fee. Once you have mastered repair techniques, you need only contact a few office equipment dealers and offer your services, or place an advertisement in the business pages of local newspapers.

Servicing Computers

As mentioned in a previous chapter, the newest equipment repair field open to entrepreneurs is the servicing and repair of computers and related computer hardware. While most large corporations and industries have their own company service arrangements for repair of computer hardware, there are thousands of professionals who have purchased "off the shelf" minicomputers and larger models. When there are electronic or mechanical breakdowns, these professionals find they are unable to get manufacturers' mechanics or specialists in repair to service their machines. As a result, many company computer programmers with good mechanical and electronic backgrounds, now "free-lance," or "moonlight" their services in the repair areas for as much as $50 per hour!

Here is a growing field of opportunity for entrepreneurs who are mechanically inclined and have a basic knowledge of electronics. Obviously, it requires four to eight weeks of intensive instruction in computer hardware repair, obtained either at schools conducted by leading computer manufacturers, or at specialized training schools. These courses can range in price from $500 to as much as $3,000 if the course runs longer than two months.

While the initial training investment might be substantial, including money to pay for living expenses while in school, the computer repair specialist has *no overhead* except for a bag of tools! The specialist can also adjust rates flexibly, depending upon the amount of work involved and the size of the hiring firm.

With inflation pushing labor costs higher, and the recession burdening business and industry, the need for "free-lance" computer repair specialists will increase dramatically over the next five years.

Security Services

Increased labor costs have seen the introduction of a new one-person security service in many smaller communities. These security entrepreneurs, trained and state-licensed to carry weapons in the course of their work, charge hourly rates to prevent thefts and vandalism at plants. They use radios, cameras, and electronic "gear" to apprehend thieves. Some are private detectives, while others are former law enforcement officers.

People who enter the security field as surveillance and patrol specialists must obviously be in excellent physical condition, and have a proof of their integrity in terms of a clear record. If they are not former law enforcement officers, they can still take criminology courses at city colleges and institutions. In the process of getting their state licenses and city gun permits, their fingerprints and photographs will be checked by the F.B.I. and state police at the time of their examinations.

An investment as a private security officer or specialist will cost about $10,000 for transportation, office space, firearms, and radio equipment.

Food Shopping Services

Some college students earning extra money, and homemakers who are only able to devote a few hours per day to part-time work, have inaugurated a new type of "food shopping" service for older people unable to get out of their houses; for professional people who, because of the press of their work, do not have time; and for mothers who cannot leave infants unattended. These people receive an hourly wage, plus 10% of the total shopping bill. These paid shoppers must have impeccable references because they handle their customers' cash. Investment required: *none*.

Hunting Guides

Enterprising people in southern states who have experience gained through fishing or hunting in area lakes, swamps, and streams, are now planning to establish a new venture, approved by authorities. State conservation departments in South Carolina, Alabama, Georgia, and Texas, have decreed that the hunting and harvesting of alligators for hides and meat is now permitted because of the high number of alligators located in these areas.

Alligator hunters' only investment is a flat-bottomed boat. Motors, nets, and nooses are supplementary. Hides are demanding excellent prices in Europe: $12 per linear foot. These are used in the manufacture of handbags, shoes, belts, and other products. The European market for alligator-hide products is a better one than the United States. The reason is a continuing campaign related to "endangered species" animals and wildlife being conducted in this country. The restriction on alligators has now been lifted after fifteen years of protection.

It is estimated by these states that millions of dollars will be realized annually by thousands of entrepreneurs from hunters to processors, for the sale of alligator hides and meat. Some hard-hit communities in these states are said to benefit from the recent action.

Mail Forwarding Services

Another field which has attracted some people who prefer to work from their homes, basements, or garages, and who have invested $250 to about $1,000, is the "private post office" activity. Essentially, this venture is a form of "mail drop" and mail forwarding service for people who, for known or unknown reasons, do not want mail sent to the home or office.

By establishing post office box numbers as collection points (which is legal), or by having all mail sent to a fictitious name location ("Ajax Letters, Ltd." for instance, registered with the state), and advertising this service in newspapers and national magazines at monthly fees, these people can earn a good income on a spare-time basis. Letters, magazines, folders, or cards are then placed into special manila envelopes and remailed if requested. Or they can be picked up by messenger for the recipient.

Mail collection boxes, in the form of racks, must be constructed, along with the installation of a small equipped office. Mail scale, address directories, zip code information, and materials for re-mailing are needed. Large cities are ideal for this purpose.

Buying Out An Existing Business

A former salesman for a plastic container manufacturer in the Midwest, located a small firm which was liquidating due to the passing of its owner. Since the firm employed less than six people, making plastic parts (chair rollers) and plastic arm supports for furniture manufacturers, the widow wanted an immediate sale at a low cost, with the provision that its new owner retain the employees.

The salesman discovered the selling price was only $80,000. His knowledge of production revealed to him that the machines were worth more than the selling price! He made an immediate move to make a down payment to the firm's treasurer, who accepted the offer.

With the funds from a bank loan and the sale of some property, the entrepreneur took over the small firm. Within a few weeks, he had developed several new plastic products which had been proposed to his former firm several times, but which were not accepted. His products included: cut-away scale models of the human organs for school biology classes, medical doctor office practices, and medical school application; small replicas of mammals which can be dissected manually by "peeling off" layer upon layer of plastic units; and miniature skeleton frames for use in hospitals, by physicians, schools, art classes, and for sale by hobby shops in "kit" form.

Within a two-year period, this entrepreneur moved his gross volume to more than one million dollars in product sales! His staff of employees has doubled, and five new related products are being sold through distributor firms.

The lesson to be learned here is that you can recognize an investment opportunity that promises substantial rewards. Your knowledge of a field, and the ability to finance a purchase, indicate good management, since your goals are well-planned. A product need, in this case, was met successfully.

Catering Services

The high cost of eating in restaurants has already resulted in the establishment of thousands of one-person "catering" operations. Restaurant owners in large cities have seen a perceptible drop in business because of inflation affecting personal incomes, and those of salespeople who normally entertain customers.

Couples have discovered they can order "in-home meals" for as many as six. brought to the house by caterers for as little as $20! Numerous small firms purchase "brown bag" lunches which are served or delivered daily by a catering enterprise. This costs half of what buying a sandwich lunch at nearby restaurants would. The same woman catered a small wedding reception in a client's backyard for under $500!

Investment for this type of operation requires a starting figure of about $350. This covers meats. vegetables. baked bread and rolls. and collateral items. A large freezer is necessary. and these are usually purchased from second-hand dealers. Also needed is a sufficient amount of kitchen equipment. ranging from food grinders to large utensils.

One individual who works from her home, reports that with rising food costs, starting investment can now reach $1.000 if a full line of foods must be handled for customers. Weekly expenses are running as much as $200. Her monthly gross food sales are topping $2.500 with only one helper. She discourages catering requests from distances greater than ten miles from her home. because of the amount of time involved. She also feels that her business will improve considerably as the inflation rate continues, and that her business is inflation-proof.

Other entrepreneurs have established inflation-proof food-related operations. Each fills a need and markets a product or service for specific segments of the population.

15 Opportunities Requiring No Investment (And A Few Requiring Small Investment)

For the readers of this book, this chapter is a bonus! In many of the previous sections, we have proposed entrepreneurial opportunities which either required a small investment or a substantial amount of capital, in order to get a business venture "off and running." Now, however, we have carefully gathered information and data on a number of entrepreneurial ventures which require *no capital investment*!

Going back to earlier advice in previous chapters, you should not be misled. *There really aren't any easy roads to a lucrative business venture*. The desire to create an income-producing business without the help of financing with cash or credit, will usually require massive doses of personal mental and physical effort. This is opposed to significant financial aid required in obtaining advanced education in the case of medicine, law, accounting, or in such skilled trades as electrician, plumber, carpenter, or mechanic.

Here are opportunities for you to consider which require no capital investment, or very little.

1. *Demonstrator*.

You can work as a company representative, appearing in department stores, showing how to use an appliance or product. You will demonstrate what the product will do for the buyer. Minimum training is required. You are paid either by salary, or a salary and commission on the number of products sold through your demonstration efforts.

2. *House cleaning*.

Personal contacts will present numerous opportunities in this area. You will be paid hourly rates, or a total price for the project.

3. *Catastrophe cleaning*.

This is a relatively new field, but a lucrative one for hard workers. You would be required to clean, wash-down, and scrub out areas such as restaurant kitchens, offices, and home interiors which have been smudged or smeared as a result of fires, smoke damage, or water-soaking. This would include heater back-up, broken water pipes, storm-damaged interiors, and vandalized schools or offices. Payment is by contract arrangement, or by *high* hourly rate.

4. *Window washing*.

There are many opportunities here. You need to be in good physical condition. Payment is by job or by hourly rate.

5. *Janitorial service*.

This can be a "second" job for most people, since it is usually done after business hours. Payment is through a contract arrangement, or hourly rate.

6. *Insurance appraiser*.

There is a large demand for these services in the automotive insurance field, as well as in the accident, residential, industrial, and in the aviation industries. Training is required and is usually furnished by the companies. Salary is usually combined with payment for the number of cases investigated.

7. *Sales work*.

This is selling on consignment, in which you are paid only after the product has been sold. This can include used cars, real estate, motor homes, utensils, vacuum cleaners, and publications.

8. *Auctioneer*.

Training is usually required to be effective. Payment is based on a percentage of the income produced by the auction, or on a hourly basis.

9. *Free-lance writing*.

This is a competitive field, but can be quite lucrative for the person with writing skills, especially on a local basis. Payment is on a per-word basis, or a flat rate per article. Check with local businesses and weekly papers who might need your services.

10. *Installation worker*.

Manual dexterity is required for this job opportunity, as in the installation of wood stoves, carpeting, insulation, or electrical and gas stoves and appliances. This is normally a salaried job, but it can also be an independent venture.

11. *Cutting and selling firewood*.

Basic tools are required, in addition to whatever transportation you might have at the moment (a pickup truck is ideal). You collect from your customers with each delivery made.

12. *Cleaning, repairing, servicing* tennis courts, swimming pools, driveways. Payment is on contract or on an hourly rate.

13. *Lawn care, trash and snow removal*.

You need to be in good physical condition and have basic homeowner's tools. Payment is by job completed or by contract.

14. *Broker*.

You locate buyers for new and used cars, homes, or businesses, machinery, equipment, find sources for investment funds, or locate buyers for a new product. Payment is by fee *from seller*, amounting to 7% to 10% of sales price.

15. *Printing broker*.

Locate business people who need any kind of printing. You review the work needed, then call printers for estimates on the jobs. Make sure to advise the printer that you are a broker. When the job is delivered, you receive up to 15% of the cost for your part.

16. *Attic and basement cleaning*.

When people begin to prepare to sell their home, or when the owner dies, they, or the family, often hire attic or basement cleaning workers. You are paid by the hour, but the bonus is that you often get to sort through the "junk" you have removed, and keep anything of value. Sometimes small fortunes can be made in discovered antiques.

17. *Telephone collector*.

You call delinquent accounts to speed payment of overdue bills. Department stores and businesses will furnish you with names. A knowledge of local and federal laws on past-due collection activities is mandatory. You are paid a percentage of the amount collected by you.

18. *Recycling materials pickup*.

This is a relatively new job. You gather aluminum cans, plastic products, glass jars, and empty containers, for sale to industrial buyers. Aluminum cans are sold to either Reynolds Aluminum Recycling Centers (check your telephone book) or to metals buyers at $20 per 100 pounds, or $200 per ton. You receive payment at the time of delivery.

19. *Sampler*.

You distribute samples of new products at shopping malls, supermarkets, at large gatherings at clubs, sports arenas, etc. A daily rate is paid by client companies.

20. *Survey interviewer*.

Full time or spare-time work opportunities are available from companies marketing to consumers. Work assignments are provided. Payment is on a per-unit basis.

21. *Food taster*.

Work in your own home, tasting new types of cooked foods, meats, vegetable preparations, and desserts. Contacts with advertising agencies are required to offer your services. Payment is by contract rate.

22. *Consultant*.

This is an extremely lucrative field once you are established in an industry or a specific commercial field. Expertise in one or more fields is a requisite. Contact companies in your field to assist in solving problems, making recommendations for improving production, reducing costs, advancing safety, or increasing profits. Compensation is through contract arrangement, and the length of time your services are needed.

23. *Heir locator*.

This is a good field for retired people since a great deal of time is needed to pore through newspaper files where notices have been placed by banks looking for missing heirs. Also, many attorneys have lists of people named in estates, who cannot be located. It is similar to detective work, but once you have located the particular person, your percentage is rewarding!

24. *Real estate appraiser*.

Some training in real estate activity is required, particularly in the area of building and property values. Contact Realtors and brokers for work in this specific field. Also contact county and township authorities for manuals and data available.

25. *Rare coin analyst*.

Here is an excellent entrepreneurial opportunity for someone who has a great deal of numismatic knowledge. You must know historical coin values, markets, sources where you can verify data, and should be affiliated with collector groups. You are paid on a fee basis from either the coin owner or the coin dealer.

26. *Employment counselor*.

You can work from your own home in this area, reviewing job resumes, preparing these for job applicants, and calling personnel departments. You contact job applicants through "Jobs Wanted" columns in newspapers, and by word-of-mouth advertising. Payment comes from counselling fees and resume preparation.

27. *Pet care specialist*.

Many people who work full time have pets in their apartments or homes, but are concerned about their welfare. This can be a lucrative field for the individual who likes animals and knows how to handle them properly and safely. You will feed and exercise dogs and cats, in addition to grooming, if your contract arrangements specify this. Payment is by monthly or weekly fee in contract form.

28. *House sitter*.

This is a relatively new field. It involves taking care of a house while owners are away on vacation or business trips. It offers opportunities for retired people. Payment is made by the number of days the sitter remains at the house.

29. *Car cleaner*.

You specialize in getting a used car or truck into clean, presentable condition for a dealer at his facility. It involves washing, cleaning, brushing the interior, washing and waxing the body surfaces, and polishing and cleaning the windows. Payment is made on a per-car basis.

30. *Fast food delivery service*.

Some fast food restaurants do not have delivery service for customers, and would welcome this extension of service. You negotiate payment on an hourly, weekly, or contract basis. This is a spare-time opportunity, and an excellent chance for retired people to supplement their incomes.

31. *Artist's representative*.

You arrange for exhibits of all types of artwork in banks, shopping malls, business office lounges, and other public areas, for marketing creative artwork. You receive a 20% commission on all artwork sold. You should have a good working knowledge of painting, sketches, and other art mediums. This can be a very lucrative field if pursued aggressively.

32. *Dinner Theatre talent coordinator*.

With the tremendous growth of dinner theatres, the problem of discovering talent for plays and musical presentations becomes difficult for owners and operators. By scouting colleges, universities, offices, and plants, and by using cards on bulletin boards and notices in company publications, you act as a "clearing house" for amateur talent. Payment comes from dinner theatre owners for "traffic" generated.

33. *Tour guide*.

This is a seasonal type of entrepreneurial opportunity in which you accompany people visiting your state or community for the first time. You accompany them to camp grounds, historical sites and points of interest in *their* transportation. Payment to you is on a fee-per-trip-made basis. Contacts through motor home dealers, travel agents, weekly newspaper editors, service stations, and restaurants will be a tremendous help.

34. *Car valet service*.

You take cars for business people to airports, bus and train stations, and office buildings. You also return the vehicles to an appointed place, agreed upon earlier. This is not a parking attendant job because you must take the vehicle to any number of locations. Frequently you accompany the business people on several of the stops. You must be available at least ten or twelve hours per day, which would cover evening hours where business socials are concerned. Compensation to you is by day, week, month, or for longer periods, developed in a contract. You might also combine this service with a complete car cleaning service, where you deliver to the owner a polish and waxed version of his previously dirty car.

The opportunities presented here are by no means complete, but fall within the "no or low investment required" category. There is a difference between a job opportunity and a business venture, either on a part-time or full time basis. You create the opportunity and carry it through profitably. It is your creation, and its success, obviously, depends on what you do with it in terms of hard work and continuity.

The Energy Problem

With the energy problem now uppermost in the minds of everyone, there will be numerous venture opportunities for you. Many of these new activities do not exist at the present time, since no one has pioneered in the energy "spin-offs" area as yet. But the important thing to remember is that these venture opportunities will not require capital investment. Your contribution, as in all the other areas, will require tremendous spurts of effort, organization, and intelligent application.

Chimney Sweeping

One aspect of the "conserve energy" syndrome which will prove profitable to entrepreneurs, is that of cleaning chimneys. Remember that you will need to be in good physical condition and health, and cannot suffer from acrophobia! The increased use of wood and coal will have a serious physical effect on chimneys, depositing layers of soot and residue on flue interiors. Unless these deposits are removed, they can cause a back-up of smoke or gas and can ultimately result in chimney fires.

European residents are accustomed to seeing "chimney sweeps" at work on roofs of hotels and homes on a regular basis. This is particularly so in late summer and spring months, when wood and coal stoves are not in use. This unique trade, dating back to the 16th Century, is highly romanticized, but it is a vital service as it saves lives and property.

Chimney cleaning experts are highly-paid, since it is a somewhat hazardous occupation. However, with modern electrical cleaners and the use of special vacuum lines, many jobs can be handled in a day's time. For people who like the out-of-doors and a variety of activity with their own working hours, here is a field which will grow tremendously in the years ahead. It will result in a highly profitable return. Investments can range from a few dollars for basic tools to a significant amount for special vehicles, hose vacuum lines, and scaling ladders.

Energy Efficiency Services

Some people have already established "energy evaluation" services where they will visit home, offices, warehouse, garages, and rural buildings to make recommendations on steps to be taken to reduce fuel consumption. People who have a background in construction and who are now retired, for example, can carry out building inspection activities with a degree of authority. Work of this type includes checking windows, window frames, and doors of all types, with various instruments from small scale smoke ejectors to pressure meters. In addition, heating systems must be checked for conversion possibilities. Air conditioners will also need to be re-evaluated in terms of output and capacity for reduction of energy use. Roofs and ceiling vents will need inspections for conversions. And the use of solar heating panels will be increasingly important to the big companies, apartments, and hotels where fuel costs are significant. These and other energy-saving ventures will prove to be "inflation-proof" business opportunities.

This new and growing field will require many skills from the basic construction worker to highly-skilled engineering talent, in making intelligent judgements and recommendations. But it will open the door to millions of new business ventures geared to saving energy.

Mobile Auto Repair Services

While the inflation and recessions will take down millions of workers in the construction and automotive industries, perhaps many of these people will be able to find new positions with emerging firms. The gasoline crisis, which is causing new car sales to drop sharply, will provide novel opportunities for new, mobile-oriented ventures. One of these might be a "door-to-door" automotive repair and tune-up service. Skilled mechanics will come to *you at your convenience,* rather than you having to drive to an independent shop miles from your home! These new auto mechanics will have fully-equipped trucks complete with tools, parts, and manuals to take care of nearly everything on wheels.

Produce Vending Services

We will see the return of the neighborhood "peddler" who vends fruits and vegetables from a modern van. This service will cater to the food requirements of residents living in apartments, condominiums, and outlying suburban areas. Here again will be opportunities for entrepreneurs to make excellent profits while performing a necessary and welcome service. None of us will relish those "luxurious" drives to distant supermarkets and food outlets in the coming years!

Woodstoves And Fireplace Equipment

The energy-saving era has produced a new field of endeavor: the marketing of used woodstoves, used fireplace screens, iron log racks, and used fire brick. These items are being sold to people who cannot afford some of the high prices being asked for them in new condition. Some of these ventures operate from a truck, from small storage yards, or from converted retail store buildings.

Insulation Business

Insulation materials are now in great demand by home builders and by other operators in the industry. Many new ventures have been established during the past year, specializing in the application of several forms of insulation materials (bats, granules, and metal foil paper). Both organic and scientifically-produced materials are now in wide use, including converted sawdust. Numerous entrepreneurs have moved into this field because of the minimum amount of start-up capital required. There remain thousands of new opportunities for your efforts in this field.

Firewood Suppliers

Perhaps the most basic and profitable segment of energy-saving activities is that of chopping, splitting, and delivery of cords of firewood. Cords of wood being delivered to some Manhattan sites bring operators as much as $125 per cord! There are even "middle men" handling retail sales in cities who purchase wood in cord lots ranging in price of up to $80, delivered. Truckers also profit from hauling wood in cord lots.

Coal Dealers

We are seeing the re-emergence of the "neighborhood" coal dealer who is selling hard coal, primarily in the Northeast. The coal comes in heavy paper sacks of twenty-five and fifty pounds. It is predicted that "fuel stores" will be appearing in many states in the nation's Northeast corridor, since coal mining is performed in this area. This is another field of opportunity for you.

Carriage Manufacturers

One unique business venture is beginning to show signs of vitality: the manufacturer of horsedrawn carriages. While there have been modest carriage sales made over the years to such religious sects as the Amish, new sales are being made to fairs, schools, institutions, and people living in rural areas.

With energy-saving as a motivation, great interest is being shown in various styles and sizes of horse-drawn carriages available from this manufacturer. The sales manager also suspects that some companies are exploring the possibility of moving into this specialized field "whole hog." One of the problems, he told us, is in finding skilled carriage builders, many of whom are elderly. Like many of our country's skilled crafts, the art of carriage making seems to be a fast-vanishing art.

Aircraft Modifications

With fuel costs for aircraft moving higher every month, many flying enthusiasts are selling gasoline-powered aircraft and are moving into soaring gliders in an effort to maintain this sports activity. Sales of "hang gliders" and soaring glider kits are now at an all-time high, report aviation product manufacturers. If the interest in this sport continues, there will be an expansion of manufacturing these types of aircraft along with the introduction of new designs and models. The field is wide open for new ideas, designs, and ventures that will bring individuals a profitable return for ingenious ideas.

Alternative Transportation Dealers

Also during this period, we have seen bicycle makers and dealers making record sales, totalling millions of dollars on new bicycle models. Shortages of bicycles have been reported in some cities on specific designs and sizes. The truly energy-saving vehicle has also produced huge second-hand bicycle markets, and another one for parts and supplies.

There has also been a spurt of new ventures related to use of bicycles as a substitute for cars. Several manufacturers are producing both electric and gas-operated power units for propulsion sources. This field is being developed for people who are retired or physically unable to expend the energy required for long trips, or where roads are steep. Despite fairly high prices for power units these have been selling extremely well nationally.

Here again is a new area where you can develop alternate power sources and unique driving devices; new electrical motors; and new types of gasoline-powered engines in a reduced size. The market for these products now exists, and offers new sources of profit for the individual who is properly motivated and will seize an opportunity and run with it.

Keeping In Tune With The Times

When you are looking for spare time, no-investment opportunities, keep the current situations facing us in mind. Anything that you can do for someone else which will ultimately save them money, time, or energy will be a business venture almost guaranteed to succeed!

16 Study Today's Market Needs

The energy crunch of the 1970's had a devastating impact upon a score of industries and businesses, ranging from new car and truck manufacturing, to the hotel and motel industry. It has literally re-shaped much of the nation's industrial profile and economy. Despite inflation's future effects, venture capitalists studying today's and tomorrow's market needs, point out that many entrepreneurs will prosper because they will develop alternative programs and techniques. This will bridge the gaps and vacuums resulting from industry's massive shift toward new energy sources.

Woodstoves

Investors are watching the dramatic development of a new multi-million dollar industry which grows almost daily—the manufacture and marketing of wood stoves and new types of wood-burning fireplaces. Already, more than fifty new companies and older firms are producing and selling a variety of stoves that burn wood and cost from $50 to as much as $1,500. These firms also import thousands of deluxe, foreign-built stoves from Scandanavian countries, and in Germany, France, and Belgium.

In Pennsylvania, a former automotive design engineer, living in a large, two-story rebuilt farm house, purchased an imported wood stove since he had a quantity of firewood. He discovered that one load of wood in the stove would burn for more than eight hours, heating his entire home! Some wood stoves burn for two days. When compared to oil heating costs, the savings were significant.

Checking The Demand For The Product

Checking with neighbors and friends, he found an interest and need for similar wood-burning stoves. Beginning with an investment of $5,000 and an empty barn on his property, he purchased twenty-four stoves of various types, both domestic and imported. He then launched a modest newspaper advertising campaign, working on a part-time basis. All of the stoves sold within a three-week period to people coming from as far as forty miles away! Several stoves were sold at more than $400.

He resigned from his design position and established an office in his home, securing a $20,000 loan from a friend, with an additional bank loan for $10,000. He then purchased 100 stoves at wholesale prices. Developing his own stove design, he incorporated a new heat-cycle system and sub-contracted the manufacturing of the unit to a small plant located twenty miles from his site.

The entrepreneur's operation has now grown to a profitable venture, grossing $700,000 annually. There are four buildings on his farm property now, including a stove display room with a full-time salesperson, a huge barn jammed with stove supplies, and two buildings loaded to the rafters with stoves in cartons. All of this includes his own designs, which now account for more than one-half of his sales.

Doubling The Sales

By keeping his staff small, and utilizing all of his own buildings, this young man reports his business will be doubled now in its third year of existence. Buyers journey to his location from cities as far as fifty miles away. He is now chairman of the two corporations which own this venture.

People who would like to move into a new, exciting field that promises rapid growth, despite inflation, should investigate the burgeoning laser industries and fields, ranging from communications to cutting high strength steel, wood, and plastic, to medical surgery. It is controlled lighting emitted from a tube, usually filled with helium and neon gas, which produces the laser beam. And laser beams are powerful enough to cut a diamond in half! However, lasers are so precisely accurate, surgeons now use this controlled form of electronic power to perform eye surgery.

Fiberoptics

Perhaps related to controlled forms of light are developments coming out of a mushrooming industry being built around "Fiberoptics." This scientific industry development comes from the concept of manufacturing bundles of plastic or glass fibers through which a laser's light is conducted, at times over a considerable distance. The fibers are protected with a special coating, a reflective material, which prevents the light from escaping through the surfaces of the fiber.

Fiberoptic products and applications are being used in the medical field, manufacturing industry, nucleonic related activities, aviation industry, and other areas. Investment to launch a new business can run as low as $10,000, to as much as $500,000. And experts point out there is plenty of room in the industry for new applications, such as those in unique lighting effects seen in discos and in theatres. Entrepreneurs can learn light generation techniques and the state-of-the-arts quickly.

Emergency Air Ambulances

The use of light aircraft and medium-weight aircraft for the transporting of people needing specialized medical assistance (or who need immediate medical aid), has developed into a sophisticated field of business activity for pilot/entrepreneurs. These "air ambulances" range from four-place, single-engine aircraft bringing in patients from remote Dakota farms to large city hospitals when they become seriously ill, to high-powered, twin-engine aircraft equipped with life-support systems and a nurse, flying the patient across the country to a large clinic.

Pilots holding commercial rating certificates and who own or lease light aircraft, can build a lucrative income by supplying "air ambulance" services, particularly if they are based in remote or rural communities far from metropolitan areas. By making their services known to hospital directors, heads of large clinics, and to state and county medical societies, these pilots can be called upon to transport seriously ill people when ground transportation is impractical in terms of time. Hourly rates, plus operation costs, are usually billed for "air ambulance" services.

Air Delivery Services

Despite the flurry of television commercials on the part of large aircraft carriers with fleets of aircraft ready to carry packages across the country, there is a growing need for smaller air courier service. The age of computers and the resulting tons of print-out material, floppy discs, magnetic tapes, and such, has spawned a need to move these items from small communities to large cities where corporate headquarters are situated.

Small enterpreneur/pilot courier service owners report that, in some cases, they have added three and four new aircraft to their facilities to take care of demands! In addition, the daily flights carrying cancelled checks, financial reports, and in some cases, bags filled with cash, are necessary for some areas of business.

Helicopters are also being used in remote, mountainous regions for transportation of cash, records, and data. These aircraft are also being used successfully by banking institutions in large cities on daily flights.

One pilot in an eastern community, which is almost fifty miles from the nearest large city, uses two small aircraft, alternately, to service about ten small companies and large commercial farm operations. He picks up machinery parts in cities about 200 miles away for his commercial customers, delivers high-priority parcels and packages, collects new parts at manufacturing plants, insecticides for farm operators, and flies executives (on special occasions only) to meetings. His high rates are justified, state his customers, because the flights slash days and weeks off regular delivery schedules.

Since his overhead is low and schedules are extremely flexible, with his prime concern being weather, this entrepreneur will prosper despite inflation.

Aerial Photography & Survey Work

Other activities, some of which are spare-time, involving people who own and operate aircraft, include aerial photography and aerial survey work.

Flying from his own airstrip which he built on his 200-acre dairy farm, a Pennsylvania pilot has managed to add about $8,000 to $10,000 annually to his regular farm income by photographing farms, forest lands, townships, and small towns from the air for a list of customers. These include real estate brokers, auctioneers, county and township governments, utility representatives, and real estate developers.

The pilot/photographer owns several excellent aerial cameras and collateral equipment. He has also built his own photo-developing laboratory and dark room, which saves him a considerable amount of money, since negatives would have to be sent away for processing. He is able to deliver enlargements within a week's time to customers. His aircraft is a two-place, high-wing monoplane and is valued at about $10,000. He feels his entrepreneurial activity will continue despite inflation, and there is no conflict with his regular farm operation.

The market for low-cost light aircraft (both new and second-hand) is fairly large across the country, with several hundred thousand licensed private pilots devoting spare time to this activity. This growing interest in aviation has spurted the development of numerous entrepreneurial operations on both the coasts.

Supplying Home Builders Of Aircraft

Two former airline aircraft mechanics in southern California discovered that hundreds of pilots were building their own light aircraft from F.A.A.-approved plans in sheds and garages, including the welding of fuselages and construction of wings. (Most were members of Experimental Aircraft Association, Inc., an aircraft "homebuilder" organization.) The majority of the aircraft required small piston aircraft engines under eighty horsepower; however, this component,

the most important one of all, was in short supply. None were being manufactured.

The two mechanics, who had been on a European tour the previous year, inspected small airfields and amateur-built aircraft equipped with Volkswagon engines converted to aircraft powerplants. They decided to secure second-hand VW engines for rebuilding. Five engines were removed from "totalled" VW cars at a dealer's yard. The engines were in excellent condition.

Within several weeks, the engines had been modified for aircraft use and were tested. These eighty-two-horsepower engines were sold for $800 each to pilots. They were used successfully and safely in later flights.

Today, new VW engines secured from the German builder are modified for aircraft use at the rate of twenty-five per month, with some of these selling for $2,200 each. Also, numerous aircraft parts are made in the small plant, making it a profitable operation.

Around the country, about five expert wood-crafters carve custom-made wooden propellors for aircraft use, and for utilization on air boats and ice sleds, providing these craftsmen with excellent incomes and another market source for their wood products.

Like most other specialists and craftsmen, these people advertise in aviation magazines, primarily those aimed at private pilots. Ads are also placed in "Sport Aviation" magazine and in publications which cater to the amateur aircraft builders and mechanics. "Trade-A-Plane," a ninety-two page tabloid, published three times each month in Crossville, Tennessee, is another publication widely-read by both commercial and private pilots and by representatives from all segments of the aviation industry. Numerous entrepreneurial opportunities can be found in each issue of this publication.

Using Your Hands: Craftmaking

Craft-making as a source of primary and part-time income, has been widely publicized over the years. There are dozens of good books on the subject found in libraries and bookstores. Such magazines as "Craft Horizons," aimed at professional craftspeople, artists, teachers, architects, designers, decorators, collectors, connoisseurs, and the consumer public, includes articles on ceramic, weaving, stitchery, jewelry, woodwork, and other arts. Technology, materials, and new ideas are covered.

Other magazines such as "Creative Crafts," "Gems and Minerals," "Popular Handicraft Hobbies," and "Working Craftsman," are quite definitive in terms of making and marketing craft products. "Craft Horizons" and "Working Craftsman" are published primarily for serious craftspeople who make and sell handcrafted items.

Handcrafted items made for sale to the public, offer numerous opportunities for retired people, since work can be done at home, and for modest expenditures. Of course, some handcrafts require ceramic baking kilns, spray equipment, or expensive shop tools, and can involve a substantial investment.

Many retired people living in California, Arizona, Florida, and other areas have supplemented their retirement incomes by becoming seriously involved in various craft areas. One woman in her '70's, who has become an accomplished landscape artist in oils, has sold numerous paintings to business officers, banks, and wealthy patrons for as much as $500 each! This income is significant. she reports, because of her inflation-eroded retirement income consisting of Social Security.

Banks and institutions across the country have become "salons" for the exhibit of many forms of art executed by both professional and amateur painters, artists. and sculptors. Thousands of art work have been successfully sold this way.

The entrepreneur who is thinking of making an income through some form of crafts, should study the market carefully if he/she intends to offer a product for sale to the public.

A printer. travelling in the South, saw a farmer displaying huge Cypress tree roots on his lawn. The printer. whose hobby is woodworking, noticed the fascinating grain of a tree root which had been sawed into a large. thick slice of wood. He purchased one of the roots and loaded it into his station wagon.

Weeks later. he carefully cut several slabs from the root. sanded and polished them. Finishing the surface with a special preservative, he bored several holes and built four coffee tables. One neighbor saw the tables and told a furniture dealer about them. The dealer bought all four tables for $200! Since the furniture builder had only paid $20 for the root. he had grossed a profit of $180! He began to give serious consideration to the making and selling of larger coffee tables that could be sold at premium prices. When not occupied with his regular printing plant efforts, he toured furniture display houses, talking with dealers. He also spent a lot of time with wholesalers of furniture.

Convinced there was a large market for expensive Cypress root and Redwood slab tables with high-gloss surfaces, the entrepreneur made a decision to purchase the raw and dried roots and stumps in large quantities. He spent several thousands of dollars on this material. Then realizing that his return would be higher if he sold directly to consumers, he rented an empty former retail food store building.

Within several months, with the help of two part-time wood workers, he displayed more than a dozen attractive Redwood and Cypress tables priced from $250 to $500 each. He had also placed advertisements in area Sunday supplements and local magazines. Within two weeks, he sold out all of the tables, and took orders for fifteen additional units! He also received requests from hobbyists to purchase slabs without any finish on the surface.

The spare-time furniture-making venture now grosses three times the business volume of the entrepreneur's printing business. And he has opened a third store in a town visited by thousands of area tourists because it is basically an "art colony" community. Other wood items have been added to the line to sell at lower costs as a hedge against inflation. And he has added a pre-fabricated electric organ building kit which consists of finished cherry wood, transistorized electronic wiring and control systems.

Other craftspeople who have made a successful living from the manufacture of wood products by handcraft, include two retired railroad conductors who now purchase "Grandfather Clock" kits by mail and then assemble these for sale to area stores and to customers. The wood components are sanded, fitted, glued and fastened, according to the drawings of the style and model ordered. Prior to installing the clock works, the frames are stained and finished.

The two craftsmen average about $100 profit on each clock completed and sold. In some cases, where larger models were requested, the profit has been higher. This income is well-received as a supplement to Social Security.

Several Texas entrepreneurs, one of whom is a technical training instructor, build and market five "butcher chopping block" units each month at $220 each. Each block, made of laminated hardwood, is carefully sanded, with gluing done in a special jig design by part-time workers. Stack-shelves made of wood are also produced in the trio's workshop whose products are advertised in regional magazines.

A retired art teacher in Wisconsin has built a flourishing mail order business which employs four full-time people manufacturing wooden decoy ducks and geese. Some of the decoys are sold from a low price of $65 to more than $100 each! Manual labor and power machines are used to produce the quality decoys. The completed, painted decoy fowl are shipped to a Maine mail order house which purchases the entire output.

Furniture Refinishing

Another growing business for entrepreneurs is the "wood stripping and finishing" venture. Using converted garages and small service station offices, these specialists convert horribly scratched, dented, and discolored tables, chairs, cabinets, and chests into attractively stained and finished pieces with gleaming surface coatings.

With family budgets "bent" beyond repair by inflation, new household furniture becomes an out-of-reach luxury for millions of Americans. However, many families purchase second-hand furniture from Goodwill Stores and the like. For a minimal fee, the small furniture stripping firms will remove old finish mechanically or chemically, down to the original wood surface. Then the piece will be sanded, filled, cleaned, and refinished to the customer's requested stain and surface coating.

These furniture refinishing entrepreneurs predict that young, growing families across the country will use these services to get needed furniture for their homes at a fraction of the cost of new articles. They also forecast a good business future despite a recession, since they are filling an important need, and at an affordable cost.

It is a field in which a minimum of capital is required to start, along with a basic knowledge of wood, furniture design, and the urge to work hard to achieve financial success.

Scale Model Building

Five retired office machine repair mechanics in the Chicago area who were interested in naval history, had formed a club to study early naval and commercial sailing vessels. Several had built accurate, scale models of several sailing vessels. When these were exhibited at a hobby fair at an area shopping mall event, three people made bids as high as $100 per model! These were not sold, but orders with cash deposits were taken for duplicate scale models to be built.

More than one year later, this group of entrepreneurs is now building and marketing eight to ten scale models of sailing ships and vessels per month, for a crafts distributor. The combined, spare-time income adds several hundreds of dollars per month to each of the men's retirement incomes.

Blacksmithing

Other lucrative handcraft enterprises which offer many financial opportunities include those of blacksmithing and metal work.

With the increase in the number of thoroughbred racehorse tracks and harness tracks around the country in the past decade, the need for "farriers," people who shoe horses (blacksmiths), has grown considerably. There is such a shortage of farriers, that three of these specialists travel the entire country during spring and summer months to shoe racehorses at high fees. Some are reported to earn as much as $600 per week. Most own camper trucks equipped with portable forges and tools, plus the expensive metal shoes required by these horses.

There are only two known farrier schools in the United States, located on the East Coast! With hundreds of thousands of people owning horses and riding almost daily and in numerous shows, the need for farrier service is vital, offering many opportunities.

However, the "Smithy" who pursues the trade must obviously be in excellent physical condition, and have a love for horses. He/she must understand the handling of horses and temperaments of these animals. An inexperienced person who attempts to shoe a skittish horse will risk serious injury!

For those who qualify, expense is moderate, including a truck or camper, and knowledge of the proper shoes, in addition to a complete line of equipment needed to do the job.

Blacksmithing, an ancient handcraft going back to the Holy Wars and "Knights of the Round Table," is still a profitable and exciting art. Hundreds of modern blacksmiths who have installed small forges and avils (and have all of the tools required), are producing and selling a wide variety of forged products, including fireplace grates, replica Indian axes, hardware for chests, fancy fence gates, massive lantern fixtures, stair rails, and other crafted items.

One auto mechanic, who earns as much from spare-time blacksmithing as he does on his regular job of car repair, has outfitted his outlying two-car garage with a forge, anvil, and all other shop equipment needed to build everything from huge door hinges to rugged shoe scrapers, all purchased by several craft shops.

"I used to think about my blacksmithing as an avocation," said the mechanic/entrepreneur. "But it's really insurance against inflation–and offers me a good income in a recession if I should lose my present job. And the way this economy is headed–that could happen!"

There are a number of good textbooks available on the art of blacksmithing, and courses are available at technical schools in some sections of the country. Since most of the work is manual–use of hammers on the anvil and lifting hot iron out of coal fires–one must be in good physical condition. It is "sweaty, dirty, and tiring work," reports one blacksmith, "But there's no other job like it anywhere!"

An investment here would be less than $1,000, unless equipment purchased is new. Air pumps for the forge can be easily secured. Special hammers, pincers, and a variety of other equipment are the most expensive items, plus the cost of malleable iron.

Metalsmithing

Metalsmiths who work in a variety of techniques with wrought iron and welding equipment (making fences, post lanterns, gates, fireplace equipment, and furniture), earn good incomes. Many specialize by building articles out of certain types of metal only (copper, aluminum, or galvanized steel) to meet the need for specific types of products. These jobs can be handled on a part-time or full-time basis with only modest investment required.

These artisans are precise workers–those who have years of experience making kitchen utensils, drinking vessels and containers, lanterns, serving plates and trays. The work is tedious and demanding. And it is a field filled with opportunities for retired people who have the time to work at making metal articles. Skill comes with experience and time.

Products made by these artisans are generally sold to wholesale or distributor buyers, to customers by mail answering advertisements, and directly from stores owned by these specialists.

Cottage Industries: The Bright Future

For years, workers in the "cottage industries" in the southern parts of the United States, stayed in their homes to earn a weekly or monthly income. They worked at home, making quilts, blankets, and fancy bedcovers. Others worked on sewing machines, turning out a wide variety of apparel and sewn materials for household use. There are still hundreds of these cottage industries in operation.

Entire industries emerged from these small operations. It has been reported that inflation has forced small manufacturers in the garment trade and textile industries to return to cottage workers for production. This eliminates expensive plant overhead, the need for lunch rooms, salary-structured bookkeeping, and facilities for employees. Workers are paid by the unit completed, almost like sub-contractors. Insurance and pension plans are eliminated for the employer. Workers must handle their own Social Security deductions and hospitalization, which most do.

A recession will see a dramatic return to cottage industry manufacturing methods. In fact, in this age of so-called "big business," the reality is that there is a quiet, but growing, trend in small cottage industry-type businesses, most of which are inflation-proof. Now may be the best time in U.S. history for an intelligently-directed small business of the cottage industry variety.

Sub-contracting

There are numerous "at home" opportunities available on the entrepreneurial market. Interested people should contact small plants and firms and offer their services as *paid sub-contractors*. A check of local business directories can help here.

Established small business owners point out that if your interests lie in any of the four basic areas–food, housing, transportation, and clothing (which take most money from the average person's take-home pay)—and you develop alternative programs to meet these needs, the possibilities are great for your financial success.

Food Co-ops

Establishing a food cooperative venture as a manager can earn you a good income, and a source of food. There are thousands of food co-ops established in the United States and more are being added to the list. Some were in existence as far back as forty-five years ago, set up by Quaker-backed organizations which provided residents of specific communities with food at lower prices than prevailing retail rates. Communes and colonies are built around food cooperatives.

In larger cities, food co-ops have been established since the early 1960's. In low income neighborhoods, this is perhaps the only way (outside of welfare funds, food stamps, and donations from religious and citizen groups) for residents of these communities to survive.

But now, the so-called "middle class" blue- and white-collar families have had to seek this means of purchasing food from depleted incomes. Cooperatives in the food distribution area are based on paid memberships, which form the financial base of the unit. Monthly fees are related to food credits, or points. Each type of food—meat, baked goods, canned vegetables and fruits, fresh produce—is "priced" at credit points. Buying is by invitation on a specific day, according to alphabetic listing or the size of the family.

The co-op member brings his/her cartons and bags to a building (sometimes nothing more than a three-car garage) where a selection of food is made. Meat, which is refrigerated, is limited in terms of the number one member can have. For example, a ten-pound ground meat package, one five-pound chicken, and a package of bacon are available for one family. Other items are also limited by quantity under the rules established. But the savings, in terms of family food expenditures, are impressive.

Other food co-ops charge semi-monthly or annual memberships, and issue cards which must be presented at the small store—and in some cases larger supermarket operations. These are "no-frills" outlets. You will not see any fancy displays with advertisements and colorful backgrounds, or hear any muzak! The places are clean but austere, with the customer doing the "bagging" or "boxing." Savings are, on the average, 20% to 35% less than at regular supermarkets.

You would be wise to spend at least a week visiting wholesale food distribution centers, and noting the spread between wholesale and retail prices. If you purchase a crate of lettuce, the cost at wholesale level will be about $10. The retail marketer will probably gross abut a $15 profit on the crate. The same is true if you purchase a crate of eggs at sixty cents per dozen, wholesale rate.

Meats and other products can be purchased at wholesale, but you will have to pay cash in advance, unlike the retailer who puts everything on his monthly credit account with the wholesaler. Factor in the cost of store space, license fees, rental of refrigeration units, and your salary. Estimate the size of gross sales needed to cover these expenses. A modest advertising program will (if you are located where people can reach you) bring in all the customers you can handle! Your co-op sales prices will determine the amount of gross business you can serve.

"Rent-A-Wreck" Business

Entrepreneurs are now renting five- and ten-year-old cars to customers in areas where weather is a factor. Many people don't want to risk damaging their newer cars on icy and snowy roads. So they will pay from $5 to $10 per day for rental of an older car with dents. These entrepreneurs report brisk business, particularly in all kinds of inclement weather and on weekends. The cars they own have been purchased, in some cases, for less than $500, but are in excellent mechanical condition. Some of the paint has worn off hoods and fenders, and upholstery is worn, but these cars offer excellent alternative transportation at a profit to their owners!

"Club" rental vans are growing in vogue among suburbanites where transportation is lacking. With gasoline costs at their highest point in history, workers are leaving cars at home. This has inspired some entrepreneurs to trade in their cars for vans and "mini-buses" with room for six to eight passengers. Daily, weekly, or monthly transportation fees are charged passengers. As a "club" or "organization," high state tariff fees are avoided, although insurance coverage is mandatory.

The rental reference makes licensing easier in many states. It is, however, profitable, and in several cases operators run as many as four vans to take care of "members."

If vans are operated much like a bus or taxi, public utility commission approval is required to pick up and transport anyone for a paid fare.

Second-hand Shops

Many people, primarily women, have opened second-hand clothing stores. Coats, dresses, skirts, suits, jackets, and other items are obtained from organizations and from families that move out of state. All items are dry cleaned, repaired, and refurbished where possible. These are sold at as much as 60% to 75% under new retail prices. Children's clothing shops featuring cleaned, refurbished garments are also becoming numerous, particularly in the inflation-hit areas of the Northeast, Midwest, and in all large metropolitan areas.

Filling Needs At The Right Prices

Find out what people need today from food to home entertainment, and *what they can afford to pay*. Fill that need successfully and you have yourself a business which, properly planned and directed, will be inflation-proof.

17 Everyone A Winner

An interesting merchandising technique has developed in large supermarkets, shopping malls, department stores, and in small shops: the creation of an attractive atmosphere in which surroundings are pleasing in color and setting. Even soft, lilting music is piped-in to make potential customers feel good. All of this, obviously, is for a reason; to make you, as a possible customer, relax your inherent restraints and buy the products on display.

Creating An Atmosphere

This is an extension of the modern sales philosophy: "If the prospective customer *feels good,* he/she will buy!" Even the salesperson plays an important role in this orchestrated scene. The person may be cheerful and pleasant, showing you the item you are interested in examining. When a decision to buy is made by you, the salesperson finally gives you the package. You are thanked for making the purchase.

The retailer has benefitted from your sale, and you have benefitted as well because the product was something you wanted. Seller and buyer should always benefit from a mutual transaction. Otherwise, the seller will not be in business for long.

The Entrepreneur's Creed

"Find a need on the part of a customer, then *fill that need* successfully!" Most business owners are honest, hard-working, successfully serve the needs of their customers, pay their bills, create jobs for others, and meet their obligations. Our attention is rarely drawn to these people, because they don't make "news" very often. It's only the scoundrels and tyrants who appear in news stories.

The Consequences Of Ill Will

It has been our experience that unless both the buyer and the seller benefit to their satisfaction, the transaction in question is not a good one. Unscrupulous people who intentionally defraud others in a business transaction will, in the long run of events, get caught up in their own web of dishonesty. As mentioned earlier, no one is going to be able to stay in business for long who makes a practice of ripping off its customers. The business will die through any of the following, or a combination: (a) overwhelming customer ill-will passed along through word-of-mouth, (b) bad press, (c) constant "hassles" with the Better Business Bureau and other consumer protection agencies, (d) conflicts with local and state law officials arising from consumer complaints, and (e) trouble with the Federal Trade Commission or the United States Postal Service, both of which can put a stop-and-desist order on a business almost overnight. So you can see where a shady operator simply won't last long. Without lasting long, a business can never establish a strong customer base, a sense of respectability, or turn a profit which will provide a comfortable lifestyle for its owner.

There are hundreds of good business opportunities for both the beginning entrepreneur and the seasoned operator, despite the inflationary economic turmoil now in effect. There are hundreds of opportunities, as well, for making a profit honestly and with hard work.

One occasionally hears the comment. "Yeah. he made *his* pile by ruthlessly *crushing* a lot of people–but he made it!" The end *doesn't* justify the means. And there are a number of former business executives of large corporations and small business owners who are either confined to jail or are fugitives from justice. They seemed to believe that the only way to a financial fortune was through employing every devious trick or deception to take money from those who did business with them! Being incarcerated or fleeing from authorities has never been our idea of a satisfying lifestyle.

Where Lack Of Ethics Leads

Certainly there were unethical business practices transacted in the sale of worthless desert land in western areas of the United States over the past decade. One such real estate firm, whose total sales of worthless property reached $35 million, was forced by the federal authorities to refund all money, with *interest*, to all of the buyers who trusted advice of salespeople. Executives were jailed and heavily fined in this particular case. It was a sorry lesson for thousands of trusting individuals who will probably never purchase any land of any kind they cannot first inspect!

Business in the United States is really not divided into the "good guys" group and the "bad guys." In a nation where there are hundreds of thousands of different business organizations, companies and corporations, there will probably always be a narrow, unethical "fringe" of people who will use dishonest and fraudulent means of making money at the expense of others. This, unfortunately, is a quirk of human nature.

How Everyone Can Benefit

Here's an inspirational example of one of the "good guys" who benefitted his fellow human, along with himself, in business transactions:

A Philadelphia entrepreneur, whose income came from several ballet dance schools established from scratch several years before, was attracted to opportunities offered by the city's rebuilding program. Rundown, dilapidated townhouses, many of which were abandoned or completely vandalized, were sold to buyers at minimal cost. The buyers had to agree to live in these houses or rent them to families with modest incomes.

Following the purchase of three of these townhouses. the investor borrowed funds from a financial institution for rebuilding operations. Working with two friends. he replaced all the wiring, plumbing. and fixtures. installed partitions. re-plastered. papered. and painted. New flooring. steps. and windows were also installed. The work took months before the townhouses were ready for occupancy.

He moved his family into one of the rebuilt homes while he rented the other two to families with small incomes. Everyone in the transaction benefitted from the arrangement. The city began to collect new taxes. As the owner, he collected rents to repay his loans. He lived virtually rent-free, and began to build equity in a townhouse now worth *ten times* its original cost!

His success with his homes inspired five other people to do the same thing in the very same block, creating a new environment for a number of families thus improving their lot.

Financial And Other Benefits

I was actively involved in a recreational project which benefitted a group of people in various ways, some of whom profited financially. Others profited physically and mentally from the operation.

There was an investment opportunity presented to a group of business and professional people, in the form of a proposed racquetball court venture. The location was a small community in which about 25,000 people lived. The residents' income came from a wide range of diversified activities. The community was located at a considerable distance from two larger cities, which meant that sports and cultural activities were limited.

Like most Americans, residents there were receptive to athletic recreational functions–football, hockey, basketball, golf, and bowling. A survey indicated that genuine interest in a new racquetball activity existed. As a result, a partnership was formed to raise the necessary funds for construction. Within several months, land was purchased, and a building erected according to racquetball standards and requirements.

The response from the community was excellent, with club memberships being filled, while others were able to use courts during daylight hours on a staggered basis. Within a relatively short time, investors saw a good return from their funds. Family members became involved in a wholesome recreational activity. Others strengthened their bodies, improving their outlooks and mental attitudes.

Here again, a new environment was created, improving facilities, and providing new jobs where none had existed before. Good profits were achieved honestly, with others enjoying benefits as well.

Let's not forget the original landowner, who also made a profit in the transaction, and deserved it!

When I was involved in the nursing home project mentioned earlier, it became a new, pleasant environment for many elderly people, in addition to other patients who needed attentive care. All of the partners involved made certain the facilities were the best that could be obtained within the established budget. In some cases, the facilities were *better* than those found in other nursing centers. From the rooms to the quality of food and nursing care, patients benefitted from their residence at this center.

Emotional Benefits

The partners made a profit, of course, on their investments following the sale of the facility, but again, both buyers and sellers *all gained* from the transaction. The high standards established initially were continued for the benefit of everyone involved.

Everyone *wins* in a situation such as this one. In reflection, there is an emotional reward as well when a mutually beneficial transaction is completed.

Several years ago, when one of my converted farm houses was rented to a family in a small town where housing was scarce and expensive, benefits were in evidence again. The husband had a limited income from his job, which narrowed the selection and choice of a house for his family. The houses in the small town were much too expensive for him to afford. Yet, he obviously needed a residence close enough to his place of employment, but large enough to house his four children.

When a real estate broker told him about my farmhouse which had just been completely remodeled in terms of heating, wiring, plumbing, new window installations, and new paint, the worker contacted me.

A rental figure was proposed that fell within his budget, and he was able to move into the house shortly thereafter.

A new source of income was generated for me while the worker and his family gained a pleasant home environment in a tree-studded setting. The owner/renter relationship was a good one.

Have you ever been involved in a partnership arrangement which was either *poorly planned and executed, badly financed* or whose market expectations were totally *unrealistic?* New entrepreneurs who volunteer funds, then back away from any interest in the daily, weekly, or monthly transactions, or fail to investigate the proposition carefully, generally find themselves in an unexpected, compromising situation!

The reactions to the scenario described range from shock and anger, to embarrassment, when the operation "caves in" financially. If a close friend was involved in drawing you into the arrangement, the agonizing results are further aggravated. Loss of money is always hard to take, particularly when it has represented an investment, no matter how speculative!

When a post-mortem is conducted to determine the reasons for the financial fiasco, it is important to know that failure came about because of *lack of experience* in the leasing partner; poorly-handled records; underfinancing; underestimation of competitive strength; bad management; no one being available to "mind the store"! Any of these can be, and are, valid reasons for business failure.

However, when a business proposition fails because one or more partners has "milked" the assets illegally and intentionally, this is deceptive, dishonest, and immoral! The remaining defrauded partners have every reason to become angered and to take legal means to recover their share of investments. No one wins in a situation like this one. No one benefits. A bad experience will mark a "conspirator" or "co-conspirator" for life.

This is not meant to be a moralistic compendium of ethics to be observed in business. It is simply a plea to consider your fellow human in your business transactions, regardless of present or past business conditions or climate. Regardless of whether the individual involved with you is unsophisticated in business relations and its ramifications, you owe him/her a fair shake. The sincere desire to *earn* a profit and pursue that objective aggressively, is not the same as sheer greed. Nor is it the same as deceptive business practices to gain an advantage.

A Story With A Moral

There is a story which still circulates in some bank offices in California. This concerns a series of investment events in which a prominent motion picture personality became involved. According to sources, the wealthy actor was intrigued with the idea of purchasing and operating a midwestern carbonated beverage company.

While the company was making a modest profit from retail outlets in a series of cities, it did little in the way of promoting its product.

After several trips out to the company, meetings were held in strictest secrecy to prevent the media from discovering the proposed plan, prior to any official announcement. Owners of the plant held out for a $4.5 million price for a buy out. But the wealthy actor, accompanied by his attorney, finally negotiated a $2.5 million sales figure. Payment was to be in cash, and settlement would take place within sixty days of signing the agreement.

Back at his San Francisco study, the wealthy actor gathered ten of his closet friends and business acquaintances and laid out his plan. They would form a corporation, pooling $100,000 each to match the actor's $1 million investment for the purchase of capital stock. The actor would then raise $500,000. In addition, an amount of $500,000 would be secured from a local bank, on a loan for working capital.

The actor's strategy, in purchasing the carbonated beverage company, was a complete change of products. He would feature faces and names of well-known show business personalities on the cans. These would be marketed in theatre lobbies across the country. He also had an option to buy a small potato chip and pretzel firm in New Jersey, which would also be patterned after the beverage can idea. These products would also be marketed in the theatre refreshment areas.

Initially upon ownership, the actor began making decisions relative to marketing programs, manufacturing, advertising, and packaging–areas about which he knew little. He also hired a former Hollywood publicity executive to function as a key man at the firm. With a busy filming commitment, the actor remained away

from the plant for several months at a time, depending upon the judgement and decisions of the former publicity man to carry the company forward.

Pay Attention To Advice From Experts

The publicity man discovered quite late that he was out of his element in the carbonated beverage production operation. Still he would not accept recommendations made by seasoned and experienced beverage salespeople. When his choices of products, colors, and methods of marketing were criticized as "not right for the market," he overrode their negative votes and directed his judgement on the products be followed without questions.

One year later, the operation was in deep financial trouble due to lack of customer acceptance of the product, badly-timed promotions, and unrealistic pricing. Truckloads of the canned beverages were returned every week because competitive brands were of better quality and were priced lower! The novel "star" beverage cans had never caught on with theatre patrons because of age differences! Younger theatre-goers (the biggest buyers of soft drinks) did not identify with the actors on the packages.

Operations were curtailed when losses virtually wiped out the original investment. The actor discovered, after a final accounting, that a total of $2.8 million had been lost on the venture, plus an additional amount in residual costs. When the news of the business failure reached his friends and acquaintances through financial publications, the actor had little to add to the sad saga of mismanagement.

Only two of the original group of investors were sympathetic in terms of the loss. The others left his presence, vowing never to speak to him again. They held him personally responsible for the loss.

Making Good On Investors' Money

Two months later, each of the ten investors received checks in the amount of $100,000 each, plus interest, from the actor's attorney! While he was not legally obligated to repay these losses, it was his decision to do so, out of a sense of moral obligation. Banker friends viewed his action with admiration. He had accepted his own loss of $1 million, but could not allow the others to do the same! He is held in high esteem by these individuals, and has never invested in any venture since that time, despite the fact that he is now more financially secure than he had been when the ill-found acquisition was first proposed.

On the negative side, there are numerous show business personalities who have lost fortunes through "bad" investment advice and through fraudulent schemes ranging from non-existent oil wells to ginseng farms. There were never any winners in those events. One of the nation's largest mail order houses, whose annual sales volume reached $18 million, was recently fined $350,000 in a U.S. Court on criminal mail fraud charges. The company advertised a line of 100 products, ranging from flower seeds to ceramics. They were forced to repay thousands of customers the cost of a specific product, which the conpany had "willfully and fraudulently" misrepresented! Its officers were severely reprimanded by the federal judge.

Later, the judge told one of his aides, "I can't understand the management of that company. They have been selling products *honestly for years*-and could have continued to make good profits. But they elected to gamble on a fraudulent product-and they have failed! *They will never live that one down!*"

When greed motivates management, look out! The risks taken pursuing this type of business are studded with disasterous curves. The "fast buck" artist will eventually bump into another of his ilk, and both will be destroyed in their desperate attempt to gain the upper hand.

The Winning Situation

The United States is a nation of interdependent people. It has been that way since its inception more than 200 years ago. Look at some of the basic industries: steel, mining, lumbering, chemical production, and transportation. Until someone somewhere *wants* their products for a specific reason to *fill a need,* nothing happens. Everyone in a long chain of events eventually benefits from these industries and services! And everyone makes a profit of some kind in each of the transactions, which is the nature of our free enterprise system.

Even in this brutal inflationary period, when costs are completely out of kilter due to government monetary philosophies, the financial exchanges (or even barter) between individuals must still benefit *both* parties.

Because it will take at least *five* to perhaps *ten* years to get the nation's economy onto a new rational standard of living, most of the present population will need to plan on solving financial problems through his/her entrepreneurial planning and business operations. This means that you will have to learn how to develop good working relationships with "the other guy" to get the things you need, and to give him/her the things they will need. This will include products, services, knowledge, and recreational activities.

Getting yourself into an isolated situation will not solve your financial problems, according to some economic advisors. This will not take care of your total living needs. Certainly lifestyles will change radically over the next decade. The passenger car, once a status symbol and a "toy," will be relegated to its primary role: dependable transportation at infrequent periods. Ride-sharing will be mandatory with larger vans used by commuters. The "lone-rider" in a single car will be a thing of the past on highways, since riding interdependence will be the rule.

Even suburban "isolation" of families will vanish because of transportation pooling and neighborhood barter. Many fragile values will change for the better! Family ties will become vastly stronger in the years ahead because of mutual needs and fulfillment.

Working Together

At this very moment, you may have a new idea or plan that will help thousands of other people solve a problem. This could involve financial problems, physical needs, housing, food consumption or preparation, or personal safety. Your solution will not only reward *you* financially, but will reward others through its implementation. You may make an important contribution to society that will bring you both financial and emotional profit!

One business executive, whose absence from organization lunches, golf course dates, and cocktail parties, aroused much speculation in the business community. A devoted family man, a non-drinker, and frequent church-goer, he had inherited a family business and fortune, but did not live on a scale many others would have with his money. He was a bit embarrassed by his family wealth.

His concern for the welfare of his company's workers frequently got him into "hot water" with members of his Board of Directors. He would make "insurance payments" on the part of the company, to a widow whose husband had little or no family insurance coverage! Every employee is now protected.

His compassion for his fellow human was revealed almost accidentally when a company treasurer (through some fluke at the same bank which handled both the corporation's and the executive's checking accounts) found his cancelled check for $5,000 made out to a haven for destitute persons. The shelter, housing and feeding hundreds of people in a month's time, received that amount every month of the year! He would also spend a lot of spare time at the center, inspecting facilities. This meant he had to forego other activities.

The Philanthropist's Position

This man's company's reputation is widely-known for its honesty in product quality. Vendors are quite often amazed at the rapidity with which bills are paid by this company. And its total business volume in dollars now exceeds $200 million. It's still growing. Its success is based largely upon the president's personal philosophy, which is "Everyone should benefit from our products and business transactions at all times." And they do.

Part Five:

The Forecast:
The Encouraging Words

18 What Is Ahead For Small Business?

We have attempted, in the preceding chapters, to give you an experienced guide to many ways of beating back inflation, and supplementing your depleted finances, and recommended numerous opportunities for making money. These suggestions can give you a strong hedge in the economic battle in which all of us are involved. If you are able to implement any one of these ideas, it will help you survive inflation. In addition, you will have made both a financial and a moral victory!

Predictions

Now that we are in the 1980's, we have been asked to probe the blackened skies of the U.S. economy. We have been asked to try to predict what is ahead for the small business, and the owner's family. We join with the scores of economic theorists, private and government economists, the econometricians, noted bankers, and securities analysts, all of whom are grappling with the same fundamental question. Forecasting, like life, is totally uncertain.

We are at the most critical economic crossroads in the history of the United States. Which road is right for us? Our options have been severely curtailed because of cataclysmic financial events which have been brought about by past and present U.S. Administrations. Our politicians' fiscal irresponsibility over a twenty-year period has placed this nation's economy in jeopardy. The mounting deficits have weakened the dollar domestically and in every major foreign capital. And for the past two decades, many conservative economists and financial advisors have been pleading with each Administration to *stop printing more currency!* The purchase of gold has become a *hedge*.

Implications Of A Tight Money Policy

Recently, the Federal Reserve Board tightened banking credit policies, which panicked the housing industry and many lenders. Its impact rocked the real estate market and many savings institutions. For the first time in history, we have a prime rate higher than it has ever been dreamed of reaching, and it will most likely go higher!

Let us look at some startling precedents related to our present economy, as we attempt to place events in a proper perspective for critical analysis and guidance.

Developments In The Near Past Which Will Affect Our Future

Energy shortage linked to dramatic increase in the cost of imported oil has further deepened the U.S. balance of payment problems. The domestic spin-offs of related energy problems include: gasoline prices crippling new U.S. car sales; unemployment at auto and truck plants; high heating oil prices burdening homeowners with depleted incomes.

* *Dealers report* thousands of people have bought a total of $6.3 billion in *gold* bullion, coins, and wafers in a recent year, for *investment* and *hoarding*.

U.S. government sees fit to guarantee loans of up to $1 billion for major industries, with the acknowledged goal of saving hundreds of thousands of jobs.

Eurodollars coming into the U.S. via California for investments in western states' thrift institutions' mortgage funds.

Stock market plunges more than ninety points on Dow Jones Index in one day at Federal Reserves credit move, causing hundreds of millions of dollars in losses.

Highest rate of inflation in the modern history of the United States. Double-digit inflation, with no hope of lessening.

Airlines beginning layoffs of personnel due to lack of business and the cost of fuel.

Suppliers of products selling to retail dealers now making payment demands of fifteen to thirty days. In some cases, collect-on-delivery payments are required.

Large department store chains report drop in sales and profits. Some encourage any type of credit card purchase.

Signs of the times? Storm flags rising on the horizon to warn of impending danger? Our politicians tell us of the possibility of a "weak" recession ahead as they campaign for re-election.

Jobs Which Will Be Spared

They know, as do millions of civil service workers, members of the Armed Forces, government servants at every level, and indentured teachers, that their incomes will be literally guaranteed under any circumstances. This salaried group will, by the nature of their job structures, *survive* both inflation and recessions.

But there are millions of workers in various sections of the country who will be "strung-out" economically, when plants and businesses close because of the financial whiplash resulting from inflation's recoil. The Northeast, Midwest, and central states will suffer the most economically in the near term.

The Future Of Auto Manufacturers

A number of new car manufacturing plants will close because sales will continue to drop off sharply.

People employed in these plants, plus those of parts and raw materials suppliers, will lose their jobs because of lack of product demand. Credit tightening and lack of mortgage money in these states will bring the construction industry (residential) to its knees, causing widespread unemployment in many areas.

Appliance Manufacturers

Manufacturers of freezers, refrigerators, "big ticket" appliances such as color T.V. sets, microwave ovens, washers, and dryers, will curtail production sharply since product demand will fall off.

Home Prices

The price of used homes will drop slowly, and in some areas there will be hundreds of houses for sale. This will be because of mortgage foreclosures brought about through loss of jobs.

The Food Industry

The last area to be affected by inflation's economic squeeze will be the food industry. Food product manufacturers, along with union organizations and supermarket chains, will attempt to keep food prices high artificially. Serious food boycotts and possibly some rioting in cities where unemployment is high, will cause food prices to drop off almost weekly on a national basis.

"Sunbelt" Workers

Workers living in the "sunbelt" states will have better job protection than workers in northern and central states. The reason for this is because sunbelt states, and such states as California, Arizona, Texas, and Washington are highly diversified industrially and commercially. These states have vast stores of natural resources, plus rich agricultural bases. These states will fare better than the rest of the nation in terms of the economy. The nation's largest percentage of wealth is represented in these states.

The Entrepreneur Will Prevail

While all of this economic convulsion is occuring, what will be happening to the small business owner? If he/she is service-oriented and is meeting the public's demands in food, housing, transportation, medical assistance, or agriculture-related activities, the entrepreneur will not only survive, but will earn a good income. The buzz word here will be *flexibility*.

The 1980's will be a period of much upheaval; sharp revision of values; a streamlining of the federal government bowing to tremendous pressures from taxpayers; new leaders in government who will be able to speak four or five languages to command international respect and admiration; and there will be curious changes in the relations between labor and industry.

Our Forecast

* American *lifestyles* will be totally different within the next decade because of numerous culture and economic "shocks" and "after shocks." These will be related to a radical shift in the economy.

* *A new monetary system* will be introduced by the end of the 1980's, conceived by a brilliant new breed of economists at the request the federal government. The "Money Card" will replace paper currency with the exception of the $1 and $5 coins for use in special areas. Computer technology and the swift movement of funds will wipe out the federal deficit through the use of an intricate financial "model."

* The International Monetary Fund will be completely *reorganized* for a compatible match with U.S. monetary policies. The twenty-nation group will be in full agreement on the matter.

* *The American home,* once the center of family activity in years past, will once again become the family core. This will be due to the return home of millions of women who are now working only to supplement depleted family incomes.* Families will spend more time in their homes than in any other place,

except on-the-job. Most American homes will have central entertainment, including circular three-dimensional color television, music areas, and controlled-circuit television for church and special cultural programs. Homes will be fully utilized–a far cry from today's motel concept of home–eating and sleeping and storage. The "quality of life" will be greatly enhanced.

* *Houses will be built in clusters* at the edges of cities to take advantage of solar heating and lighting. These will have modular designs for quick additions and inexpensive remodelling. The custom built house will almost vanish from the American scene, except in outlying areas. All houses will be factory-built for quick, inexpensive assembly.

* *Big labor unions will be broken up* into regional, autonomous organizations for better assimilation with local industries. Four- and three-day work week will prevail, with millions returning to colleges or pursuing avocations in their spare time.

* *Retired people will be free of any type of taxes.* Because of their reduced incomes, they will be able to purchase any commodity at one-half of the cost, including food. They will be permitted to travel free anywhere, on any type of vehicle or aircraft.

* *Prisons will undergo a radical change.* Manpower will be used to clean up polluted streams and areas, and to rebuild areas damaged by natural disasters. With the exception of those prisoners incarcerated because of capital crimes and facing the death penalty, prisoners will be paid fairly for their work. Married prisoners will live in trailer-like vehicles on prison property for conjugal visits with wives and visits by family members.

* *High-speed electronic mail service* from coast to coast and from city to city, will replace the present archaic mail delivery handled manually.

*Of course, the women who *choose* to work for their own fulfillment will continue to do so. We are referring only to those who are forced to work in order to meet family obligations.

* *The large car manufacturers will be in competition with smaller companies* with greater financial flexibility, and quick technological adaptability. Power sources will change from gasoline and diesel fuel, to electrical and nuclear powered battery driving devices.

* *The motion picture industry will be absorbed by the new television corporation conglomerates* because movie theatres will be outmoded by virtue of home entertainment centers. Television sets will have several adaptable screens for viewing up to six feet in height.

* *Church services will change from weekly to monthly and even quarterly.* Services will be channeled to each home of members over private television lines. This will aid in suppression of diseases spread through group contact as it occurs now.

* *Crime will be sharply curtailed* because of restructured police departments. Wide employment opportunities, particularly among low income groups will be available. These low income groups will be "tapped" for training in construction work, primarily the rebuilding of inner cities.

* *Three distinctly new types of police officers will appear on the scene:* (1) The Police Agent, a college-trained, highly-motivated officer. He would patrol so-called "high crime" areas, investigate, and make difficult arrests. (2) The Police Officer would be well-trained, but involved only in routine patrol work and traffic law enforcement. (3) The Community Service Officer would be specially trained to work in disadvantaged areas, have empathy with community leaders, and assist both the Police Agent and the Police Officer in communicating information and making minor arrests. They might also arbitrate in domestic clashes.

As part of this chapter on economic forecasting, and the changes in American lifestyles as it will affect the small business owner over the years ahead, you need to be aware of what other economic theorists are predicting in their books and newsletters.

A number of experts are predicting a series of unsettling events which may scare you. Their prognostications range from, "Conditions will be mildly disturbing with gold in use as currency," to the more vehement, who forecast such things as "riots in the streets, looting, and total disaster unless you prepare for the worst."

Being Aware Of What Others Are Predicting

While we are not in agreement with these conflicting stories of warnings and advice, we believe that all information relative to the future U.S. economy, American lifestyles, comments on capitalism, and personal theories about the federal government's programs should be reviewed, studied, and evaluated by every business person. This is part of your educational process in business planning.

Since we cannot reprint each nationally-known financial and business advisor's theories in its entirety, we will include pertinent excerpts for your review.

Here are some informative thoughts on the future of the U.S. economy from Ted Nicholas, nationally-known business author of many books, an entrepreneur, and a corporate executive.

Ted Nicholas' View

"It appears that inflation will be with us for the foreseeable future. After all, politicians find it an appealing method of paying bills created by their over-spending. They simply print more money.

"Inflation will probably last for decades until one of two things happens:

(a) The budget is balanced, bringing on recession, or depression at first, then a leveling off.

(b) The currency eventually collapses.

"No one knows what the scenario will be, but the prudent person prepares for all emergencies. While presently unlikely, a currency collapse could occur as soon as sometime in the next decade. If certain circumstances occur, and deficits become even greater, it will create a runaway inflationary period similar to the Weimar Republic in Germany. The things that will keep you going are gold coins, silver coins, paid-for buildings (especially in smaller towns), and a sound small business, that fills needs. Because of a possible collapse of our currency...a prudent person should take certain steps which could assure survival during disruptions. The following steps should be considered in the form of *insurance:*

1. Purchase one year's supply of dehydrated food for all family members.

2. Maintain a supply of vital medicine for family members.

3. Put at least 10% of your liquid assets in gold coins of non-numismatic type (e.g. S. African Kruggerands).

4. Obtain at least one bag of pre-1966 silver coins of $1,000 face value. During a currency collapse of paper money, gold and silver coins may be the best unit of exchange.

5. Maintain a bank account and safe deposit box in Switzerland, the Cayman Islands, or the Bahamas, which consists of Swiss francs and gold coins to the extent you can afford.

However, the greatest protection is a small flexible business of your own. And there are and will continue to be great opportunities for the entrepreneur.''

Noted investment advisor Eliot Janeway reports:

Eliot Janeway's View

''There can be solutions, not just cataclysmic ends, to inflation and other problems. There will be a severe slump, plus runaway inflation marked by record high interest rates for 1980 (and beyond).''

Harry Browne, investment advisor, and author of two books on the U.S. monetary crisis reports:

Harry Browne's View

''The future may be unpredictable, but there are expectations that may have overwhelming probabilities. Gold and silver will triumph; gold-backed currencies will be worth far more than unbacked paper promises. When you've decided that the investment provides the right long-term protection, or opportunity for you, that is the time to buy. Not before then–and certainly not after then.

''The governments have created their own problems. They'll have to deal with those problems themselves. Unfortunately, governments have no resources except those they take from you–and that's where they'll turn as problems become more critical. Your duty now is to prevent further confiscation of your wealth.''

Howard Ruff, former securities broker, and now editor of a financial newsletter, a controversial author, writes:

Howard Ruff's View

''Store enough food for one year. Survival starts here. It is the insurance you can eat in your country refuge with your family. The future is a grisly list of unpleasant events: failure of the federal banking system, collapse of Social Security, a breakdown in our food distribution system, a possible war with the Arabs or the Russians.

''Buy guns and ammunition. Ammunition may be the best possible investment you could make because it can be bartered for things you need. Buy diamonds, gold, and bags of silver coins for hoarding. Buy some real estate in the country, or a place in a small town away from large cities where trouble will be expected.''

There are some candid opinions about the future of the U.S. economy and some world events, by some well-known persons.

The Three Possibilities For The Future

Now let us give you another aspect of future economic possibilities within the broad framework of perspective. We pose the following three scenarios for consideration:

#1. The future will be *much like* conditions today.
#2. The future will be *better* than it is today.
#3. The future will be *far worse* than it is today.

Although we could arrive at statistical chances as to which of these will actually occur, we know that when it does occur, it will be a *100%* situation! In medicine, the terms "always" and "never," for example, do not exist. By the same token, we must temper the blanket assertions in terms of a prediction because *at the worst*, some of the ideas will succeed, and in the *best possible situation*, someone will manage to fail!

Everything Stays The Same

#1. If the world and the business climate *remain* as we currently know them to be, the predictions of the previous authors will prevail.

Things Improve

#2. If conditions *are better* than they are today, the individual entrepreneur who is aggressive, has kept abreast of technological advances, and is able to utilize this technology a manner which is not being used, he/she will achieve success with the same certainty as death and taxes. SINE wave cycles will occur these should be programmed into your concepts. The SINE wave is *real*, and it occurs because of human patterns based on social and psychological makeup. We cannot hear these influences, so we should learn to recognize the SINEwave and use it.

Things Get Worse

#3. If the future will be *far worse* than it is today, what factors will prevail?
(a) A tax revolt would occur nationally.
(b) Rampant inflation would sweep unchecked.

(c) A deep industrial depression could occur.
(d) Massive unemployment would prevail.
(e) Increased social unrest would prevail.
(f) Insurrection might occur.
(g) A complete breakdown of governmental authority might occur.

What To Do If Things Get Worse

In the case of Situation #3, you should plan to acquire one to five acres of wooded, as well as open land, on which to live with your family. If it would be impractical to move a house onto this land, or the material for building a home would be impossible to obtain, secure all of the basic steel tools possible: axes, crow bars, picks, shovels, hatchets, and woodworking tools. With these, and the help of your family members, you could fell some trees and construct a cabin. Also, your family could secure a complete library of reference volumes on subjects, ranging from planting vegetables to home medical care. Fuel for cooking and heating would come from the wood lot.

With seeds and plants, you can store food. You can cure meats from game animals. You can preserve foods as the earlier settlers did. You can build furniture. All of these things can be bartered for your family's needs. Life would be primitive indeed, but it could be sustained.

We have shown you several levels of future economic possibilities which could occur. The last alternative presented is based on the premise that the United States government and our capitalistic system would fall apart.

We do not believe this will happen.

Why Things Will Get Better

It is inconceivable that a great nation such as ours, which at one period *marshalled* the most powerful sea armada, air force, and armies to defeat a tyrannical Nazi army and the Japanese Armed Forces–a nation that *developed* the first atomic bomb, and later *harnessed* nuclear power, and which later put several men on the moon in a brilliant technological project which *no other nation has duplicated*–a nation of the most intellectual academicians, scientists, engineers, medical specialists–a nation which developed the *first* electronic computer that revolutionized industry and commerce–and whose agricultural production *supports* more than a dozen nations with food, would slide into oblivion because of political financial dereliction!

How The Energy Problem Will Be Solved

The key question is, "Will the energy problem be solved?" Our answer: "Yes." But not in terms of what we are doing today. New technological advances–nuclear power; power generated under nuclear units in massive seawater desalting plants on the West Coast; solar power and heating; natural gas piped from Canada over new lines; gas cells converted into electricity for transportation; and other more dramatic developments are coming. Two decades will be needed.

The Triumph Of Free Enterprise

The United States will never be the same again in terms of today's lifestyles, monetary standards of exchange, recreation, or industrial activity. Capitalism will prevail in this country, but in a more refined concept to improve the lives of its residents. And the world will change with us, as it has done in the past.

Part Six:

Suggested Readings and Resources

Suggested Readings and Resources

BOOKS

Investigate Before Investing
International Franchise Association
1025 Connecticut Ave., Suite 1005
Washington, D.C. 20036

Franchise Opportunities Handbook
U.S. Government Printing Office
N. Capital & H. Street
Washington, D.C. 20550

You Can Profit From a Monetary Crisis
by Harry Browne
Bantam Books
666 Fifth Avenue
New York, NY 10019

Where The Money Is & How To Get It
by Ted Nicholas
Enterprise Publishing, Inc.
Two West Eighth Street
Wilmington, DE 19801

How To Get Rich and Stay Rich
by Fred Young
Frederick Fell Publishers
386 Park Avenue
New York, NY 10016

Financing for Small and Medium Sized Businesses
by Harry Gross
Prentice-Hall
Englewood Cliffs, NJ 07632

The Managerial Woman
by Margaret Henning and Anne Jardin
Anchor Press/Doubleday
245 Park Avenue
New York, NY 10017

1001 Job Ideas for Today's Woman
by Ruth Lembeck
Dolphin Books
2743 Broadway
New York, NY 10020

The Retirement Handbook
by Joseph Buckley
(Revised by Henry Schmidt)
Harper & Row
10 East 53rd Street
New York, NY 10022

Not Quite Ready to Retire: 351 Jobs and Businesses for Older Workers
by William David
The Macmillan Company
866 Third Avenue
New York, NY 10022

*Investing On Your Own: How To Find Winning
Stocks in Your Own Backyard*
    by Richard L. Thorsell
    McGraw-Hill Book Co.
    1221 Avenue of the Americas
    New York, NY 10020

1980 Wood Stove Directory
    (lists all stove and wood
    furnace manufacturers)
    P.O.Box 230
    Manchester, NH 03108

How To Turn Your Idea Into a Million Dollars
    by Don Kracke
    Doubleday & Co.
    245 Park Avenue
    New York, NY 10017

Dozens of Ways to Make Money
    by Anne Michie
    Harcourt Brace Jovanovitch
    757 Third Avenue
    New York, NY 10017

*Building & Buying the High Quality House
at the Lowest Cost*
    by A.M. Watkins
    Doubleday & Co.
    245 Park Avenue
    New York, NY 10017

The Only Investment Guide You'll Ever Need
    by Andrew Tobias
    Bantam Paperbacks
    666 Fifth Avenue
    New York, NY 10019

New York Times Book of Money
    Revised and updated by
    Richard E. Blodgett
    Quality Paperbacks
    Middletown, PA 17057

Wind and Windspinners
    (Building Wind-driven Electrical Systems)s)
    Peace Press
    3828 Willat Avenue
    Culver City, CA 90230

Design and Build Your Own Electric Vehicles
    Peace Press
    3828 Willat Avenue
    Culver City, CA 90230

The Solar Cookery Book
    Peace Press
    3828 Willat Avenue
    Culver City, CA 90230

Survival Greenhouse
    Peace Press
    3828 Willat Avenue
    Culver City, CA 90230

Buying & Renovating a House
    Alfred A. Knopf, Inc.
    210 East 50th Street,
    New York, NY 10022

The Art of Blacksmithing
    by Alex Bemer
    Funk & Wagnalls
    666 5th Avenue,
    New York, NY 10016

Blacksmithing
    F.S. Drake Co.
    801 Second Avenue
    New York, NY 10017

PERIODICALS

Collecting:
Antique Cars and Parts
    114 E. Franklin Avenue
    Sesser, IL 62854

Sport Aviation Magazine
    Experimental Aircraft Assn., International
    P.O.Box 229
    Hales Corner, WI 53136

Acquire: The Magazine of
Contemporary Collectibles
    170 Fifth Avenue
    New York, NY 10010

American Collector
    Crain Communications
    740 Rush Street
    Chicago, IL 60611

Antique Trader Weekly
    Box 1050
    Dubuque, IA 52001

Trade-A-Plane
    Crossville, TN 38555

Financial:
Barron's National Business and Financial Weekly
    22 Cortlandt Street
    New York, NY 10007

Business Weekly
    221 Avenue of the Americas
    New York, NY 10020

Black Enterprise
    295 Madison Avenue
    New York, NY 10017

Coin World
    Box 150
    Sidney, OH 45367

Forbes
    60 Fifth Avenue
    New York, NY 10011

Money
    Time Life Building
    Rockefeller Center
    New York, NY 10020

Journal of Commerce
    99 Wall Street
    New York, NY 10005

Fortune
    1271 Avenues of the Americas
    New York, NY 10017

Free Enterprise
    800 Second Avenue
    New York, NY 10017

Dun's Review
    666 Fifth Avenue
    New York, NY 10019

Wall Street Journal
    22 Cortlandt Street
    New York, NY 10007

Crafts:
Craft Horizons
    44 West 53rd Street
    New York, NY 10019

Creative Crafts
    Carsten's Publications, Inc.
    Box 700
    Newton, NJ 07860

Gems and Minerals
    Box 687
    Mentone, CA 92359

Popular Handicraft Hobbies
    Tower Hobbies
    Box 428
    Seabrook, NH 03875

Working Craftsman
Box 42
1290 Shermer Road
Northwood, IL 60062

Craftworkers Market (annual publication)
Writer's Digest Publications
9933 Alliance Road
Cincinnati, OH 45242

Profitable Craft Merchandiser
News Plaza
Box 1790
Peoria, IL 61656

Entrepreneurial:
Venture: The Magazine for Entrepreneurs
35 West 45th Street
New York, NY 10036

Free Enterprise
800 Second Avenue
New York, NY 10017

Flea Market Business Guide
Elkay, Dept. 4
70 Main Street
Farmingdale, NJ 07727

New Ventures
(newsletter)
2430 Pennsylvania Avenue
Washington, D.C. 20037

Income Opportunities
380 Lexington Avenue
New York, NY 10017

Investment Opportunities Around the World
Box 61009
Miami, FL. 33161

Toy and Hobby World
124 East 40th Street
New York, NY 10016

The Commercial Fish Farmer
P.O.Box 2451
Little Rock, AR 72203

Political and Economic
Dollars and Sense
National Taxpayers Union
325 Pennsylvania Avenue
Washington, D.C. 20003

General Business
FOCUS Business Newsweekly
1015 Chestnut Street
Philadelphia, PA 19107

Security Industry
Security World
5 South Wabash Avenue
Chicago, IL 60603

Security Management
Bureau of Business Practice
24 Rope Ferry Road
Waterford, CT 06386

Computer Industry
Data Management
505 Busse Highway
Park Ridge, IL 60068

Computer World
797 Washington Street
Newton, MA 02160

Computer Decisions
50 Essex Street
Rochelle Park, NJ 07662

Personal Computing
1050 Commonwealth Avenue
Boston, MA 02215

Food:

Family Food Garden
   Box 1014
   Grass Valley, CA 95945

Food Plant Ideas
   731 Hennpin Avenue
   Minneapolis, MN 55403

Food Technology
   221 N. LaSalle Street
   Chicago, IL 60601

Home Building

Homeowner's How-To Magazine
   380 Madison Avenue
   New York, NY 10017

House Beautiful
   717 Fifth Avenue
   New York, NY 10022

Your Home
   P.P.Box 2315
   Ogden, UT 84403

Select Home Designs
   382 W. Broadway
   Vancouver, B.C.
   Canada V5YR2

Solar Homes
   Quality Paperbacks
   Middletown, PA 17057

Mobile/Modular Housing Dealer Magazine
   6339 Northwest Highway
   Chicago, IL 60631

Real Estate
   P.O.Box 1689
   Cedar Rapids, IA 52406

Hudson Home Guides
   289 S. San Antonio Road
   Los Altos, CA 90808

National Home Center News
   425 Park Avenue
   New York, NY 10022

How-To-Build-Your-Own-Home, School
   Shelter Institute, Pat Hennin, Director
   38 Center Street
   Bath, ME 04530
   Phone: (207) 442-7938

Lumber/Wood Harvesting:

Dixie Logger and Lumberman
   210 N. Main Street
   Wadley, GA 30477

Wood and Wood Products
   300 W. Adams Street
   Chicago, IL 60606

Furniture Building:

Woodworking and Furniture Digest
   Hitchcock Building
   Wheaton, IL 60187

Tools, Woodworking Machines, Techniques

Mechanix Illustrated
   1515 Broadway
   New York, NY 10036

Popular Mechanics
   One Park Avenue
   New York, NY 10016

Science and Mechanics
   380 Lexington Avenue
   New York, NY 10017

Blacksmithing/Farrier Related Periodicals

Horseman's Yankee Peddler Newspaper
  Wilabraham, ME 01095

Practical Horseman
  The Pennsylvania Horse, Inc.
  West Chester, PA 19380

Quarter Horse Journal
  Box 9105
  Armarillo, TX 79105

Horse Illustrated
  Box A
  Lake Elsinore, CA 92330

Metalworking Digest
  20 Community Plaza
  Morristown, NJ 07960

Regional Business Publications

Capital District Business Review
  105 Wolf Road
  Albany, NY 12205
  Phone: (518) 458-7000

California Business
  406 North Golden Mall
  Burbank, CA 91503
  Phone: (213) 843-2121

Colorado Business
  1139 Delaware Plaza
  Denver, CO 80204
  Phone: (303) 573-1433

Connecticut Business Journal
  217 Harrison Avenue
  Harrison, NY 10528
  Phone: (203) 622-1220

Corporate Report
  7101 York Avenue
  Minneapolis, MN 55435
  Phone: (612) 835-6855

Crain's Chicago Business
  740 Rush Street
  Chicago, IL 60611
  Phone: (312) 649-5303

Florida Trend
  8th Avenue & 13th Street
  Tampa, FL 33601
  Phone: (813) 247-5411

FOCUS: Philadelphia's Business Newsweekly
  1015 Chestnut Street
  Philadelphia, PA 19107
  Phone: (215) 925-8545

Kentucky Business Ledger
  1215 S. Third Street
  Louisville, KY 40203
  Phone: (502) 635-5212

Long Island Business Review
  303 Sunnyside Blvd.
  Plainview, NY 11803
  Phone: (516) 681-8000

New England Business
  120 Tremont Street, Suite 420
  Boston, MA 02108
  Phone: (617) 482-7040

Northern Ohio Business Journal
  Bulkley Building, Suite 313
  Cleveland, OH 02108
  Phone: (216) 621-1644

Outlook: The Kansas City Business Journal
  4149 Pennsylvania Avenue
  Kansas City, MO 64111
  Phone: (816) 931-4541

The South
  8th Avenue & 13th Street
  Tampa, FL 33601
  Phone: (813) 247-5411

Texas Business Magazine
   3003 LBJ Freeway, Suite 115
   Dallas, TX 75234
   Phone: (214) 241-7401

Westchester Business Journal
   217 Harrison Avenue
   Harrison, NY 10528
   Phone: (914) 835-4600

Agencies and Organizations
Small Business Administration
   National Agency Office
   1141 L Street, NW
   Washington, D.C. 20416

Energy Research & Development Administration
   Washington, D.C. 20545

Federal Energy Administration
   Capitol & H. Streets, NW
   Washington, D.C. 20401

Farm Credit Administration
   400 L'Enfant Plaza East, SW
   Washington, D.C. 20401

Consumer Information Center
   Dept. 156
   Pueblo, CO 81009

Dept. of Agriculture
   Food & Nutrition Service
   14th and Independence Avenue, SW
   Washington, D.C. 20250

Government Printing Office
   N. Capitol & H Street, NW
   Washington, D.C. 20401

Department of Commerce
   14th & Constitution Avenue, NW
   Washington, D.C. 20230

United States Patent & Trademark Office
   Washington, D.C. 20231

American Entrepreneur's Association
   631 Wilshire Blvd.
   Santa Monica, CA 90401

Homebuilding Source:
"Topsider" Pre-fabricated Homes
   George T. McDonald
   Carter Construction & Engineering Co., Inc.
   P.O.Box 849
   Yadkinville, NC 27055
   Phone: (919) 679-8846

Ridge Homes, Inc.
   501 Office Center Drive
   Washington, DC 19034 (pre-cut)

Wilderness Log Homes
   Route 2
   Plymouth, WI 53073 (pre-cut)

Scandia Log Homes
   7303 222nd Street
   Woodinville, WA 98072 (pre-cut)

Miles Homes
   4500 Lyndale Avenue
   Minneapolis, MN 55412 (pre-cut)

Inventor's Associations:
AMERICAN SOCIETY OF INVENTORS
   947 Old York Road
   Abington, PA 19001
      Albert G. Fonda, Director
   Phone: (215) 885-2050

Inventors Club of America
   121 Chestnut Street
   Springfield, MA
   Phone: (413) 737-0670

Utah Innovation Center
  Salt Lake City, UT
        William Bowen, Director

Massachusetts Institute Of Technology (MIT)
  Innovation Center
  Cambridge, MA

National Science Foundation
  Tuscon, AZ

Stamp Collectors Organization:
Society of Philatelic Americans
  58 W. Salisbury Drive
  Wilmington, DE 19809

Consumer/Economic Information Sources:
Economic Facts
  The National Research Bureau
  424 N. Third Street
  Burlington, IA 52601

Buyways
  1000 Sunset Ridge Road
  Northbrook, IL 60062

Consumer's Digest
  4001 Devon West
  Chicago, IL60646

Export Financing Information
  Small Business Administration
  "Hotline" (800) 424-5201

Business Aids, Management Guide Data
  Bureau of Business Practice
  24 Rope Ferry Road
  Waterford, CT 06386
  Phone: (800) 243-0876

International Consulting or Research
  The Wharton School of Business

University of Pennsylvania
3620 Locust Walk
Philadelphia, PA 19103
        Frank Contractor
Phone: (215) 243-4838

Successful Small Farms
  Herbert T. Leavy
  Structures Publishing Co.
  Farmington, MI 48024

U.S. Forest Service
  Forest Products Laboratory
  P.O. Box 5130
  Madison, WI 53705

Fiberglas™ Car Bodies
Fiberfab, Inc.
  1000 Turner Crossroads, South
  Minneapolis, MN55416
  Phone: (800) 328-5671

Bicycles and Equipment
American Bicyclist & Motorcyclist
  461 Eighth Avenue
  New York, NY 10001

Bike Pedapower Engines
  591 Mantua Blvd.
  Sewell, NJ 08080
  Phone: (800) 257-7955

Pensions:
Pension World
  461 Eighth Avenue
  New York, NY 10001

Pensions and Investments
  740 Rush Street
  Chicago, IL 60611

Index